THE INDIAN TRIBES
OF NORTH AMERICA

THE INDIAN TRIBES
OF NORTH AMERICA

WITH BIOGRAPHICAL SKETCHES AND
ANECDOTES OF THE PRINCIPAL CHIEFS

THOMAS L. McKENNEY
and
JAMES HALL

with an Introduction by

H. J. BRAUNHOLTZ

Volume III

ROWMAN AND LITTLEFIELD
TOTOWA, NEW JERSEY

THIS EDITION FIRST PUBLISHED IN THE UNITED STATES 1972
by Rowman and Littlefield, Totowa, New Jersey

ISBN 0 87471 119 3

THIS REPRINT TAKEN FROM THE
1934 EDITION

by John Grant, Edinburgh

This edition published by
kind permission of the copyright holder,
John Grant,
31 George IV Bridge, Edinburgh

Reprinted in Great Britain by
Scolar Press Limited, Menston, Yorkshire

THE INDIAN TRIBES
OF NORTH AMERICA

ENCAMPMENT OF PIEKANN INDIANS
Near Fort McKenzie, on the Muscleshell River

THE INDIAN TRIBES
OF NORTH AMERICA

WITH BIOGRAPHICAL SKETCHES AND
ANECDOTES OF THE PRINCIPAL CHIEFS

THOMAS L. McKENNEY

AND

JAMES HALL

WITH AN INTRODUCTION BY

H. J. BRAUNHOLTZ

*Illustrated with 123 full-page Plates in Colour (chiefly from the Indian
Gallery, formerly in the War Department at Washington), Photogravure
Portraits, and two Maps*

VOLUME III

EDINBURGH: JOHN GRANT
31 GEORGE IV. BRIDGE
1934

CONTENTS

                                                                    PAGE

LIST OF PORTRAITS   vii

THE GENUINENESS OF THE PORTRAIT OF POCAHONTAS   .   .   ix

INTRODUCTORY NOTE. BY H. J. BRAUNHOLTZ   .   .   .   xiii

HISTORY OF THE INDIAN TRIBES OF NORTH AMERICA   .   .   1

THE NORTH AMERICAN INDIANS. BY JAMES HALL   .   .   83

INDEX   347

MAPS

1. The Localities of the Indian Tribes of the United States
     in 1833   .   .   .   . At end

2. The United States showing Indian Reservations, 1906   . At end

LIST OF PORTRAITS

PAGE

Encampment of Piekann Indians . . *Frontispiece*

Nowaykesugga, an Otto 11

No-Tin, a Chippeway Chief 26

Monchonsia, a Kansas Chief . . . 34

Tahcoloquoit, a Saukie Warrior 35

Tukosee Mathla, a Seminole Chief . . . 59

Pashenine, a Chippeway Chief 74

Oche Finceco, a Half-Breed Creek . . . 91

Pocahontas, the Princess who rescued Captain Smith . 106

Ledagie, a Creek Chief 114

Ongewae, a Chippeway Chief 115

Nahetluchopie, a Muskogee Chief . . . 123

Amiskquew, a Menominie Warrior . . . 138

Itcho Tustennuggee, a Seminole Chief . . . 155

David Vann, a Cherokee Chief 170

Julcee Mathla, a Seminole Chief 187

Jackopa, a Chippeway Chief 202

Keeshewaa, a Fox Warrior 219

A Winnebago, an Orator 234

Waatopenot, a Chippeway Chief 251

Peechekir, a. Chippeway Chief 266

Ohyawamincekee, a Chippeway Chief . . . 283

John Ross, a Cherokee Chief 298

Apauly Tustennuggee, a Creek Chief . . . 315

vii

THE GENUINENESS OF THE PORTRAIT OF POCAHONTAS

THE Portraits in this work are not merely pictorial, but exact like-nesses of the individuals they represent, and of the costumes in which they are attired. Many have doubted whether a genuine likeness of Pocahontas existed,—indeed, we had long abandoned all hope of procuring one, but by dint of constant effort, having got upon a trail, some years ago, one has been found. That it may be contemplated with the interest that we all take in viewing portraits of distinguished persons—an interest always greatly increased in proportion as our confidence in the fidelity of the artist, and in the close resemblance which his production bears to the individual, is established—we state that this is an exact copy of an original portrait of Pocahontas, painted between the years 1616 and 1617, during her visit to England, in company with her husband, Mr Rolfe. The remains of the original are at this time, November 20, 1843, in possession of Dr Thomas Robinson, in Petersburg, Virginia. Mr R. M. Sully, the artist who made the copy from the original, from which copy the portrait in this work was taken, employed great labour in attaching the decaying parts together, so as to bring the whole within his power, and he succeeded.

We proceed to state the proofs on which the genuineness of this beautiful picture rests. The original documents are in our possession, from which we copy the following :—

1st, A letter from Richard Randolph, Esq., of Virginia, written and dated in Washington, 1st April, 1842 :

"Pocahontas and Mr Rolfe, her husband, arrived at Plymouth on the 12th June, 1616. Their portraits were taken whilst they were in England, where their son Thomas was born. Pocahontas died at Gravesend in the early part of the year 1617 ; her husband returned to Virginia, leaving his son to the care of Mr Henry Rolfe, his brother.

"Thomas Rolfe returned to Virginia, and there married, and died leaving an only child, Jane, who married Col. Robert Bolling, and died, leaving an only child, John Bolling, whose daughter Jane married Richard Randolph, of Curles, in the County of Henrico, State of Virginia. Their son Ryland, who owned and resided on the patrimonial estate, after receiving his education in England, was informed that the portraits of Pocahontas and Rolfe were in the possession of a gentleman in England, whose name is now forgotten.

" He wrote to his friend in England, to endeavour to purchase them for him: when the gentleman was applied to, and informed that Mr Randolph was a descendant of Pocahontas and Rolfe, he presented the portraits to Mr Randolph, whose friend sent them to Virginia, where they arrived safely, and were hung up in Mr Randolph's mansion, Turkey Island.

" Mr Randolph died in the year 1784. Soon after his death, his estate was publicly sold, and these portraits were purchased by Mr Thomas Bolling, of Cobbs, in the County of Chesterfield, at twenty shillings each, that being the appraised value ; owing to the following agreement :—Mr Thomas Bolling, and four other descendants of Pocahontas, were each anxious to purchase the pictures ; and a proposition was made to decide by lot which of the five should have them, and Mr Bolling, being the nearest, was permitted to purchase them without opposition.

" This statement was made to me by my father, David Meade Randolph, who was the executor of Ryland Randolph, and sold the pictures.

" The inventory and account of sales may be seen in the office of the County Court of Henrico.

" *Washington, 1st April*, 1842.   RICHARD RANDOLPH."

2nd, Copy of a letter to Mr R. M. Sully, from Mr W. F. Simpson of Virginia :

" *Friday, 13th August*, 1830.

" Dear Sully :—You requested me a few days ago to call and see the portrait of Pocahontas you have lately been busy upon, from the one which you borrowed from her descendants at Cobbs. I did so last evening while you were from home, and feel much pleasure in bearing testimony to the style in which you have executed your trust, a task so difficult from the mutilated state of the original picture, that I really thought it almost impossible for you to succeed as completely as you have done. It is faithful to a letter, perhaps more so than is *politic*, since had you made some little alteration in her ladyship's position, and dressed her rather more in accordance with the taste of this after age, I have no doubt the picture would tell better with the majority of those who may hereafter see it. I, of course, think you quite right in sticking as rigidly to the 'letter of the law' as you have done."

3rd, Copy of a statement from Doctor T. Robinson, of Petersburg, Virginia, 20th August, 1843.

"The Indian picture copied by Mr Sully, the original of which is now in my possession, was shown to me at Cobbs, some seventeen or eighteen years ago, by Mr Bolling, as the portrait of Pocahontas; Mrs B., then proprietor of the portrait, was herself a descendant of Pocahontas, and widow of the representative of Powhattan. A slight inspection of the costume satisfied me that this was the only portrait of a female painted in the reign of James I. among the family pictures.

"With very great pleasure I bear testimony to the rigid fidelity with which Mr Sully has copied this very interesting portrait, notwithstanding the temptation to certain alterations in conformity with the romantic spirit of the history of the individual whom it represents, by which the effect might have been increased, without impairing the likeness. From everything of this kind Mr Sully has with great propriety abstained, while the likeness, costume and attitude have been preserved with great exactness.

"The original is crumbling so rapidly that it may be considered as having already passed out of existence.

"*Petersburg, August* 20, 1830.   T. ROBINSON."

4th, Copy of a statement from Mrs Anne Robinson, of Virginia:

"From my earliest recollections I have been accustomed to see the picture copied by Mr Sully in the house of my grandfather, Mr T. Bolling, of Cobbs; it was always shown as the portrait of Pocahontas. Mr T. Bolling was the representative of Powhattan; my grandmother, Mrs Bitty Bolling, equally distinct from Pocahontas; neither entertained a doubt that the picture in question was a portrait of Pocahontas. My father, also a descendant of Pocahontas, was well acquainted with the history of the picture.

ANNE ROBINSON."

5th, Extract of a letter from D. M. Randolph to R. M. Sully:

"*Yorktown, 10th September,* 1830.

"About the year 1788-9, I resided at Presque Isle, one mile from Bermuda Hundred. Occasionally interchanging visits of hospitality with the masters of vessels while in that port, it was my good fortune to become intimate with a captain Joseph Watson, of the brig *Jane*, of Washington.

"This captain Watson brought Mr Randolph a parcel of books.

"These books were accompanied by a long letter from Jonah Wheeler, of the respectable commercial house of Gerard, Preston Winder & Wheeler, then existing in Liverpool. The books were presented by Mr Wheeler, from his having understood my character as a farmer, and my name as a descendant of Pocahontas.

"Mr Wheeler stated that he had heard 'his mother relate the circumstance of a Mr Randolph or Bolling, having in their day been over to England and going down into Warwickshire, one hundred and fifty miles from London, in pursuit of the portraits of Mr Rolfe and Pocahontas'; the gentleman, he said, offered a large price for the pictures, but the family who had them, themselves not descendants from Pocahontas, but from Rolfe, disdaining a *premium*, generously gave the same to Ryland Randolph, who satisfied them of his better pretensions to so valuable a possession. I retain a perfect recollection of their being brought over from England by my uncle, their first appearance at Turkey Island, and lastly their sale, by myself, acting as clerk to my father, the administrator, in the month of March, 1784. Our estimable fellow-citizen, Fayette, were he now among us, would, I believe, identify the pictures and confirm their history, from the fact of his intimacy with Ryland Randolph, whose house served for his headquarters a considerable time in the memorable campaign of 1781.

"Yours, &c.,

"D. M. RANDOLPH."

There are additional documents before us; but we rest the genuineness of the copy taken by Mr Sully, as also that of the original, upon the above proofs, with the assurance that the picture in this work is a perfect copy by Sully from the original.

INTRODUCTORY NOTE

By H. J. BRAUNHOLTZ

INTENSIVE research in the ethnology of the American
Indians during the last fifty years has done much to
remedy the state of ignorance of their aboriginal
culture complained of by the authors in their opening
paragraphs. Indeed, so far as the survival of this
culture has permitted, the aborigines of North America
may now be regarded as the best known and most
fully described of all primitive peoples. This research
has necessitated a considerable revision in our estimate
of the Indians' position in the scale of human culture,
and has rendered untenable many of the general
conclusions arrived at on inadequate evidence by the
authors of this work. It should also be noted that
their remarks refer, for the most part, only to the
tribes of the Central and Eastern States (the so-called
"Plains" and "Eastern Woodlands" areas), and not
to the Pacific seaboard or the settled "Pueblo" peoples
of the south-west to whom the term "roving barbarians"
is quite inapplicable. Moreover, even in this limited
field the authors' general conclusions, which seem to
have been partly influenced by a desire for rhetorical
effect, are not entirely consistent with the more detailed
circumstances which they themselves describe. Archæo-

logical study, which was hardly in its infancy at the time when this work was published, has thrown a flood of light on the prehistory of America, more particularly with respect to the higher civilisations of Mexico, Central America, and Peru.

To correct in detail the numerous erroneous statements, so as to give a true picture of Indian life as we now know it to have been, would involve a more extensive commentary than appears practicable or desirable in a work which can never be regarded as an ethnological text-book. It may, however, be briefly noted that the aborigines had in fact developed the arts of making stone tools, pottery and basketry to a considerable, and in some localities to an exceptionally high degree, and that the handicrafts were by no means confined to the womenfolk, in spite of the authors' statement to the contrary. Nor were the Indians devoid of medical and surgical science of an empirical kind, including such therapeutic methods as bone-setting, cauterizing, cupping, sweat-baths and dieting.

On the other hand, the authors' view that the American Indians are of Asiatic origin is in agreement with modern ethnological opinion, which is based chiefly on their proved physical affinities with the Mongolian races. Their main route of immigration was almost certainly *via* the Bering Strait, and this movement probably began at a time corresponding broadly to the last palæolithic phase of Europe, perhaps about 12,000 B.C., since there is evidence that the earliest inhabitants of America possessed neither pottery nor polished stone implements. No certain evidence of early or middle palæolithic cultures or of a human species, such as "Neanderthal Man," differing essentially from the modern inhabitants, has been found on the American Continent.

For an introduction to the ethnology of North America, the reader may be referred to the following general works :—

J. C. Wissler. *The American Indian* (2nd ed., 1922).

F. W. Hodge. *Handbook of American Indians North of Mexico*. Bureau of American Ethnology, Bull. 30 (1907).

Handbooks of the American Museum of Natural History, New York.

And for Archæology, to the following :—

W. H. Holmes. *Handbook of Aboriginal American Antiquities*. Bureau of American Ethnology, Bull. 60 (1919).

W. H. Holmes. *Mexican and Central American Antiquities*. Bureau of American Ethnology, Bull. 28 (1909).

T. A. Joyce. *Mexican Archæology* (1914) and *Central American Archæology* (1916).

For more special studies, the following should be consulted :—

Annual Reports and Bulletins of the Bureau of American Ethnology. Washington.

Annual Reports of the U.S. National Museum. Washington.

Anthropological Papers and Bulletins of the American Museum of Natural History. New York.

Publications (Anthropological Series) of the Field Columbian Museum, Chicago.

Publications of the Museum of the American Indian (Heye Foundation), New York.

The American Anthropologist (Quarterly Journal). Washington.

For an account of the "reservations" and present condition of the North American Indians, *see*—

G. B. Grinnell. *The Indians of To-day.* (New York, 1900.)

Extensive bibliographies are supplied in—

W. I. Thomas. *Source-book for Social Origins.* (Boston, 1909.)

G. Buschan. *Illustrierte Völkerkunde*, Vol. I. (Stuttgart, 1922.)

HISTORY OF THE INDIAN TRIBES OF NORTH AMERICA[1]

THE earlier historians, who recorded the efforts and progress of the European adventurers that sought in the New World those favours which fortune had denied them in the Old, have not left us much precise information respecting the condition of the Indian tribes who then occupied this part of the continent. The external appearance of the Indians, and their mode of life, differing so widely from everything which Europeans had previously seen, seem to have arrested their attention, and withdrawn it from objects of inquiry, which, to us, are so much more important.

Could we bring back the three centuries that have elapsed since the discovery by Columbus, how much might we hope to recall of the history, tradition, and institutions of the Indians which have for ever passed away! Still much remains—and if all who have opportunities for observation would devote themselves to these researches, a race of men not more insulated in their position, than peculiar in their opinions and customs, would be rescued from that comparative oblivion in which we fear they are destined, under present circumstances, speedily to become involved.

Whence the Indians of America derived their origin, is a question long discussed[2]; and although the particular causes, and route, and circumstances of their migration can never be ascertained, yet there is little doubt, at this day,

---

[1] See Note 1, end of this Section, p. 82.   [2] See Note 2, *ibid.*

that they are branches of the great Tartar stock. In arriving at this conclusion, we do not give much weight to any casual coincidences that may be discerned between the Asiatic and American dialects. Of all the sources of information by which the descent of nations can be traced, we consider the deductions of comparative etymology, when applied to a written language, the most uncertain. It is difficult in such cases to fix, with accuracy, the true sound of words; and it is well known that coincidences exist in many languages, radically different from one another, and spoken by communities whose separation from any common stock precedes all historic monuments. Such coincidences are either accidental, or the analogous words are the common relics of that universal tongue which was lost in the miraculous interposition upon the plains of Shinar.

There is a fact illustrative of this position, within our own knowledge, which demonstrates the futility of any conclusion drawn from such premises. It is well known that the practice of dividing fields in England, by ditches, was introduced in the last century. When it was first adopted, the common people were suddenly arrested in their walks upon the brink of these ditches, without being aware of their existence, until they approached them. Their surprise was manifested by the exclamation, "*ha, ha,*" and eventually the ditches themselves were denominated *ha, ha*. Among the *Sioux*, the Falls of St Anthony are called *ha, ha*. These Falls, approached from below, are not visible, until a projecting point is passed, when they burst upon the traveller in all their grandeur. The Indians, no doubt, struck with the sudden and glorious prospect, marked their surprise, as did the English peasants, with the same exclamation—*ha, ha;* and this exclamation has become the name of the cataract.[1] But he who would

---

[1] For the term *Minnehaha*, see Note 3, end of this Section, p. 82.

deduce from this coincidence the common origin of the
English and Sioux, would reason as logically as many of
those who arrange the branches of the human family into
classes because a few doubtful resemblances in their
vocabularies are discovered.

Some curious observations on this topic were made by
the celebrated American traveller, John Ledyard. The
wide extent of his travels among savage nations in almost
every region of the globe, together with his remarkable
sagacity in discriminating, and facility in recording, the
peculiarities of savage manners and character, gives a
value to his opinions and remarks on this subject, which
those of few other persons can claim. The following
extract is from his *Journal*, written in Siberia :

" I have not as yet taken any vocabularies of the Tartar
language. If I take any, they will be very short ones.
Nothing is more apt to deceive than vocabularies, when
taken by an entire stranger. Men of scientific curiosity
make use of them in investigating questions of philosophy
as well as history, and I think often with too much
confidence, since nothing is more difficult than to take a
vocabulary, that shall answer any good ends for such a
purpose. The different sounds of the same letters, and of
the same combinations of letters, in the languages of
Europe present an insurmountable obstacle to making a
vocabulary, which shall be of general use. The different
manner, also, in which persons of the same language would
write the words of a new language, would be such, that a
stranger might suppose them to be two languages.

"Most uncultivated languages are very difficult to be
orthographized in another language. They are generally
guttural; but when not so, the ear of a foreigner cannot
accommodate itself to the inflection of the speaker's voice
soon enough to catch the true sound. This must be done

instantaneously ; and even in a language with which we are acquainted, we are not able to do it for several years. I seize, for instance, the accidental moment, when a savage is inclined to give me the names of things. The medium of this conversation is only signs. The savage may wish to give me the word for *head*, and lays his hand on the top of his head. I am not certain whether he means *the head*, or *the top of the head*, or perhaps *the hair* of the head. He may wish to say *leg*, and puts his hand to the calf. I cannot tell whether he means *the leg*, or *the calf*, or *flesh*, or *the flesh*. There are other difficulties. The island of Onalaska is on the coast of America, opposite to Asia. There are few traders on it. Being there with Captain Cook, I was walking one day on the shore in company with a native, who spoke the Russian language. I did not understand it. I was writing the names of several things, and pointed to the ship, supposing he would understand that I wanted the name of it. He answered me in a phrase, which in Russ meant, *I know*. I wrote down, *a ship*. I gave him some snuff, which he took, and held out his hand for more, making use of a word which signified in Russ, *a little*. I wrote, *more*."—See Sparks' *Life of John Ledyard*, p. 148, first edition.

The claims of our primitive people to an Asiatic descent are founded upon other and stronger testimony ;—upon the general resemblance which they bear, in many points of character, manners, customs, and institutions—circumstances not easily changed, or easily mistaken—to the various tribes occupying the great table-lands of Tartary. We feel no disposition to examine the details of this question. It has been long before the literary world, and all the facts and considerations connected with it have been carefully investigated, discussed, and considered. To revive it were idle, for its interest can never be revived, nor is there reason to suppose that any new or more accurate views of the subject will ever be presented.

After stating many curious particulars and striking facts on this subject, Ledyard adds, by way of conclusion from the whole—

"I know of no people among whom there is such a uniformity of features, (except the Chinese, the Jews, and the Negroes) as among the Asiatic Tartars. They are distinguished, indeed, by different tribes, but this is only nominal. Nature has not acknowledged the distinction; but, on the contrary, marked them, wherever found, with the indisputable stamp of Tartars. Whether in Nova Zembla, Mongolia, Greenland, or on the banks of the Mississippi, they are the same people, forming the most numerous, and, if we must except the Chinese, the most ancient nation on the globe. But I, for myself, do not except the Chinese, because I have no doubt of their being of the same family."

Again, he says: "I am certain that all the people you call *red* people on the continent of America, and on the continents of Europe and Asia, as far south as the southern parts of China, are all one people, by whatever names distinguished, and that the best general name would be *Tartar*. I suspect that *all* red people are of the same family. I am satisfied that America was peopled from Asia, and had some, if not all, its animals from thence." —*Life of Ledyard,* pp. 246, 255.

Equally idle would it be to indulge in speculations concerning the causes, or motives, or circumstances, which led to this exodus from the Eastern to the Western continent. How long it had occurred previously to the discovery, is, and must remain a matter of conjecture—the facts in our possession are not sufficient to enable us to form even a plausible conjecture upon the subject. It is evident, however, that many ages must have passed away between the first settlement of America and its discovery by Europeans. With the exception of the half-civilised empires of Mexico and Peru, the aboriginal inhabitants were roving barbarians, little advanced from a state of Nature, and depending solely upon the chase for the means of subsistence. They seem to have been spread pretty equally over the continent, leaving no portion of the country without inhabitants, nor any with a dense population. Barbarous tribes, under such circumstances, increase slowly. The life of a hunter is not favourable to a rapid increase of population. If he sometimes possesses an abundance, he is often exposed to famine.

In forming a correct estimate of the early condition of the Indians, much allowance must be made for the spirit of exaggeration visible in the narratives of the first travellers and adventurers. They seem to have surveyed the objects before them under the influence of a mirage, which not only distorted the features, but increased their numbers and proportions. In addition to this predisposition, the fault in some measure of the age, the soldiers of fortune who hazarded life and fame in their efforts to subdue the native inhabitants, were led, in the statement of their own claims and services, to overrate the number, and power, and resources, of their enemies. There are many evidences of this spirit, particularly among the Spanish conquerors, and he who reads the account of their expeditions, and compares them with the habits and condition of the people they describe, as these are now known to us, must be satisfied, that if the leading facts are true, the details are entitled to little credit. It is difficult, at this distance of time and place to point to particular instances of this habit of misrepresentation. The conclusion must be deduced rather from a general view of the subject, than from single facts.

But there is one gross exaggeration which we are able to detect, by a comparison of the descriptions which have come to us, with the actual customs of the Indians of the present day.

Everyone must recollect the wonderful accounts which have been given of the hieroglyphical pictures of the Mexicans, and these have been often referred to, as evidence of the advances made by those people in knowledge and civilisation. In Dr Robertson's *History of America*, accurate representations are given of those paintings; and they resemble, in every particular, the rude drawings made by the *Sioux*, and other Western Indians, upon the fleshy side of their buffalo skins. The exact resemblance cannot be mistaken, as everyone may satisfy himself who will compare the reduced facsimiles given by Dr Robertson, with those which accompany Dr James's account of Colonel Long's travels to the Rocky Mountains.

In the region extending from the Atlantic Ocean to the Rocky Mountains, and from the Great Lakes to the Gulf of Mexico, there were numerous tribes wandering over the country and dividing it among them by very indefinite boundaries, and an imperfect possession. It is impossible to form an enumeration of these tribes, as they existed at the era of the discovery. We have ourselves collected not less than two hundred and seventy-two names * of different tribes which are found in the early narratives and histories;

* Dubois,	Tomeas,	Nez percez.
Cheveux relevez,	Abchas,	Kareses.
Quatoghies,	Talapenches,	Mousonis.
Adnondecks,	Conchakus,	Cawittas.
Capiga,	Pakauds,	Tallpoosas.
Bull heads,	Kaoutyas, or Cowetas,	Coosas.
Mussisakies,	Ouanchas,	Apalachias.
Esopus,	Chenakisses,	Coushaes, or Coosades.
Cheveux ou Port leué,	Escaamba,	Oakmulgis.
Andata honato,	Souriquois,	Oconis.

Oneidas,
Canastoga,
Calmawas,
Arogisti,
Sinodouwas,
Dewagamas,
Lenehas,
Onondagos,
Cayugas,
Wayanoak,
Chictaghicks,
Iwikties,
Utawawas,
Ouyslanous,
Kaskaskias,
Mitchigamuas,
Renais,
Outagamies,
Sioux,
Sauks,
Kickapoos,
Tamawas,
Chactas, or Choctaws,
Peauguicheas, or Pea-
  hushaws, supposed
  to be Peanguicheas,
  or Piankeshaws,
Alibamous,
Taskikis,
Outachepas,
Assinais,
Adaies, or Adayes,
Pammahas,
Epesengles,
Avoyelles,
Chatots,
Thomez,
Chacci Oumas,
Oufe Agoulas,
Tapoussas,
Bayouc Agoulas,
Oque Loussas,
Avoyels,
Otheues,
Wampano,

Cambas,
Peskadaneeoukkanti,
Twightwes,
Salanas,
Shawanoes,
Outagamies,
Kehabous,
Maskuticks,
Mahekandes,
Pottawatimies,
Walhominies,
Puans,
Dionoudadie,
Owenagungas,
Ouiagies,
Ponacocks,
Schahooks,
Agonnousioni,
Canabas,
Etecheneus, or Etch-
  mins,
Malicetes,
Baisimetes,
Papinachois,
Oumamioucks,
Eves, or Chats,
L'Ecureuil,
Mohingaus, supposed
  to be Mohingans or
  Mohicans,
Aisnous,
Tangibao,
Ouabaches,
Biscatonges,
Chininoas,
Choumaus,
Nassonis,
Quanoatinos,
Tarahas,
Palaquessous,
Nabari,
Montagnes, supposed
  to be Montagnard
  or Montagues,
Ochasteguins,

Ockhoys.
Alibam.
Weetumkees.
Paleanas.
Tacusas.
Chacsihoomis.
Alickas.
Odsinachies.
Aunies.
Tuscaroras.
Nehkereages.
Tahsagroudie.
Conestogoe.
Canoyeas, or Nanti-
  hokes.
Conoyucksuchroona.
Cochnewwasroonaw.
Tehoanoughroonaw.
Sachdagughroonaw.
Catawbas.
Chenkus.
Conoy, living among
  the Tuscaroras.
Aquelon pissas, or
  Colla pissas.
Tiaoux.
Oaktashippas.
Wyogtami.
Shogleys.
Musquakees.
Sahohes.
Amikones, or Castor.
Malecites.
Poualakes.
Onyapes.
Apineus.
Mattaugwessawacks.
Nihanticks.
Nepnet.
Dassa Monpeake.
Chickahominies.
Yamassecs.
Nipmuck.
Nianticks.
Norredgewock.

Wamanus,
Chihokokis,
Wapingeis,
Connecedegas,
Rondaxes,
Wasses, mentioned by Long,
Hawoyazask, or Musquash,
Minisuk,
Shawendadies,
Wateree,
Eano,
Charah,
Chowan,
Nachee,
Yamasee,
Coosah,
Callapipas,
Oumas,
Tomkas,
Natches,
Anhawas,
Pehenguichias,
Pr,
Casco,
Pigwachet,
Piscataquas,
Newickawanacks,
Wiscasset,
Passamaquoddy,
St. Francois,
Quinaquous,
Ipati,
Hannetons,
Oua,
Tentouha,
Nadouesteaus, supposed to be Nadowessies,
Arsenipoits,
Chougaskabees,

Ontaouonones,
Andastonez,
Bussenmeus,
Altihamaguez,
Gaspesiens,
Iroquets,
Nation neuht,
Sokoki,
Abenaquis,
Ozembogus,
Tangeboas,
Ostonoos,
Mausalea,
Mousa,
Ossotoues,
Chachachouma,
Yataches,
Onodo,
Napgitache,
Quonantino,
Epicerinis, or Sorciers,
Kiscakous,
Mosookees,
Ouachas,
Caouachas,
Chitimachas,
Hoomas,
Mobilians,
Pasca Oocolos,
Hattahappas, supposed to be Atakapas,
Uchees,
Biloxis,
Ybitoopas,
Mistapnis,
Pascagoulas,
Bayagoulas,
Quinnepas,
Mongontatchas,
Tonicas,
Otchagras,

Wewenocks.
Androscoggins, or Anasaguntacooks.
Tomez.
Corrois.
Offogoulas.
Teoux.
Castachas.
Atakapas.
Ounontcharonnous.
Plats cotez de chiens.
Savanois.
Gaspesiens.
Bersiamitts.
Papenachois.
Montagnez.
Naausi.
Naichoas.
Ouadiches.
Cabinoios.
Mentous.
Ozotheoa.
Dogenga.
Panivacha.
Pera.
Panaloga.
Malatautes.
Tichenos.
Nepissings.
Tamescamengs.
Têtes de boule.
Nation du Castor.
Tetes plates.
Octotates.
Aïouez.
Omaus.
Montagnais.
Torimas.
Topingas.
Sothoues.
Kappas.

It is highly probable that duplicates occur in this list. Montagnes, for example, may mean the same as Montagnais, etc.

and how many more would have been disclosed by further research, we presume not to say. Upon what principle these appellations were originally given, it is impossible to ascertain. They far exceed any actual divisions among the Indians, either social or political, which could have existed; and it would be vain to inquire to what tribes or bands many of them were given. Then, as now, the Indians were doubtless separated into many communities, occupying different regions, and with interests which were, or were supposed to be, various and sometimes adverse. Whether they all descended from a common stock is a question not easily answered. Even at this day, our information concerning the Indian languages is very imperfect. The principles which regulate them are but partially known, and much more severe investigations into their construction will be necessary before we are enabled to ascertain all the points of resemblance which they bear to one another, and all the anomalies they exhibit when compared with the more methodised and finished tongues of the Old World. Many of the Indian languages are evidently cognate dialects, but in attempting to ascend to their common origin, we soon become involved in uncertainty.

The great division of the French writers was into the Huron, or Wyandot, the Algonquin, and the Sioux stocks. These comprehended almost all the tribes known to them, and they yet comprehend much the larger portion of the tribes known to us. But besides these, the present state of our information upon the subject leads to the conclusion that there are three primitive languages spoken by the southern tribes. Of these the Choctaws and the Chickasaws form one; the Creek, or Muskogee, another; and the Cherokee a third. West of the Mississippi the primitive dialects appear to be the Minataree, the Pawnee,

NO-WAY-KE-SUG-GA
An Otto

the Cheyenne, the Blackfeet, and the Padouca, making eleven original stocks between the Gulf of St Lawrence, and the Rocky Mountains.   But it is by no means certain that all these great families are radically different one from another.   Further investigations may exhibit resemblances not yet discovered, and reduce to cognate dialects, languages now supposed to be radically dissimilar.

This great diversity of speech among a race of men presenting in other respects features almost identical, is a subject of curious and interesting speculation.   Everyone who has surveyed the Indians must have been struck with the general resemblance they bear to each other.   In all those physical characteristics which divide them from the other great branches of the human family, they form one people.   The facial angle is the same, and so is the colour, general stature, form of the face, appearance, and colour of the eyes, and the common impression which is made, by the whole, upon the spectator.   These facts indicate a common origin.   But we find among a people occupying the same general region, and with similar habits and modes of life, and unbroken communication, eleven languages, among which no verbal resemblance has been discovered.   And yet, as far as we are acquainted with them, one common principle of construction pervades the whole.   Whence this unity of form and diversity of expression ?   Are they to be traced to the facility with which the words of unwritten languages are changed, and to the tenacity with which we adhere to the process by which our ideas are formed and disclosed ?   If so, these languages have descended from a common origin, and the tribes must have separated from one another at periods more or less remote, as their dialects approach, or recede from, each other.   But this conjecture does not accord with the local relations and established intercourse between many of the tribes. Some of those speaking languages radically different live, and have lived for ages, in juxtaposition, and the most confidential relations have been established among them. This is particularly the case with the Winnebagoes speaking a dialect of the Sioux stock, and the Menomines speaking a dialect of the Algonquin stock; and such is also the case with the Hurons, or Wyandots, and the Ottawas. And it is well known that the Shawanese, whose language is similar to that spoken by the Kickapoo, and other northern tribes, emigrated from the South, and were, when they became first known to the Europeans, planted among the Creeks upon the streams flowing through Florida. The patronymic appellations used by the various tribes indicate a connection very different from that which we should be led to deduce from a comparison of their dialects. We cannot trace these claims of affinity to any known source; but like many usages which have survived the causes that gave birth to them, they were doubtless founded upon established relations existing at the time. The Wyandots claim to be the uncle of all the other tribes; and the Delawares to be the grandfather. But the Delawares acknowledge themselves to be the nephew of the Wyandots, and these two tribes speak languages which have not the most remote resemblance. Whether we shall ever be able to settle these questions is doubtful. At any rate we can only hope to do it by observation, and by a rigid abstinence from idle speculations until our collection of facts shall be greatly enlarged.

In looking back upon the condition of the Indians previously to the arrival of the Europeans, and to the introduction of their manufactures among them, we shall find that He who "tempers the wind to the shorn lamb" had provided them with means of subsistence, and sources of enjoyment suited to their situation and wants. They were divided, as we have seen, into many different tribes, subdivided into various bands or families. This sub-division was an important branch of Indian polity. It would be idle to recount the traditions respecting the origin and objects of this institution. We must be satisfied with surveying them, as they are, or rather as they were, leaving the causes which induced them, whether accidental or designed, among the mysteries of the fabulous period of their history.

The number of these bands among the various tribes was different, and perhaps indefinite. They usually extended, however, from five or six, to twelve or fifteen. Each had a distinct appellative, derived from some familiar animal, as the bear tribe, etc. ; and the figure of the animal giving name to the tribe became the *totem*, or armorial bearing of every individual belonging thereto. When it became necessary to identify a person in any of their rude drawings, or to affix his mark to any instrument prepared by the white man, his totem was first made, and then any particular characteristic added which might apply individually to him. The animal itself thus selected for a *manitou*, or guardian spirit, or at least certain parts of it, were not used for food by any of the tribe, although free for any other person. All those belonging to the same tribe were considered as near relations, and intermarriage among them was strictly prohibited. Among some of these Indian communities, the village or peace chiefs of one tribe were chosen by the other tribes ; and these subdivisions had an important operation upon their government and institutions.

In the autumn, when the flesh and furs of the animals used by the Indians became in season, the various bands

or families separated, and repaired to their proper districts
for hunting. Huts were erected of bark, or logs, in
favourable and sheltered situations, and here the families
resided, the different individuals following their respective
employments. The men devoted themselves to the chase,
with zeal and assiduity. And while the game was
abundant they provided a surplus, which in cold weather
was preserved by freezing, and in moderate weather by
drying or jerking it. No man was excused from this first
and great duty. Boys were anxious to become hunters,
and old men to remain hunters. The pride of both was
enlisted, for both were despised, if unequal to the task.

With the necessary supply of food, however, the labour
of the men ceased. All other duties devolved on the
women. These, as may well be supposed, were arduous
enough. Such has always been the fate of the weaker
sex among barbarous tribes, and it was probably never
more severe than among the North American Indians.
They procured the fuel, which was cut with stone toma-
hawks, and transported it to the camps upon their backs.
They cooked the provisions, dressed the skins, made the
canoes, and performed all the labour not directly connected
with those hunting or hostile excursions which constituted
the occupation of the men. In these employments the
winter was passed away, and industrious and provident
families generally accumulated a considerable stock of
dried meat, and a quantity of furs and skins sufficient for
their wants during the year.

As the spring approached the hunting camps were
evacuated, and the various families collected together in
their villages. These were generally situated upon small
streams, where the land was of the best quality. Here
corn was planted, rudely, and in small quantities, but still
enough to supply them with food for a short time in the

latter part of the summer, and the beginning of autumn. The corn was cultivated entirely by the women. Indelible disgrace would have attached to the warrior who could so far forget himself as to aid in the performance of this, or any other duty requiring manual labour. As they had no domestic animals, no fences were necessary; and the rude instruments then in use allowed them to do little more than plant and cover the seed.

This was the principal season for amusements, for business, and for warlike expeditions. Their whole population was brought together. Days and nights were frequently devoted to feasts, to dances, and athletic games. The young men were engaged in these pastimes, and the others in the discussion and consideration of affairs involving the general interest or security. Difficulties and feuds in the tribe were terminated. If war existed it was prosecuted with vigour, or proposals for peace were made or received. These few months formed, indeed, the social life of the Indian. At all other periods he was a solitary animal, engaged like most other animals in the great duty of self-preservation.

It is easy to conceive that this annual round of employment might be occasionally interrupted—it, no doubt, was so. A successful or a disastrous war changed essentially the condition of a tribe, stimulating or depressing them. An unfavourable season for hunting increased the labour of the men, and added to the privations of their families. There can be little doubt also that all tribes, before the discovery, lived in a state of great insecurity. No fact in their whole history is better established than the universal prevalence of war among them; and their wars were too often wars *ad internecionem*. They fought, like the animals around them, to destroy, and not to subdue. The war-flag **was**

always flying, and the war-drum sounding. Their
villages were generally enclosed with palisades, composed
of the trunks and limbs of trees, burnt at the proper
length, and secured, not by being placed in a ditch, but
by having earth carried and deposited against them.
This earth was doubtless taken from the soil around,
equally, and not by making holes, (because in these
an enemy could shelter himself), and was carried to
the place of deposit by the squaws in skins. And in
this way, by an accumulation of earth for a succession
of ages, we are satisfied, that the earthen parapets, which
so often strike the traveller with wonder in the solitary
forests of the West, have been formed. They are
certainly monuments of aboriginal labour, but of labour
expended for safety and existence during many generations. In the narrative of Cartier's voyage to the
St Lawrence, is a minute description of one of these
fortified villages, occupying the present site of Montreal,
and there called *Hochelaga*. The process of attack and
defence is stated, and the whole corresponds with the
account we have given, and with all we know of the
manners and condition of the Indians.

Their government was then, as it is now, essentially
a government of opinion. It is not probable that any
punishments were ever judicially affixed to crimes. But
their circumstances were such, that few crimes could be
committed. Ardent spirits, the bane of civilised and of
savage life, were unknown among them. No facts have
come down to us indicating that any intoxicating liquor
was ever used by them, consequently their passions were
never excited or inflamed, as they now are, by this
destructive habit. Of real property they had none—for
theirs was a perpetual community in the possession of
their lands; and their personal property was of very

trifling value, consisting of little more than the skins in which they were clothed. There were no motives, therefore, to violate the rights of property, and few to disturb the rights of persons. Murder was almost the only offence which, by universal consent, was followed by punishment; and this punishment, if such it can be called, was the right which the friends of the deceased person possessed to take the life of the offender, or to commute, by receiving some valuable article.

Each tribe had two descriptions of officers, performing different duties, and acting independent of one another. The village, or peace chiefs, directed the civil concerns of the government. They were usually hereditary, or elected from particular families. Among some of the tribes the descent was in the direct line from father to son; among others it was in the collateral line, from the uncle to the nephew—the son of his sister—and where this was the case, the reason given was to insure the succession to the blood of the first chief, which object was certainly attained by selecting the sister's son to succeed each chief. Women were sometimes, but not often, eligible to authority. All these elections and successions were regulated by established rules, as were the ceremonials attending them. The rank of these chiefs was fixed, and generally one of them was the acknowledged head of the tribe, and the others were his counsellors. The external form of the government was arbitrary, but in its practical operation it was a democracy. No question was decided but upon full discussion and deliberation among the chiefs, and doubtless the public opinion produced its effect upon them. These chiefs adjusted any disputes existing among the individuals or families of the tribe; assigned to all their proper hunting districts; received and transmitted messages from and to other tribes; conducted and controlled their great feasts and religious festivals, and concluded peace.

But with the declaration of war terminated these duties, and all the authority of these conscript fathers. Like the decree of the Roman senate, which declared the republic in danger and prostrated all other power before the dictator, the commencement of hostilities suspended all the authority of the village chiefs, and substituted that of the war chiefs. In the selection of these warriors the accident of birth had no influence. Reckless valour; the ability to do and to suffer; the power to lead and command, all proved and displayed in many a bloody combat, could alone elevate an Indian to the command of his countrymen, which dignity conferred little else than the right to lead, and to be the first in every desperate enterprise. Their tactics embraced no combination of movement, none of that system of manœuvres which teaches every combatant that he is a part of a great machine, ruled and regulated by one presiding spirit. Their battles, like those described by Homer, were single combats, in which physical force and courage prevailed.

It is not easy to ascertain their mythological opinions, or their religious doctrines. Almost all the tribes have been more or less the objects of instruction by the missionaries sent among them by various religious societies, established among the Christian nations who have planted colonies on the continent. The effect of the doctrines taught by these missionaries upon the traditions and opinions of the Indians is visible; and it is difficult to separate what they have thus received, from what they have inherited from their forefathers. Nothing can be more crude than these fables and notions, which are certainly their own, and which constitute their system of theology. They probably had an indistinct idea of a future existence, but it was doubtful, shadowy, unproductive, the mere wreck of a revelation made in the early ages of the world, adhered to without knowledge, and without hope. Every object in Nature had a familiar spirit, some for good and some for evil. And the Creator, in their view, seems to have been a gigantic undefined being, contending with the elements, sometimes subduing, and sometimes subdued by them.

It is impossible to reconcile the inconsistent opinions of his power and other attributes, to be deduced from the traditionary fables which they repeat and believe. Under the name *Nanibujo* or some similar appellative, he is known to the tribes of the Algonquin stock, and the idlest and wildest tales are told of his prowess and contests, sometimes with the Deluge, which seems to form an era in all traditions, and sometimes with the imaginary animals with which the water and the land were filled.* We feel no disposition to repeat these stories here. They would scarcely serve the purpose of amusing the reader, and only add to the many existing proofs of the folly to which man is prone in an unenlightened state.

The intellectual acquirements of the Indians were as low as they are recorded to have been among any people on the face of the earth. They had no letters and no learning. Not the slightest rudiments of a single science were known among them. The sun, and moon, and stars, were balls of light set in the heavens. The earth was an island. Their pathology referred every disorder to a spirit which was to be driven out by the noise and incantations of the jugglers, which constituted their

* See McKenney's *Tour to the Lakes*, pp. 302-5, etc.

whole medical science. Their arithmetic enabled them
to count to a hundred, and here, generally, their power
over numbers ceased. Their arts consisted in making
a bow and arrow and canoe, and in taking their game
upon the land and in the water. We presume there was
scarcely an Indian on the continent who could
comprehend an abstract idea, and at this day the
process is neither common nor easy. The great business
of their lives was to procure food, and devour it; and to
subdue their enemies, and scalp them.

Such, in general, was the condition of the Indians
when the Europeans arrived among them. Their sources
of enjoyment were few and simple, and it is possible,
notwithstanding the state of their society was such as we
have depicted it, that they enjoyed some proportion of
happiness. Why they had advanced so little in all that
constitutes the progress of society, it is not easy to
conjecture. The question presents one of the most
difficult problems to be found in the whole history of mankind. Here was a people in the rudest condition, knowing
nothing, and attentive to nothing but their physical
wants; without metallic instruments, agriculture, manufactures, or education; and with the means only of
supplying their most indispensable animal necessities.
Such, doubtless, had been their condition for ages. It
certainly could not have been worse at any period of their
previous history; if it had been, they must have been
more helpless than the animals around them, and from
entire improvidence, and the absence of power to protect
and perpetuate existence, have become extinct.

What then prevented their advancement? Why was
experience lost upon them? Knowing that the alternations
of the seasons would bring with them abundance and
scarcity, why did they not provide for the one when they

possessed the other? The accumulation of knowledge forms the distinguishing characteristic between men and brutes. The boundary which divides reason and instinct is not always well defined, nor easily ascertained. Indeed, who can determine where instinct terminates and reason begins? In some important respects instinct is a less fallible guide than reason. But as instinct was at the Creation, so it is now. It exerts the same influence over the same varieties of living beings and under the same modifications now as heretofore :—whereas reason is now, and has always been, susceptible of indefinite, perhaps infinite improvement. The treasures of knowledge accumulated by those who have gone before us have descended to us. Their experience has become our experience, and we are taught by it what to embrace and what to avoid. But of all this the aboriginal inhabitants of America exhibited no example. They were stationary, looking upon life as a scene of physical exertion, without improving, or attempting to improve. With the exception of the half-civilised empires of Mexico and Peru, the condition and improvement of which we are satisfied were grossly exaggerated by the early adventurers, all the primitive inhabitants, from the Straits of Magellan to Hudson's Bay, were in this state of helpless ignorance and imbecility. Whether they inhabited the mild and genial climates, were burned by the vertical sun of the tropics, or by a still harder fate were condemned to the bleak and sterile regions of the North, all were equally stationary and improvident. Ages passed by and made no impression upon them. The experience of the past, and the aspiration of the future, were alike unheeded. Their existence was confined to the present. We confess our inability to explain this enigma, and we leave it without further observation.

Their previous history and progress are utterly lost—lost in that long interval of darkness which precedes authentic history amongst all nations—it rests, and probably will ever rest, upon the Indians.

In what direction the current of emigration traversed the continent, and when and where it sent out its lateral branches to form distinct communities, and eventually to speak different languages, we have no means of ascertaining. Some of the Indian traditions refer to an Eastern, and some to a Western origin, but most of the tribes trace their descent to the soil they inhabit, and believe their ancestors emerged from the earth. Nothing can be more uncertain, and more unworthy, we will not say of credit, but of consideration, than their earlier traditions; and probably there is not a single fact in all their history, supported by satisfactory evidence, which occurred half a century previously to the establishment of the Europeans. It is well known that important incidents are communicated, and their remembrance preserved, by belts of wampum formed of strings of beads originally made of white clay, in a rude manner, by themselves, but now manufactured for them from shells. These beads were variously coloured, and so arranged as to bear a distant resemblance to the objects intended to be delineated. The belts were particularly devoted to the preservation of speeches, the proceedings of councils, and the formation of treaties. One of the principal counsellors was the *custos rotulorum;* and it was his duty to repeat, from time to time, the speeches and narratives connected with these belts; to impress them fully upon his memory, and to transmit them to his successor. At a certain season every year they were taken from their places of deposit, and exposed to the whole tribe, while the history of each was publicly

recited. It is obvious, that by the principles of associa-
tion these belts would enable those whose duty it was,
to preserve with more certainty and facility the
traditionary narratives; and they were memorials of the
events themselves, like the sacred relics which the Jews
were directed to deposit in the Ark of the Covenant.
How far the intercourse between the various tribes
extended, cannot be known. There is reason to believe
that the victorious Iroquois carried their arms to Mexico.
It has been stated by Mr Stickney, an intelligent observer,
well acquainted with the Indians (having been formerly
Indian agent at Fort Wayne), that he once saw a very
ancient belt among the Wyandots, which they told him
had come from a large Indian nation in the south-west.
At the time of its reception, as ever since, the Wyandots
were the leading tribe in this quarter of the continent.
Placed at the head of the great Indian commonwealth by
circumstances which even their tradition does not record,
they held the great council fire, and possessed the right of
convening the various tribes around it, whenever any
important occurrence required general deliberation. This
belt had been specially transmitted to them, and from the
attendant circumstances and accompanying narrative, Mr
Stickney had no doubt but it was sent by the Mexican
emperor, at the period of the invasion of that country by
Cortez. The speech stated, in substance, that a new and
strange animal had appeared upon the coast, describing
him like the fabled centaurs of antiquity, as part man and
part quadruped; and adding, that he commanded the
thunder and lightning. The object seemed to be to put
the Indians on their guard against this terrible monster,
wherever he might appear.

Could a collection of these ancient belts be now made,
and the accompanying narratives recorded, it would afford

curious and interesting materials, reflecting, no doubt, much light upon the former situation and history of the Indians. But it is vain to expect such a discovery. In the mutations and migrations of the various tribes, misfortunes have pressed so heavily upon them, that they have been unable to preserve their people or their country, much less the memorials of their former power. These have perished in the general wreck of their fortunes—lost, as have been the sites of their council fires, and the graves of their fathers.

When the French first entered the St Lawrence, the great war had commenced between the Wyandots and the Iroquois, which terminated in the entire discomfiture of the former, and produced important effects upon all the tribes within the sphere of its operation. The origin of this war is variously related, but the more probable account refers it to the murder of a small party of Iroquois hunters by some of the young Wyandots, jealous of their success. Previously to this event, the Iroquois had been rebuked by the superior genius and fortune of their rivals, and lived peaceably in their vicinity, without competition, if not without envy, and devoting themselves to the chase. This unprovoked outrage roused their resentment, and finding that no satisfaction could be obtained, that their representations were slighted, and themselves treated with scorn, they took up arms. No contest at its commencement could have appeared more hopeless. Experience, character, influence, numbers, all were in favour of their enemies. And yet this war, commenced under such inauspicious circumstances, ended in the utter prostration, and almost in the extinction of the Wyandots; entailed upon them a series of calamities unexampled in any history, and elevated the Iroquois to the summit of aboriginal power and fame. It produced,

also, the most important consequences upon the whole
course of Indian events during more than a century of
desperate valour and enterprise.   Little did they think,
who commenced this war with arrows pointed with flints,
and with war-clubs rudely made from the hard knots of
trees, that before its termination a new race of men would
arrive among them, destined to exert a final and decisive
influence upon their fate, and bringing with them new
weapons, terrific in their appearance and sound, and more
terrible still by their invisible operation and bloody
effects.

In the sunlight of the Indian condition, there were
redeeming circumstances which did much to balance the
evil resulting from their peculiar condition and institutions.
Their solemn assemblies and grave deliberations around
their council fires presented imposing spectacles.   From
some of the facts incidentally stated by the early French
historians, it is obvious that the chiefs were then treated
with much more respect than is now paid them.   It was
the duty of the young hunters to provide them with the
food and furs necessary for the support and clothing of
their families.   It was, in fact, a tax levied under the
conciliatory name of present.   The sieur Perrot, who was
sent in 1671 with messages from the Governor-General of
Canada to many of the western tribes, states that the
great chief of the Miamies then lived at Chicago, upon
Lake Michigan.   That he was constantly attended by a
guard of forty young warriors, as well for state as for
security, and the ceremonies of introduction to him were
grave and imposing.   All this evinces the consideration
then attached to the chiefs, which gave to them much
personal influence, and to their opinions much weight
and authority.   This deference served to counteract the
democratic tendency of their institutions, and operated in

the same manner as the more artificial checks in civilised
governments. Age, and wisdom, and experience, were
thus protected from rude interruption, and the rashness of
youth, as well as from those sudden tempests of passion,
to which they are as easily exposed as their own lakes to
the tempests that sweep over them.

In comparing the present situation of the Indians with
their condition before the discovery, great allowances must
be made for the changes which have been produced, and
for their general deterioration in manners, in morals, and
in extrinsic circumstances. There are, and no doubt
always have been, radical defects in their institutions—
defects peculiar to themselves, and which have made them
a phenomenon among the human family. That there are
varieties in the human race, is a physiological truth which
will not be questioned. The controversy begins only when
the causes of this diversity are investigated, and their
extent and effects are estimated. This wide field of
discussion we shall not enter. And it must be left to
future inquirers to ascertain whether the physical
differences so obviously discernible in comparisons between
the Caucasian, Mongolian, Ethiopian, Malay, and other
varieties, are the cause or the consequence of the peculiar
moral characteristics by which the various races of men are
distinguished.

The aboriginal inhabitants of America are marked by
external features peculiar to themselves, and which
distinguish them from all the other descendants of Adam.
They are marked too by peculiar opinions, habits, manners,
and institutions. The effect of the coming of the Europeans
among them cannot be doubted. They have diminished
in numbers, deteriorated in morals, and lost all the most
prominent and striking traits of their character. It were
vain to speculate now upon the position they would have

NO-TIN
A Chippeway Chief

occupied, had they abandoned their own institutions, and coalesced with the strangers who came among them.

But these more general observations can give but an indefinite idea of the circumstances and situation of the Indians. We must not only survey them as one people, possessing similar characteristics, but we must view them also in detached groups, as they actually lived, and occupied different portions of the country, each pursuing their course independent of, and too often at war with, their neighbours. But in this general sketch we shall not attempt to trace the history of all the tribes whose names have come down to us. Such a task would be alike hopeless and unprofitable. We shall confine ourselves to the more prominent divisions, whose progress, condition, and fate are best known to us.

The tribes occupying that part of the United States east of the Hudson River, were known to the other Indians under the general name of *Wabenauki*, or men of the east. Their languages were cognate dialects, branches of the Algonquin stock, and bearing a very perceptible resemblance to one another. It cannot be doubted that all these tribes had one origin ; and that their separation into distinct communities had taken place at no very remote period when our acquaintance with them first commenced.

Heavily indeed have time and circumstances pressed upon them. They may all be considered as extinct, for the few wretched individuals who survive have lost all that was worth possessing of their own character, without acquiring anything that is estimable in ours. As the great destroyer has thus blighted the relations which once existed between these Indians and our forefathers, it does not fall within our plan to review their former condition, and to trace the history of the numerous small bands into

which they appear to have been divided. Little besides
the names of many of them is now known, and these have
probably been multiplied by the ignorance and carelessness
of observers but imperfectly acquainted with them. The
Narragansets and the Pequods are the two tribes with
whose names and deeds we are most familiar. The former
from their skill in the manufacture of wampum, earthen
vessels, and other articles, originally used by the Indians ;
and the latter from their prowess in war, and from the
desperate resistance they made to the progress of the white
men. Their principal chief, known to us by the English
name Philip, appears to have been an able and intrepid
man, contending under the most discouraging circumstances
against invaders of his country, and falling with the fall of
all that was dear to him, when further resistance was
impracticable. His name, with the names of Pontiac
and Tecumthe, and a few others, seem alone destined to
survive the oblivion which rests upon the forest warriors
and upon their deeds.

The Mohegans occupied most of the country upon the
Hudson River, and between that river and the Connecticut.
Conflicting accounts are given of their language and origin,
but since more accurate investigations have been made
into the general subject of our Indian relations, we know
that they are a branch of the Delaware family, and closely
connected with the parent stocks. So far as our information
extends, this was their original country, for the wild
traditions which have been gravely recorded and repeated,
respecting the migrations and fortunes of this great
aboriginal family, are unworthy of serious consideration.
A few hundreds of this tribe are yet remaining, but they
abandoned their primitive seats many years ago, and
attached themselves to some of their kindred bands. A
few of them have passed the Mississippi, and others are

residing in Upper Canada, but the larger portion have established themselves at Green Bay.

The Six Nations, known to the French as the Iroquois, and to the English as the Mingoes, were the most powerful tribe of Indians upon the continent. They originally occupied the country north of Lake Ontario, but after the commencement of hostilities between them and the Wyandots, and their allies the Algonquins, they removed to the south of that lake, and established their residence in what is now the western part of the State of New York. At the commencement of this contest, they were so unequal to their adversaries that they withdrew beyond the sphere of their operations, and engaged in hostilities with the Shawanese, then living upon the southern shore of Lake Erie. Their efforts were here successful, and they expelled this tribe from their country, and took possession. Emboldened by success, and having acquired experience in war, from which they had long refrained, they turned their arms against their enemies to revenge the injuries they had received. A long and bloody contest ensued, and it was raging when the French occupied the banks of the St Lawrence. They took part with the Wyandots and Algonquins, and Champlain accompanied a war-party in one of their expeditions, and upon the shore of the lake which bears his name, fought a battle with the Iroquois, and defeated them by the use of fire-arms, which then became first known to these aborigines. But the latter were soon furnished with the destructive weapon of European warfare by the English and Dutch, and their career of conquest extended to the Mississippi. The Wyandots and Algonquins were almost exterminated, and the feeble remnant were compelled to seek refuge in the Manitoulin Islands, which line the northern coast of Lake Huron. Their inexorable enemies followed them into these secluded

regions, and finally compelled them to flee among the
Sioux, then living west of Lake Superior.

During almost a century they harassed the French
settlements, impeded their progress, and even bearded them
under the walls of Quebec.   It has been thought that
Champlain and his successors in authority, who controlled
the destiny of New France, committed a great political
error in identifying their cause with that of either of the
hostile parties.   But a neutral course was impracticable.
Aboriginal politics necessarily associated with the great
contest for supremacy, then pending between the Iroquois
and their enemies.   It was the absorbing topic of discussion,
and those who were friendly to one party, were of course
hostile to the other.   Had the French declined the overtures
of both, they would have acquired the confidence of neither,
and probably have furnished another proof of the inefficacy
of temporising measures in great questions of public policy.
They naturally attached themselves to those of their own
immediate vicinity, and the others were as naturally
thrown into the arms of the English.   During the
long contest between these two European powers for
supremacy upon the continent, the Iroquois were
generally found in the English interest, and the other
tribes in the French.

History furnishes few examples of more desperate
valour, more daring enterprise, or more patriotic devotion,
than are found in these wars, first waged by the Iroquois
for that revenge which they regarded as justice, but
afterwards for conquest.

Those Indians present the only example of intimate
union recorded in aboriginal history.   They consisted
originally of five tribes, namely, the *Mohawks*, the
Onondagos, the *Senecas*, the *Oneidas*, and the *Cayugas*.
About the year 1717, the *Tuscaroras* joined the Con-

federacy, and formed the sixth tribe—from this period the Iroquois were sometimes known as the Five Nations, and sometimes as the Six Nations.

The origin of this Confederacy is unknown to us.   It existed when they became first known to the whites.   So imperfect were the investigations made into these subjects, that the principles of their union are but little understood. Each tribe probably managed its internal concerns independent of all the others.   But the whole seem to have formed an Amphictyonic league, in which subjects of general interest were discussed and determined.   The Tuscarora tribe had occupied a portion of North Carolina, but they became involved in difficulties with the people of that province, and after a series of disasters were compelled to abandon it.   Their language resembles that spoken by the other tribes of the Confederacy, and there is little doubt but at some former period they had been united by an intimate connection, and probably by the ties of consanguinity.   They must have separated from the kindred stock, and been led by circumstances, now unknown, to migrate to North Carolina; and thence perhaps after a lapse of ages, they were driven back to their ancient possessions.   Dr Williamson has observed, that "this migration of the Tuscarora Indians, and other migrations of Indian tribes, well attested, do not accord with Lord Kames' observation, that 'savages are remarkably attached to their native soil.'"   There are many instances in the history of the Indians where their primitive country has been abandoned, and a new one obtained by favour or by power.   These migrations, however, have seldom, perhaps never, been voluntary, but the result of untoward circumstances, submitted to with great reluctance.   They are certainly far from drawing in question the accuracy of the observation referred to.

Of this once powerful Confederacy, about six thousand individuals now remain. The larger portion of them live upon a reservation near Buffalo in the State of New York : a few are found in Pennsylvania, and some in Ohio, at Green Bay, and in Canada.

The Delawares were situated principally upon tide-water in New Jersey, Pennsylvania, and Delaware. Their own appellation of *Lenne Lenape,* or original people, has been almost forgotten by themselves, and is never used by the other tribes. This is the family about which so many fables have been related, and credited. Occupying the country between the Hudson and Potomac Rivers, and between the eastern slope of the Allegheny Mountains and the ocean, they became early known to the Moravians, and engaged the care and attention of the zealous missionaries employed by those exemplary Christians. The whole subject of Indian relations was fresh and new to them. They seem never to have known, or to have heeded, that enterprising, sagacious, and learned men, had long preceded them in these investigations, and had traversed the continent, surveying the condition of its inhabitants, and inquiring into the changes they had undergone. All that the Delawares told of themselves seems to have been received without suspicion, and recorded and repeated without scrutiny. It is easy for those who have formed much acquaintance with the Indians to trace the circumstances which gave to the legends of the Delawares such authority, and to the teachers of the Delawares such credulity.

The Moravians were first planted among these Indians. Their inoffensive lives, and disinterested efforts to improve them, soon created mutual confidence and attachment. The Moravians followed them in their various migrations, from the Susquehannah to the Ohio, from the Ohio to the

Muskingum, from the Muskingum to Lake St Clair, and thence in many of their wanderings, that have at last terminated in their passage across the Mississippi, which, like the fabled river, dividing the living from the dead can never be recrossed by an Indian community.

During this long, frequently perilous, and always pious intercourse, the attention of the missionaries was directed exclusively to their neophytes.   The manners, customs, and condition of the other tribes were a sealed book to them.   And when the old Delaware chief recounted their transactions, dwelling with fond regret upon the fallen fortunes of their nation, and explaining the subtle policy of the Iroquois, by which the Delawares were reduced to the condition of women, it was perhaps natural that the tale should be believed.   Its utter inconsistency with the whole course of Indian conduct, and with the authentic series of events, as they appear in the early French narratives, before this pretended self-abasement, was unknown to these unsuspecting, worthy men.   He who has heard Indian traditions, related by age, and listened to by youth, in the midst of an Indian camp, with every eye upon the speaker, and "all appliances to boot," must be sensible of the impression they are calculated to make.   And we may well excuse the spirit in which they were received.

The Delawares, at the period when our knowledge of them commenced, had yielded to the ascendancy of the Iroquois ; and were apparently contented with their submission.   The circumstances of the conquest are entirely unknown to us.   But of the result there is no doubt.   The proceedings of a council, recorded by Colden, held with the Iroquois and Delawares, at Philadelphia, in 1742, by the Governor of Pennsylvania, is conclusive upon this point.   The Iroquois appealed to the Governor, as the acknowledged, paramount authority, to remove

VOL. III.   C the Delawares from a tract of land which they had ceded to Pennsylvania many years before, but the possession of which they refused to relinquish. The complaint was made in open council, at which the Iroquois and Delawares were both present, and at the next sitting it was answered by the former in these words :—"We have concluded to remove them, and oblige them to go over the river Delaware, . . ."; and then turning to the Delawares, the speaker said :—"Cousins, let this belt of wampum serve to chastise you. You ought to be taken by the hair of the head and stretched severely till you recover your senses and become sober. But how came you to take upon you to sell land at all ? We conquered you ; we made women of you ; you know you are women, and is it fit that you should have the power of selling lands, since you would abuse it ? The land you claim is expended ; you have been furnished with clothes, meat and drink by the goods paid you for it, and now you want it again, like children, as you are. And for all these reasons we charge you to remove instantly. We don't give you the liberty to think about it. Don't deliberate, but remove away, and take this belt of wampum."

This being interpreted by Conrad Wesir into English, and by Cornelius Spring into the Delaware language, Canepitigo, taking a string of wampum, added further :—

"After our just reproof, and absolute order to depart from the lands, you have now to take notice of what we have further to say to you. This string of wampum serves to forbid you, your children, and grandchildren, to the latest posterity, for ever, meddling in land affairs ; neither you, nor any who shall descend from you, are ever hereafter to presume to sell any land. For which purpose you are to preserve this string, in memory of what your uncles have this day given you in charge. We have some other

MON-CHONSIA
A Kansas Chief

TAH-COL-O-QUOIT
A Saukie Warrior

business to transact with our brethren, (the whites) and therefore depart the council, and consider what has been said to you. "

He who can believe, after this, the idle tales related of the power and prowess of the Delawares, must be left to his credulity.

The principal portion of this tribe emigrated from Pennsylvania many years since, and established themselves in Ohio. Thence they removed to White River, in Indiana; a few years ago they crossed the Mississippi, and now occupy a reservation secured to them in the southwestern part of Missouri.

The Wyandots stood at the head of the great Indian Confederacy. How this pre-eminence was acquired, or how long it had been enjoyed, there are none to tell. They were originally established on the St Lawrence, but during their long and disastrous contests with the Iroquois they were greatly reduced, and compelled to flee before these victorious enemies. From their local position, they engaged the care and attention of the Roman Catholic missionaries at a very early period, and their history, for upwards of two centuries, is better known than that of any other tribe. After the Iroquois began to gain the ascendancy, the calamities endured by the Wyandots are unparalleled in the history of nations. Their enemies pursued them with the most unrelenting rigour, and without attempting to trace the incidents of this war, we shall merely observe, that the Wyandots were driven to seek protection from the Sioux, at the western extremity of Lake Superior. They here remained until the Iroquois were crippled by their wars with the French, when they returned to Lake Huron, and established themselves for a short time in the vicinity of Michilimackinac. Dissatisfied with that sterile region, they descended the Detroit River about the period when the French formed their first settlements in that quarter, and afterwards took possession of the Sandusky Plains, in Ohio. A small portion of the tribe yet live upon the river *aux Canards,* in Upper Canada ; and a still smaller portion upon the river Huron of Lake Erie, in the Michigan territory. The principal part, however, occupy the country upon the Sandusky River, in Ohio. Their entire population, at this period, is about seven hundred.

This tribe was not unworthy of the pre-eminence it enjoyed. The French historians describe them as superior, in all the essential characteristics of savage life, to any other Indians upon the continent. And at this day, their intrepidity, their general deportment, and their lofty bearing, confirm the accounts which have been given to us. In all the wars upon our borders, until the conclusion of Wayne's Treaty, they acted a conspicuous part, and their advice in council, and conduct in action, were worthy of their ancient renown.

They possessed the right to convene the several tribes at the great council fire, always burning at the lodge of their principal chief, called *Sarstantzee,* who lived at Browns-town, at the mouth of the Detroit River. Whenever any subject involving the general interest of the tribes required discussion, they despatched messages to the country, demanding the attendance of their chiefs, and they opened and presided at the deliberations of the council.

The ingenuity of vengeance has perhaps never devised a more horrible punishment than that provided among this tribe for murder. The corpse of the murdered man was placed upon a scaffold, and the murderer extended upon his back, and tied below. He was here left, with barely food enough to support life, until the remains of the murdered subject above him became a mass of putridity, falling upon him, and then all food was withheld, when he perished thus miserably.   There were no traces of a similar punishment among any other tribe.

The Ottawas were the faithful allies of the Wyandots, during all their misfortunes, and accompanied them in their various peregrinations.   They are now much scattered, occupying positions upon the Maumee, upon the Grand River of Lake Michigan, upon the eastern and western coasts of that lake, and upon the heads of the Illinois River.   Their number is about four thousand.

To this tribe belonged the celebrated Pontiac.   He was born about the year 1714, and while a young man distinguished himself in the various wars in which the Ottawas were engaged.   He gradually acquired an ascendancy over his countrymen, and his name and actions became known to all the tribes in the north-west.   He was a faithful adherent to the French interest, and a determined enemy of the English.   During many years of the long contest between those powers, which terminated in the utter subversion of the French empire in America, he was present in all the important actions, stimulating his countrymen by his authority and example. Major Rogers states in his narrative, that when he marched into the Ottawa country with his first detachment, which took possession of the posts in the north-west, Pontiac met him with a party of his warriors, and told him he stood in his path, and would not suffer him to advance.   By amicable professions, however, Major Rogers conciliated him, and for a short time he appeared to be friendly. But his attachment to the French, and hostility to the British, were too deeply rooted to be eradicated, and he concerted a scheme for the overthrow of the latter, and for their expulsion from the country.   No plan formed by the Indians for defence or revenge, since the discovery of the continent, can be compared with this, in the ability displayed in its formation, or in the vigour with which it was prosecuted. The British had then eleven military posts covering that frontier : at Niagara, at Presque Isle, at Le Bœuf, at Pittsburgh, at Sandusky, at the Maumee, at Detroit, at Michilimackinac, at Green Bay, and at St Joseph. Pontiac meditated a contemporaneous attack upon all these posts, and after their reduction, a permanent confederacy among the Indians, and a perpetual exclusion of the British from the country. Like Tecumthe, he called the superstition of the Indians to the aid of his projects, and disclosed to them the will of the Great Spirit, which he prevailed on them to believe had been revealed to him by the various prophets over whom he had acquired an influence. One great object was to render his people independent of the white men, by persuading them to resume their ancient mode of life.

To follow the history of Pontiac in his eventful career, would lead us too far from the course we have prescribed for ourselves. Some of the principal facts are recorded in the journals of that day, but these are the mere outlines. All that gives interest to the picture lives only in the Indian and Canadian tradition, and in the few manuscript notices of these transactions, which have been accidentally preserved.

Eight of these posts were captured. But Niagara, Pittsburgh, and Detroit, were successfully defended. The siege of the latter is by far the most extraordinary effort ever made by the Indians in any of their wars. It commenced in May, 1763, and continued with more or less vigour, until the place was relieved by General Bradstreet in 1764. During this period many of the events seem more like the incidents of romance, than the occurrences of an Indian campaign. Among these were the attempt to gain possession of the town by treachery, and its providential disclosure; the attack upon one of the British armed vessels by a fleet of canoes, and the precipitate retreat of the assailants, after gaining possession of the vessel, in consequence of orders being given by the captain to fire the magazine, which were overheard, and communicated to the Indians by a white man, who had been taken captive by them early in life; the battle of the "Bloody Bridge," well named from this sanguinary action, in which an aid-de-camp of Sir Jeffrey Amherst commanded and fell, and the desperate efforts twice made by blazing rafts to set fire to the armed vessels anchored in front of the town—these, among many events of subordinate interest, give a character of perseverance and of systematic effort to this siege, for which we shall in vain look elsewhere in Indian history. If contemporary accounts and traditionary recollections can be credited, all these were the result of the superior genius of Pontiac, and of the ascendancy he had gained over his countrymen.

The subsequent fate of this warrior chief did not correspond with the heroic spirit he displayed in his efforts against the British. After their power upon the frontier was re-established, he left the country and took refuge among the Indians upon the Illinois. From some trivial cause a quarrel arose between him and a Peoria Indian, which terminated in his assassination.

Such was the respect in which his memory was held, that the other tribes united in a crusade against the Peorias to revenge his death, and that tribe was, in effect, exterminated.

The Chippeways (or Ojibways) reach from Lake Erie to the Lake of the Woods, possessing a country of great extent, much of which, however, is sterile in its soil, and bleak in its climate. They possess the coasts of Lake Huron and Lake Superior, the heads of the Mississippi, some of the western coast of Lake Michigan, and have a joint interest with the Ottawas and Pottawatimies in the country of the Fox and Des Pleines Rivers in Illinois. Their numbers are computed at fifteen thousand.

These Indians live generally upon the Great Lakes, and upon the streams flowing into them. Fish forms an important article of their food, and they are expert in the manufacture of bark canoes, the only kind used by them, and in their management. In cleanliness, in docility, and in provident arrangement, they are inferior to many of the other tribes; and those in the immediate vicinity of our frontier posts and settlements, furnish melancholy examples of the effect of the introduction of spirituous liquors among them. All the bands extending to the Arctic Circle, and occupying the territories of the Hudson's Bay Company, appear to be branches of this great family. The principal seat of their power and government was formerly at Point Chegoimegon upon Lake Superior, and from the accounts of the Catholic missionaries stationed among them, they were then a prosperous and influential tribe.

The Pottawatimies are situated principally in the northern parts of Indiana and Illinois, in the southwestern section of Lake Michigan, and in the country between that lake and the Mississippi. They are estimated at about six thousand five hundred.

This was formerly the most popular tribe north of the Ohio. They are remarkable for their stature, symmetry, and fine personal appearance. Their original country was along the southern shore of Lake Michigan, but they extended themselves to the White River in Indiana on the south, to the Detroit River on the east, and to the Rock River on the west. And they first interposed an effectual barrier to the victorious career of the Iroquois.

Between these three last named tribes, the Ottawas, Chippeways, and Pottawatimies, a more intimate union existed than between any of the other tribes, not actually forming a strict confederacy. Their languages approach so near, that they understand one another without difficulty. They have but one council fire, in other words, but one assemblage of chiefs, in which their important business is managed. And until recently they were unwilling to conclude any important affair, unless around this common council fire. But this institution, like many of their other peculiar customs, is fast mouldering away. Many of the circumstances which gave influence and authority to these grave convocations, have long since disappeared. The ashes of their council fires are scattered over the land, and the plough has turned up the bones of their forefathers.

The Shawanese for more than a century have been much separated, and their bands have resided in different parts of the country. A considerable portion of them live upon a reservation at Waupaukonetta in Ohio, but a majority have crossed the Mississippi, and have recommenced the life of warriors and hunters, in hostile attacks upon the Osages, and in the pursuit of the buffalo. This transmigration commenced during our revolutionary war. They made their first settlement, on their removal, near Cape Girardeau. This position they have since relinquished, and they are now much dispersed in Louisiana, in Arkansas, and in Missouri. The tribe numbers about two thousand persons.

Much obscurity rests upon the history of the Shawanese. Their manners, customs, and language indicate a northern origin, and upwards of two centuries ago they held the country south of Lake Erie. They were the first tribe which felt the force, and yielded to the superiority of the Iroquois. Conquered by them, they migrated to the south, and from fear or favour, were allowed to take possession of a region upon Savannah River, but what part of that river, whether in Georgia or Florida, is not known—it is presumed, the former. How long they resided there, we have not the means of ascertaining; nor have we any account of the incidents of their history in that country, or of the causes of their leaving it. One, if not more of their bands removed from thence to Pennsylvania, but the larger portion took possession of the country upon the Miami and Sciota Rivers in Ohio, a fertile region, where their habits, more industrious than those of their race generally, enabled them to live comfortably.

This is the only tribe among all our Indians who claim for themselves a foreign origin. Most of the aborigines of the continent believe their forefathers ascended from holes in the earth, and many of them assign a *local habitation* to these traditionary places of nativity of their race. Resembling, in this respect, some of the traditions of antiquity, and derived, perhaps, from that remote period, when barbarous tribes were troglodytes, subsisting upon the spontaneous productions of the earth. The Shawanese believe their ancestors inhabited a foreign land, which, from some unknown cause, they determined to abandon. They collected their people together, and marched to the sea-shore. Here various persons were selected to lead them, but they declined the duty, until it was undertaken by one of the Turtle tribe. He placed himself at the head of the procession, and walked into the sea. The waters immediately divided, and they passed along the bottom of the ocean, until they reached this *"island."*

The Shawanese have one institution peculiar to themselves. Their nation was originally divided into twelve tribes or bands, bearing different names. Each of these tribes was subdivided, in the usual manner, into families of the Eagle, the Turtle, etc., these animals constituting their *totems*. Two of these tribes have become extinct, and their names are forgotten. The names of the other ten are preserved, but only four of these are now kept distinct. These are the Makostrake, the Pickaway, the Kickapoo, and the Chilicothe tribes. Of the six whose names are preserved, but whose separate characters are lost, no descendants of one of them, the Wauphautha-wonaukee, now survive. The remains of the other five have become incorporated with the four subsisting tribes. Even to this day, each of the four sides of their council houses is assigned to one of these tribes, and is invariably occupied by it. Although, to us, they appear the same people, yet they pretend to possess the power of discerning, at sight, to which tribe an individual belongs.

The celebrated Tecumthe, and his brother *Tens-kwau-ta-waw*, more generally known by the appellation of "The Prophet," were Shawanese, and sprung from the Kickapoo tribe. They belonged to the family, or *totem*, of The Panther, to the males of which alone was the name *Tecumthe*, or *Flying across*, given.

Their paternal grandfather was a Creek, and their grandmother a Shawanese. The name of their father was Pukeshinwau, who was born among the Creeks, but removed with his tribe to Chilicothe upon the Sciota. Tecumthe, his fourth son, was born upon the journey. Pukeshinwau was killed at the battle at Point Pleasant, at the mouth of the Kenhawa, in 1774, and The Prophet was one of three posthumous children, born at the same birth, a few months afterwards.

We shall not here relate the incidents of the lives of these two men, who exercised, for many years, such a powerful influence over the minds of their countrymen— one by his prowess and reputation as a warrior, and the other by his shrewdness, and by the pretensions to a direct intercourse with the Great Spirit, and to the character and qualifications of a prophet. The elevation and authority of Tecumthe resulted from the operation of causes which are felt among all nations, and at all times—resource and energy in war, and success in battle.

This is the Tecumthe who fell in the late war between the United States and Great Britain, in the memorable battle of The Thames, in Upper Canada, and, as we believe, by the hand of Colonel Richard M. Johnson, of Kentucky.

The influence acquired by The Prophet arose from circumstances peculiar to the Indians, characteristic of the state of their society, and of the superstitious notions prevalent among them. The title of Prophet, as conferred by us upon this sagacious impostor and fanatic, conveys a very inadequate idea of his pretensions. Every tribe has its prophets, who perform distinguished parts in all public transactions. Their celebrity and influence are sometimes confined to their own tribe, and sometimes extended to those which are circumjacent, depending upon the success of their power of vaticination. But of all these magicians or prophets, no one ever attained equal fame, or exercised equal authority with the Shawanese prophet, at first called Sau-te-was-e-kaw, but afterwards Tens-kwau-ta-waw, or the *Open Door*. His name, and the accounts of his miracles, spread from Lake Superior to Florida, and there was not a tribe of Indians in all this vast extent, that did not steadily direct their attention to this man, looking for some signal interposition to check the ascendancy of the whites, and to restore the Indians to their former and better condition. During a few of the first years of this century, great agitation prevailed among the Indians, and they were evidently looking for some great and immediate crisis in their affairs. This feeling was manifested in the alarm upon the frontiers, and, united with other causes, the most prominent of which was foreign influence, led to the battle of Tippecanoe, and eventually to the co-operation of some of the tribes with the British.

The history of this paroxysm of fanaticism would exhibit many curious and interesting traits of human character, and might be compared with similar delusions which have prevailed in more civilised communities. The Prophet established himself at Greenville, upon the Miami of the Ohio, where he was attended by delegates from various tribes. He recommended to the Indians to refrain from the use of whisky, and to free themselves from all dependence upon the whites, by resuming, as far as possible, their ancient habits of life. Under the pretence of extirpating witchcraft, he inflamed the minds of the Indians against every enemy or rival, and procured their destruction. He gathered round him a band of faithful believers, prepared to execute his orders upon friend or foe. Universal panic prevailed among the Indians, and had not still stronger apprehensions overpowered their delusion, by the critical relations between the United States and Great Britain, and the evident approach of war, the Shawanese Prophet might have become the *Mahamet* of his race.

In how much of all this he was an impostor, and how much a fanatic, it is impossible to tell, and was perhaps unknown to himself. The progress of delusion over ourselves is established by the whole history of mankind, and the confines of fanaticism and imposture are separated by imperceptible boundaries. In the relations which he gave of his intentions, opinions, and history, he appears to have been candid, and willing to disclose everything known to him. But we shall not fatigue the reader with this narrative.

The Prophet is yet living, but has removed west of the Mississippi, and joined the Shawanese of that region. Wherever he may be, his talents will give him influence over the Indians.

The Kickapoos were doubtless united with the Shawanese at a period not very distant. The traditions of each tribe contain similar accounts of their union and separation; and the identity of their language furnishes irrefragable evidence of their consanguinity. We are inclined to believe that when the Shawanese were over-powered by the Iroquois, and abandoned their country upon Lake Erie, they separated into two great divisions; one of which, preserving their original appellation, fled into Florida, and the other, now known to us as the Kickapoos, returned to the West, and established themselves among the Illinois Indians, upon the extensive prairies on that river, and between it and the Mississippi. This region they have, however, relinquished to the United States, and have emigrated to Missouri, near the centre of which State a reservation has been secured to them. This tribe numbers about two thousand two hundred.

The Miamies, when first known to the French, were living around Chicago, upon Lake Michigan. It was the chief of this tribe, whose state and attendance were depicted by the sieur Perrot in such strong colours; Charlevoix, without vouching for the entire accuracy of the relation, observes, that in his time there was more deference paid by the Miamies to their chiefs, than by any other Indians.

This tribe removed from Lake Michigan to the Wabash, where they yet retain an extensive tract of country upon which they reside. A kindred tribe, the Weas, more properly called the Newcalenous, long lived with the Miamies. But they have recently separated from them, and crossed the Mississippi. Their whole number does not exceed three hundred and fifty. Of the Miamies, about one thousand yet remain.

This tribe was formerly known to the English as the Twighwees. They appear to have been the only Indians in the West, with the exception of one other tribe, the Foxes, who at an early period were attached to the English interest. The causes which led to this union are unknown, but for many years they produced a decisive effect upon the fortunes of the Miamies.

That strangest of all institutions in the history of human waywardness, the man-eating society, existed among this tribe. It extended also to the Kickapoos, but to how many others we do not know. It appears to have been the duty of the members of this society to eat any captives who were taken, and delivered to them for that purpose. The subject itself is so revolting at this day, even to the Indians, that it is difficult to collect the traditionary details concerning this institution. Its duties and its privileges, for it had both, were regulated by long usage, and its whole ceremonial was prescribed by a horrible ritual! Its members belonged to one family, and inherited this odious distinction. The society was a religious one, and its great festivals were celebrated in the presence of the whole tribe. During the existence of the present generation, this society has flourished, and performed its shocking duties, but they are now wholly discontinued, and will be ere long forgotten.

The various tribes on the Illinois River were known to the French as the Illinois Indians, but the appellation was rather descriptive of their general residence, than of any intimate union, political or social, subsisting among them. And it is not easy to ascertain precisely the tribes which were included under this term. The Kaskias, the Cahokias, the Peorias, the Michigamies, the Tamorias, the

Piankeshaws, inhabited that region, and all spoke dialects bearing a close resemblance to one another, and nearly allied to the language of the Miamies and Weas. Some of these tribes are extinct, and others are reduced to a few individuals. The Piankeshaws are the most numerous, and they number but three hundred and fifty individuals. The whole have passed over the Mississippi.

When the French first explored the country on the Illinois, the buffalo were so numerous that they were denominated the Illinois ox. All the accounts of that early period concur in representing the aboriginal population as abundant. One of the tribes, called the Mascontires, or people of the prairie, has disappeared. They make a considerable figure in the earlier journals, and were probably a branch of the Pottawatimies.

The Illinois River furnished, for many years, the principal communication between the lakes and the Mississippi, and was the connecting ligament which held together the French possessions in Canada and Louisiana. The Indians, therefore, upon this line, were early known to the French, who devoted great care and attention to them. No circumstance ever occurred to interrupt their mutual harmony, and the Illinois Indians appear to have been among the mildest of the aboriginal race. They gathered round the French posts, anxious to secure protection—but a series of calamities pursued them, unexampled even in the aboriginal history, and which finally led to their entire destruction. Before the power of the Iroquois was broken, these fierce people carried their victorious arms to the prairies of the Illinois, as well as to the sands of Florida, the rugged hills of New England, and the deep forests of Canada. The villages and camps of these comparatively mild people were frequently attacked, and the inhabitants destroyed; and for many

years it was considered dangerous to pass along the
Illinois River, lest the *Mengue* should start from some
secret covert, or projecting point, to do their deeds of
horror.   After the decline of the confederacy, a war
commenced between the Illinois Indians and the Winnebagoes, and the latter sent many war parties into the
territories of their enemies.   In one of these, which took
the route of Lake Michigan in canoes, tradition says that
a violent storm arose, in which six hundred Winnebago
warriors perished.   Mutual exhaustion, however, led to
the decline of this contest, but peace did not visit these
fair and fertile regions.   The Sauks and Foxes, unable
to live a life of peace, after their signal discomfiture by
the French and their confederated allies upon Fox River,
took up the tomahawk against the Illinois tribes, and
prosecuted the warfare with equal vigour and fury.   They
poured their war parties over the whole country—burning,
murdering, and destroying.   The Illinois Indians were
almost exterminated.   The feeble remnant that survived
endeavoured to interest the French in their favour, and
they sought protection under the guns of their posts.
But the French did not consider it politic to interfere
between the contending parties, or perhaps felt unable to
stay the tide of victory, and these unfortunate Indians
were abandoned to their merciless enemies.

The Sauks and Foxes, known to the French as the
Saukies and Ottagamies, were originally distinct tribes.
Circumstances have produced an intimate union between
them, and in their relations with the other Indians, they
may be considered as forming but one tribe.   The distinction between them is every day giving way to time and
to mutual intercourse, and in a few years all difference
will be unknown.   Their country is upon the Mississippi,
extending from the *Des Moines* to the Ioway River, and

stretching westwardly beyond the Council Bluffs upon the Missouri, and into the immense prairies * periodically visited by the buffalo.   The Sauks and Foxes, like all the Indians occupying regions where these animals resort, annually hunt them in the proper season.   This is their harvest, yielding them abundance of meat, which they dry and transport to their villages for the subsistence of their families.   At those periods those immense level plains are literally alive with countless thousands of those animals, when the whole Indian population engages in the animating task of hunting them.   Their flesh is the Indians' food; and their skins furnish clothing and tents.   With the unconquerable aversion of the Indians to labour, it is difficult to conceive how they could subsist, were it not for these living and abundant harvests, sent in the hour of need.

The principal residence of the Foxes is about Dubuque's mines on the Mississippi; of the Sacs, near the mouth of Rock River.   The mineral region designated by the above title, extends westward of the Mississippi.   The Indians have learned the value of lead ore; their women dig it in considerable quantities, and sell it to the traders.

* Prairies, as the reader knows, are extensive, uncultivated tracts of unwooded, level country.   They abound in grass, and in flowers of every hue.   So extensive are most of them, as to present nothing but the horizon for the eye to rest upon, save here and there a grove of trees, resembling small islands in the ocean; and sometimes a tongue of woodland, looking like a cape, stretches in upon the unbroken surface.   These serve the traveller for landing places.   He rejoices at sight of them, as does the mariner at sight of land.   They shelter him from the sun and dews, and supply his fuel.

Few sights are so beautiful as these savannas, when their luxuriant crop is put in motion by the wind.   The undulations are literally flowery billows.

The growth of the prairies we have crossed, averaged in height about five feet.   Sometimes, however, it reaches to six and seven feet.

These Indians are remarkable for the symmetry of their form, and fine personal appearance. Few of the tribes resemble them in these particulars; still fewer equal their intrepidity. They are, physically and morally, among the most striking of their race. Their history abounds with daring and desperate adventures and romantic incidents, far beyond the usual course of Indian exertion. Their population is about six thousand six hundred.

By the earliest accounts of those tribes that have come down to us, they appear to have occupied a part of the peninsula of Michigan. Saginau Bay is named from the Sauks, *Saukie-now*, or Sauk Town—that having been the principal seat of their power. The Foxes, or Ottagamies, were always restless and discontented Ishmaelites of the lakes, their hand against every man, and every man's hand against them. From some cause unknown to us, probably from their own turbulent and jealous disposition, they were early dissatisfied with the French, and avowed their attachment to the English. They intrigued with the other tribes to expel the French from the country, and by their efforts a British detachment under Major Gregory, towards the close of the seventeenth century, entered Lake Huron with a view to establish trading regulations with the Indians. They were, however, attacked, though in a time of peace, by their vigilant rivals, and compelled to abandon the country.

The French commenced a permanent establishment upon the Detroit River in 1701, and the attempt was early regarded with jealousy by the Foxes. In 1712 they attacked the place, then weak, both in its defences and its garrison. They were, however, repulsed in an effort to carry it by a *coup de main;* and then endeavoured to set it on fire by discharging lighted arrows into the roofs, which were thatched with straw. In this too they were

frustrated by the vigilance of the French, but not discouraged. They took a position adjoining the town, determined to harass the garrison, and eventually to compel
their surrender. This position they fortified, and in it
secured their families and provisions. But while this was
doing, the French were not idle. They despatched
messengers to the various tribes upon whom they could
rely—to the Wyandots, the Ottawas, Pottawatimies, and
the Chippeways, stating their perilous condition, and
requiring their assistance. These tribes soon collected
their warriors, and poured them in to the assistance of the
French. The Foxes were driven into their entrenched
positions, and reduced to extremity. At the moment of
their greatest hazard, a violent storm arose, during which
they abandoned their fort and fled to a *presque isle*, which
advances into Lake St Clair. Here, however, they were
pursued, and after a vigorous resistance their enemies
overcame them, put a thousand of their warriors to death,
and led the women and children into captivity. From the
narrative of these occurrences it appears that at this time
an intimate union did not exist between these tribes, for a
part of the Sauks had joined the Foxes, and a part of
them took up arms with the allied tribes for the defence
and relief of the French.

After this severe calamity, the remainder of the Foxes,
together with the Sauks, migrated to the country between
Green Bay and the Mississippi, and established themselves upon Fox River. But it is as difficult for them to
change their habits, as it would be for the buffalo of their
own plains to submit its neck to the yoke. Their turbulent spirit accompanied them, and in a short time their
war parties were sent out in all directions, and they
seriously menaced the safety, if not the existence, of the
French power. A formidable expedition was prepared for

their reduction, and the neighbouring Indians were invited
to accompany it.   To this they cheerfully assented, and
the confederated forces invested the principal fort of the
Sauks and Foxes, at the *Butte des Morts*, or the hill of
the dead, so called from the signal chastisement they
received, and the numerous bodies of the slain that were
buried in a mound there.   The survivors were here
reduced to unconditional submission, and their power and
spirits wholly broken.

By their valour and enterprise they have secured a
desirable region for themselves.   But they are involved in
almost perpetual hostilities with the Sioux.   More than
one peace has been concluded between these tribes under
the auspices of the United States, but they have really
been but temporary terms, broken by the ever restless
disposition of the Sauks and Foxes.   Their numbers are
much inferior to those of the Sioux, but they are better
armed, and their force is more concentrated.   The Sioux
are divided into large bands, without a very intimate
political connection, and their power is spread over a very
extensive region.   The Sauks and Foxes have the further
advantage of greater courage and confidence, a higher
reputation, and greater experience in war.   It is probable,
therefore, that hostilities will long continue between them,
without any very decided advantage on either side.

The Menominies, or *Folles Avoines*, occupy the country
upon Fox River, and generally roam over the district
between Green Bay and the Mississippi, and by permission
of the Chippeways and Sioux, extend their periodical
migrations into the prairies in pursuit of the buffalo.   Few
of our tribes have fallen from their high estate more
lamentably than these Indians.   They are, for the most
part, a race of fine looking men, and have sustained a high
character among the tribes around them.   But the curse

of ardent spirits has passed over them, and withered them. They have yielded to the destructive pleasures of this withering charm, with an eagerness and a recklessness even beyond the ordinary career of savages. There is, perhaps, no tribe upon all our borders so utterly abandoned to the vice of intoxication as the Menominies ; nor any so degraded in their habits, and so improvident in all their concerns.

Their language has long furnished a subject of doubt and discussion among those engaged in investigations into the philology of the Indians. By many it has been supposed that their language is an original one, peculiar to themselves, and having no affinity with those spoken by the Indians of that quarter ; and that in their communication with the neighbouring tribes, they use a dialect of the Chippeway language, which among the north-western Indians, is what the French language is upon the Continent of Europe—a general medium of communication. We are, however, satisfied that the proper Menominie is itself but a branch of this great stock. Its mode of pronunciation among themselves gives it a peculiar character, and almost conceals its resemblance to the cognate dialect. It is accompanied by singular guttural sounds, not harsh, like that of the Wyandots or the Sioux, but rather pleasant ; and the accent is placed differently from that of all the other families of this stock. Those who are not aware of the change which can be made in a language, by changing the accent upon every word, may easily satisfy themselves by making the experiment in English. It will be found that in our polysyllabic words particularly, the accent may be so changed as to disguise them entirely, and to render it difficult to discern the original form. When to this peculiar guttural sound, and this system of accentuation, are added the other causes, constantly operating upon the Indian languages, and producing their recession from one another, we shall find all the circumstances that have contributed to the existing characteristics of the Menominie language.

These Indians derive their name, *Folles Avoines,* or false oats, from the means of subsistence furnished to them by the wild rice. Their country abounds with it. Providence has given this vegetable to the northern regions. It is sown without hands, raised without care, and gathered with little trouble. It is an annual plant which delights in the still, shallow lakes, formed by numerous streams that wind their way through the level countries of the north-west. When ripe the grain falls into the water, and gradually sinking to the bottom, remains there during the winter, when it germinates. It rises above the water to ripen, but does not possess the quality which belongs to many aquatic plants, of accommodating itself to the rise and fall of the waters, and thus coming to perfection equally well in dry and in wet seasons. It sometimes happens that the waters rise above the grain, when it perishes, which produces great distress among the Indians. This grain ripens in the last of August and beginning of September. It is gathered by the females, who move amidst this harvest in bark canoes, and bending the stalks over their sides, shake the grain from the ear, or beat it off with sticks. They separate the husk by putting the whole in a skin, where, after it is dry enough, it is trodden out.

We have traversed these lakes in the same kind of vessels employed by the Indians, when to the eye they put on the appearance of immense fields, the surface of the water being entirely invisible, except immediately around the canoe, as it was forced through this rich and waving harvest. The grain is very palatable, and makes a nutritious article of food, and when threshed out without being placed in a skin, or submitted to the action of smoke, it is as pleasant as the cultivated rice.

Although the labour of gathering and preserving this article is very little, yet such is the indolence of those to whom it has been sent, that the few bags full which each family may secure, become soon exhausted. It rarely happens, however, that anything is gained by the experience of these people, for the wants of one season never operate to produce greater exertions in gathering the rice, or additional economy in the use of it, in a succeeding one. The produce of millions of acres of this precious production annually perishes. It is allowed to waste itself upon the waters, because the Indians are too indolent and too improvident to receive it from the hand of Nature. They have less industry and provident arrangement than the beaver or the ant. He who is enamoured of savage life, or who believes that all the misery of our aboriginal people is owing to the coming of the whites among them, may easily change these opinions by surveying their condition, starving and dying during the winter, because they are too lazy to stretch out their hands in autumn, and gather the harvest which a beneficent Providence has placed before them.

The Menominies occupy the same situation now that they did when they first became known to the whites. They seem to be favourites with all the adjoining Indians, and hunt upon their own land, and upon that of others, without hesitation and without complaint. They are reduced to about four thousand two hundred persons.

All the tribes whose history we have slightly sketched, belong to two different stocks—the Wyandot, or Huron; and the Chippeway, or Algonquin. But the Sioux appear to have not the slightest affinity with either of these families, and include a separate class of tribes and languages. Their original, and even to this day their principal residence, is west of the Mississippi, but the patronymic tribe itself occupies considerable territories east of that river; and one of the cognate branches, the Winnebagoes, is entirely east of it. These two tribes, therefore, are brought within the geographical limits we have prescribed to ourselves.

The Sioux seem to occupy a similar position with relation to the tribes west of the Mississippi which the Chippeways occupy to those east of that river. Both extend over an immense region of country, and the language spoken by each appears to be the root from which the affiliated dialects of the stock have sprung. With a knowledge of the Chippeway, a traveller might hold communication with most of the tribes within the original territory of the United States; and with a knowledge of the Sioux, he might also communicate with a great majority of the tribes in the trans-Mississippi country. Their languages, however, are radically different, and in the present state of our knowledge of the subject, may be considered primitive.

The Sioux, so called by the French, from the last syllable of *Naudawessie*, the Chippeway term for enemy, and emphatically applied by the Chippeways to their hereditary enemies, are known to themselves, also, under the designation of *Dahcotah*.

This nation is now divided into two great and independent families, with no political connection, and, until very recently, engaged in a long course of hostilities. There are the Dahcotah proper, and the Assiniboins, or, as they call themselves, *Hohay*. The separation took place at no distant period, and, no doubt, originated in one of those domestic feuds to which all barbarous people, having no regular code of law, morals, or religion, are peculiarly liable. The story is very freshly remembered, and each party repeats its own version of it. The Assiniboins detached themselves from their kindred bands, and emigrated to the country upon the Assiniboin River. Here they reside, stretching into the Hudson Bay territories on the one side, and to the Missouri on the other. Their numbers are estimated at eight thousand. In their habits they are erratic. They raise no agricultural article, but subsist entirely on the buffalo, whose countless herds roam over those trackless regions, obeying the invariable laws of Nature, which impel them from south to north, and from north to south, as the great processes of subsistence and reproduction require. The mode described by travellers, of driving these animals into a kind of enclosure made by poles stuck into the ground, each pole surrounded by a piece of turf, and diverging into two lines from a point, seems to have originated with the Assiniboins, if it is not peculiar to them. These poles are placed in the ground at the distance of about six feet from each other. It is upon these the powerful and furious animal rushes, and becomes imprisoned, without any effort to pass the feeble barrier. The Indians follow on horseback, and slaughter them in immense numbers.

The Sioux, or Dahcotah proper, occupy the country between the Missouri and Mississippi, extending from the possessions of the Sauks and Foxes, to those of the Assiniboins and Chippeways, touching west upon the Omahaws, the Arichares, and Mandans. They are divided into seven great bands—the Mendewahkautoan, or Lower Sioux, or *Gens du Lac;* the Waukpakoote, or people who shoot in the leaves; the *Gens de la Feuillestirees;* the Waukpatone; the Sistasoons, or

TUKO-SEE MATHLA
A Seminole Chief

people who travel on foot; the Yanctons, or people who live out of doors; the Tetons, or people of the prairies, and the Eahpawaunetoter, or people who never fall. By others, however, these divisions are differently represented, and the names are rather indicative of local situation, or some accidental habit, than of any political associations. The Sioux are one people, perfectly homogeneous in their language, character, habits, and institutions. They are wanderers over the prairies, pursuing the buffalo as constantly as the Assiniboins. Only one of their bands, the Lower Sioux, has any fixed villages, or permanent habitations. The others are restless, reckless, and homeless, traversing a region almost as extensive and unbroken as the ocean itself. Owing to their remote position, and wandering habits, it is difficult to ascertain their numbers. They are generally estimated at fifteen thousand.

A beneficent Providence has made provision in the animal and vegetable kingdoms, under every variety of situation, suited to the climate, and adapted to the wants and support of men. Before civilisation, that great destroyer of natural distinctions, has taught them the value of industry, and the comfort of prudent foresight, barbarous tribes having few objects to engage their attention, and being chiefly engaged in the supply of their physical wants, soon acquire a perfect knowledge of the animals that roam with them over the country, and of the best methods of taking and killing them. Their own customs are strongly marked by their dependence upon these sources, and their domestic institutions partake of the character thus impressed upon them. It is difficult to conceive how the arid deserts of Asia and Africa could be traversed without the aid of the patient and docile camel; how the Laplander could subsist, if Nature had not given him the reindeer; or the miserable Esquimeau, who warms his snow hut with train oil, and subsists upon the carcasses of the aquatic monsters stranded upon his coast, could live amidst his inhospitable wilds, were not these supplies providentially sent for his support.

In like manner, the buffalo has been provided for the aboriginal tenants of our great western prairies. These animals supply houses, clothing, food, and fuel. So numerous are they as to defy the quickest eye, follow them as it may over these vast plains, to count them. Nor are they less regular in their habits and movements, than the shoals of migratory fishes, which, coming from the recesses of the deep, visit different coasts, furnishing a cheap and abundant supply of food.

The Indians of all those regions depend entirely upon the buffalo for subsistence, and are very expert in the destruction of them. Mounted on fleet horses they pursue these animals, and seldom fail to transfix them with their arrows. Thus equipped they pursue a herd until as many are killed as are wanted, when they return, and collecting the tongues, and bunches upon the back, which are esteemed the most precious parts, they leave the carcass to the beasts and birds of prey.

In stature, the Sioux exceed our other north-western tribes. They are, in general, well formed, with rather slender limbs, and exhibit, as is usual among the Indians, few examples of deformity, either natural or accidental. Until lately they were clad entirely in buffalo skins, as are yet many of their remote tribes. But those in the vicinity of our posts and settlements, have learned the superiority of woollen clothing, and the means of acquiring it by the traffic in furs. The habit which prevails among many of them of wearing the hair long, and dividing it into separate braids, gives them a singular and repulsive appearance.

Their domestic animals are the horse and the dog; of these they have great numbers. When they remove their encampments, their tents of skins, poles, and other articles are packed up by the women, and drawn by the horses and dogs. All are employed in this labour, except the men. As such business would be dishonourable to them, they precede the caravan, without labour and without trouble.

Most of their political institutions resemble those of the other tribes. They have little of either law or government. The chiefs can advise, but not command— recommend, but not enforce. There is a sort of public opinion which marks the course a person should pursue under certain circumstances. If he conform, it is well; and if he do not, except when an act is committed exciting revenge, or requiring expiation, it is equally well. In such an emergency, the law of the strongest too often decides the controversy. Much, however, depends upon the personal character of the chief who happens to be at the head of the band. If he is a man of prudence and firmness, his representations will generally have weight, and his interference will go far towards checking, or satisfying the injury. The chieftainship is hereditary, rather in families than in direct descent. If a son is well qualified he succeeds his father; if he is not, some other member of the family takes the post without any formal election, but with tacit acquiescence, induced by respect for talents and experience.

The same uncertainty, which rests upon the religious opinions of the great Algonquin family, rests also upon those of the Sioux, and their cognate tribes. Indeed, it is a subject upon which they seem not to reflect, and which they cannot rationally explain. Some undefined notion appears to be entertained that there are other beings, corporeal, but unseen, who exert an influence upon the affairs of this life, and these they clothe with all the attributes that hope and fear can supply. They are propitiated with offerings, and contemplated as objects of terror, not of love—they are feared, but never adored. The storm, the lightning, the earthquake, is each a *Wah-kon*, or spirit, and so is every unusual occurrence of Nature around them. They have not the slightest conception of an overruling Providence, controlling and directing the great operations of matter and of mind : nor do their notions upon these subjects, such as they are, produce the slightest favourable effect upon their sentiments or conduct. If the hunter sees a large stone of unusual appearance, he recognises a Wah-kon, makes an offering of a piece of tobacco, and passes on. If a canoe is in danger, he who has charge of it throws out, as a sacrifice, some article, to appease the offended spirit, and often the frail vessel glides down, leaving no memorial of the danger, or the rescue. A rattlesnake is a Wah-kon, and must not be killed : even after he has inflicted his terrible wound he is suffered to live, lest his kindred should revenge his death! It is doubtful whether any Indian, whose original impressions had not been changed by intercourse with white men, ever voluntarily killed a snake. To call this religion, is to prostitute the term. It produces no salutary effect upon the head or heart. These puerile observances or superstitions, are insulated facts. They form no part of any system, but are aberrations of the human understanding, conscious of its connection with another state of being, and mistaking the delusions of imagination for the instinctive dictates of reason.

The Sioux have occupied, since they first became known to the Europeans, much of the country where they now reside. For a long period they have been engaged in hostilities with the Chippeways, and although truces have been often made, no permanent reconciliation has been effected. In this long contest, the advantage seems to have been on the side of the Chippeways, for we are told by the French travellers, that the Sioux at one time occupied the coasts of Lake Superior. From this region they have been driven for generations, and the Chippeways have obtained permanent possession of the upper Mississippi, and will probably push their rivals still farther west. In that direction also the buffalo is receding; and where he goes, the Sioux must follow, for without these animals, the plains of the Mississippi and Missouri would be as uninhabitable to the Indians as the most sterile regions of the globe.

The Winnebagoes occupy the region between Green Bay and the Mississippi, and a considerable extent of country upon this river, above Prairie du Chien. Here seems to have been, during a century and a half, the period that they have been known to us, the seat of their power and population. The early French travellers found them at Green Bay, and they were here when Carver performed his adventurous journey. They have been long known among the Canadians by the designation of *Puans*, which has become their familiar appellation, and doubtless owes its origin to their filthy and unseemly habits, which have given them a disgusting pre-eminence among all the tribes that roam over the continent.

If their own tradition can be credited, they came originally from the south-west; and some of their peculiar manners and customs, together with their language, indicate that they are not now among the tribes with whom they have been most nearly connected. The Chippeways, Menominies, Sauks, Foxes, and Pottawatimies, by whom they are almost surrounded, and with whom they are in habits of daily intercourse, are all tribes of the Algonquin stock, speaking dialects more or less removed from that parent tongue.   While the Winnebagoes are evidently a branch of the Sioux family, their language is allied to that spoken by the numerous tribes of this descent who roam over the immense plains of the Missouri and Mississippi. It is harsh and guttural, and the articulation is indistinct to a stranger.   It is not easily acquired by persons of mature age, and there are few of the Canadians who live among them, by whom it is well spoken.

As a people their physical conformation is good. They are large, athletic, and well made—not handsome, but with symmetrical forms, rather fleshy than slender. They will bear a favourable comparison, in these respects, with any of the aboriginal family.

Their country is intersected with numerous streams, lakes, and marshes, in which the wild rice abounds.   The same subsistence is offered to them as to the Menominies, and the same use is made of it.   Equally indolent and improvident, they are the subjects of the same wants and sufferings.

The Winnebagoes are fierce and desperate warriors, possessing high notions of their own prowess, and when once engaged in warlike enterprises, reckless of all consequences.   During the difficulties upon the Mississippi, a few years ago, there were instances of daring and devotion among them, which may bear a comparison with the loftiest descriptions of Indian magnanimity that have been recorded.*   In former times they were engaged in

* Certain murders were committed at Prairie du Chien, on the Upper Mississippi, in 1827, by a party of Indians, headed by the famous Winnebago chief, RED BIRD. Measures were taken to capture the offenders, and secure the peace of the frontier.   Military movements

were made from Green Bay, and from Jefferson Barracks, on the Mississippi—the object being to form a junction at the Portage of the Fox and Ouisconsin Rivers, and decide upon ulterior measures. Information of these movements was given to the Indians, at a council then holding at the Butte des Morts, on Fox River, and of the determination of the United States Government to punish those who had shed the blood of our people at Prairie du Chien. The Indians were faithfully warned of the impending danger, and told, if the murderers were not surrendered, war would be carried in among them, and a way cut through their country, not with axes, but guns. They were advised to procure a surrender of the guilty persons, and by so doing, save the innocent from suffering. Runners were despatched, bearing the intelligence of this information among their bands. Our troops were put in motion. The Indians saw, in the movement of the troops, the storm that was hanging over them. On arriving at the Portage, distant about one hundred and forty miles from the Butte des Morts, we found ourselves within nine miles of a village, at which, we were informed, were two of the murderers, Red Bird, the principal, and We-kaw, together with a large party of warriors. The Indians, apprehending an attack, sent a messenger to our encampment. He arrived, and seated himself at our tent door. On inquiring what he wanted, he answered, " *Do not strike. When the sun gets up there,* (pointing to a certain part of the heavens) *they will come in.*" To the question, Who will come in?—he answered, " *Red Bird, and We-kaw.*" Having thus delivered his message, he rose, wrapped his blanket around him, and returned. This was about noon. At three o'clock another Indian came, seated himself in the same place, and being questioned, gave the same answer. At sundown another came, and repeated what the others had said.

The amount of the information intended to be conveyed in this novel manner, was that the Red Bird and We-kaw had determined to devote themselves, by surrendering their persons and their lives, rather than by a resistance, involve the peace of their people, or subject them to the consequences of an attack. The heroic character of this act will be more clearly perceived, when we assert, on our own knowledge, that the murders committed at Prairie du Chien, were in retaliation for wrongs which had been long inflicted on the tribes to which those Indians and their warriors belonged. It is true, those killed by them at Prairie du Chien were innocent of any wrong done to the Indians. But Indian retaliation does not require that he, who commits a wrong, shall, alone, suffer for it.

The following extract of a letter, written on the occasion of this voluntary surrender, is introduced in this place for the purpose of making the reader acquainted with the details of that interesting occurrence, and the ceremonies attending it. It was addressed to the Honourable James Barbour, then Secretary of War, though not as forming any part of the official correspondence. We have omitted parts of the extract, as published at the time, and supplied additional incidents, which, in the hurry of the preparation, were omitted.

PORTAGE OF THE FOX AND OUISCONSIN RIVERS,
Monday, 4th September, 1827.

My dear sir :—It would afford me sincere pleasure, did the circumstances, by which I find myself surrounded, allow me better opportunities and more leisure, because I could then, and would most cheerfully, enter into those minute details which are in some sort necessary to exhibit things and occurrences to you as they are seen by me. I will, notwithstanding, in this letter, from the spot on which the *Red Bird* and *We-kaw* surrendered themselves, give you some account of that interesting occasion, and of *everything* just as it occurred. It all interested me, and will, doubtless, you.

You are already informed of our arrival at this place on the 31st ultimo, and that no movement was made to capture the two murderers, who were reported to us to be at the village nine miles above, on account of an order received by Major Whistler from General Atkinson, directing him to wait his arrival, and meantime to make no movement of *any* kind. We were, therefore, after the necessary arrangements for defence and security, &c. idly, but anxiously waiting his arrival, when, at about one o'clock to-day we descried, coming in the direction of the encampment, and across the Portage, a body of Indians, some mounted and some on foot. They were, when first discerned, on a mound, and descending it ; and, by the aid of a glass, we could discern three flags—two appeared to be American, and one *white*. We had received information, the day before, of the intention of the band at the village to come in with the murderers to-day ; and therefore expected them, and concluded this party to be on its way to fulfil that intention. In half an hour they were near the river, and at the crossing place, when we heard singing ; it was announced by those who knew the notes, to be a *death song*—when, presently, the river being only about a hundred yards across, and the Indians approaching it, those who knew him said, " it is *the Red Bird singing his death song*." On the moment of their arrival at the landing,

two *scalp yells* were given ; and these were also by the Red Bird. The
Menominies who had accompanied us, were lying, after the Indian
fashion, in different directions all over the hill, eyeing, with a careless
indifference, this scene; but the moment the yells were given, they
bounded from the ground as if they had been shot out of it, and, running
in every direction, each to his gun, seized it, and throwing back the pan,
picked the touch-hole, and rallied. They knew well that the yells were
scalp yells; but they did not know whether they were intended to
indicate two scalps *to be taken,* or two *to be given*—but inferred the first.
Barges were sent across, when they came over; the Red Bird carrying
the white flag, and We-kaw by his side. While they were embarking, I
passed a few yards from my tent, when a rattlesnake ran across the path ;
he was struck by captain Dickeson with his sword, which, in part,
disabled him, when I ran mine, it being of the sabre form, several times
through his body, and finally through his head, and holding it up, it was
cut off by a Menominie Indian with his knife. The body of the snake
falling, was caught up by an Indian, whilst I went towards one of the
fires to burn the head, that its fangs might be innoxious, when another
Indian came running, and begged me for it. I gave it to him. The
object of both being to make *medicine of the reptile !* * This was interpreted
to be a good omen; as had a previous killing of one a few mornings before
on Fox River, and of a bear, some account of the ceremonies attending
which and of other incidents attending our ascent up that river, I may
give you at another time.

    By this time the murderers were landed, accompanied by one hundred
and fourteen of their principal men. They were preceded and represented by *Caraminie;* a chief, who earnestly begged that the prisoners
might receive good treatment, and under no circumstances, be put in
irons. He appeared to dread the military, and wished to surrender them
to the sub-agent, Mr Marsh. His address being made to me, I told him
it was proper that he should go to the great chief, (Major Whistler ;)
and that so far as Mr Marsh's presence might be agreeable to them,
they should have it there. He appeared content, and moved on, followed
by the men of his bands ; the Red Bird being in the centre, with his white
flag, whilst two other flags, American, were borne by two chiefs, in the
front and rear of the line. The military had been previously drawn out
in line. The Menominie and Wabanocky Indians squatting about in
groups, (looking curious enough,) on the left flank—the band of music

---

    * The noise of the rattles of a rattlesnake when excited, is precisely
that of a repeating watch in the intervals between the strokes.

on the right, a little in advance of the line. The murderers were marched up in front of the centre of the line—some ten or fifteen paces from which seats were arranged, which were occupied by the principal officers attached to the command, &c.: in front of which, at about ten paces, the Red Bird was halted, with his miserable looking companion We-kaw, by his side, whilst his band formed a kind of semicircle to their right and left. All eyes were fixed upon the Red Bird; and well they might be; for, of all the Indians I ever saw, he is decidedly the most perfect in form, and face, and motion. In height he is about six feet straight, but without restraint; in proportion, exact and perfect from his feet to his head, and thence to the very ends of his fingers; whilst his face is full of expression and of every sort to interest the feelings, and without a single, even accidental glance, that would justify the suspicion that a purpose of murder could by any possible means conceal itself there. There is in it a happy blending of dignity and grace; great firmness and decision, mixed with mildness and mercy. I could not but ask myself, can this be the murderer—the chief who could shoot, scalp, and cut the throat of *Gagnier?* His head too—nothing was ever so well formed. There was no ornamenting of the hair after the Indian fashion; no clubbing it up in blocks and rollers of lead or silver; no loose or straggling parts; but it was cut after the best fashion of the most refined civilised taste. His face was painted, one side red, the other a little intermixed with green and white. Around his neck he wore a collar of blue wampum, beautifully mixed with white, sewn on a piece of cloth, and covering it, of about two inches width, whilst the claws of the panther, or large wild cat, were fastened to the upper rim, and about a quarter of an inch from each other, their points downward and inward, and resting upon the lower rim of the collar; and around his neck, in strands of various lengths, enlarging as they descended, he wears a profusion of the same kind of wampum as had been worked so tastefully into his collar. He is clothed in a *Yankton dress,* new, rich, and beautiful. It is of beautifully dressed elk, or deer skin; pure in its colour, almost to a clear white, and consists of a jacket, (with nothing beneath it,) the sleeves of which are sewn so as to neatly fit his finely turned arms, leaving two or three inches of the skin outside of the sewing, and then again three or four inches more which is cut into strips, as we cut paper to wrap round, and ornament a candle. All this made a deep and rich fringe, whilst the same kind of ornament, or trimming, continued down the seams of his leggings. These were of the same material, and were additionally set off with blue beads. On his feet he wore moccasins. A piece of scarlet cloth about a quarter of a yard wide, and half a yard long, by means of a slit cut through its middle, so as to admit the passing through of his head, rested, one half upon his breast, and the other on his back.   On one shoulder, and near his breast, was a large and beautifully ornamented feather, nearly white ; and on the other, and opposite was one nearly black, with two pieces of wood in the form of compasses when a little open, each about six inches long, richly wrapped round with porcupines' quills, dyed yellow, red, and blue ; and on the tip of one shoulder was a tuft of red dyed horse hair, curled in part, and mixed up with other ornaments.   Across his breast, in a diagonal position, and bound tight to it, was his war pipe, at least three feet long, richly ornamented with feathers and horse hair, dyed red, and the bills of birds, &c. ; whilst in one hand he held the white flag, and in the other the pipe of peace.   There he stood.   He moved not a muscle, nor once changed the expression of his face.   They were told to sit down. He sat down, with a grace not less captivating than he walked and stood.   At this moment the band on our right struck up and played Pleyel's Hymn.   Everything was still.   The Red Bird looked towards the band, and eyeing it with an expression of interest, and as if those pensive notes were falling softly and agreeably on his heart.   When the hymn was played, he took up his pouch, and taking from it some *kinnakanic* and tobacco, cut the latter after the Indian fashion, then rubbed the two together, filled the bowl of his beautiful peace pipe, struck fire with his steel and flint into a bit of spunk, and lighted it, and smoked.   All this was done with a grace no less captivating than that which had characterised his other movements.   He sat with his legs crossed.

If you think there was anything of affectation in all this, you are mistaken.   There was just the manner and appearance you would expect to see in a nobly built man of the finest intelligence, who had been escorted by his armies to a throne, where the diadem was to be placed upon his head.

There is but one opinion of the man, and that is just such as I have formed myself, and attempted to impart to you.   I could not but speculate a little on his dress.   His white jacket, with one piece of red upon it, appeared to indicate the purity of his past life, stained with but a single crime ; for, all agree, that the Red Bird had never before soiled his fingers with the blood of the white man, or committed a bad action.   His war pipe, bound close to his heart, appeared to indicate his love of war, which was now no longer to be gratified. Perhaps the red, or scarlet cloth, may have been indicative of his name—the *Red Bird*.

All sat, except the speakers, whose addresses I took down, but have not time to insert them here. They were, in substance, that they had been required to bring in the murderers. They had no power over any, except two, and these had voluntarily agreed to come in and give themselves up. As their friends, they had come with them. They hoped their white brothers would agree to receive the horses, (they had with them twenty, perhaps,) meaning, that if accepted, it should be in commutation for the lives of their two friends. They asked kind treatment for them, earnestly begged that they might not be put in irons, and that they all might have some tobacco, and something to eat.

They were answered, and told, in substance, that they had done well thus to come in. By having done so, they had turned away our guns, and saved their people. They were admonished against placing themselves in a similar situation in future, and told, that when they should be aggrieved, to go to their agent, who would inform their great father of their complaints, and he would redress them; that their friends should be treated kindly, and tried by the same laws that their great father's children were tried; that, for the present, they should not be put in irons; that they all should have something to eat, and tobacco to smoke. We advised them to warn their people against killing ours; and endeavoured also to impress them with a proper conception of the extent of our power, and of their weakness, &c.

Having heard this, the Red Bird stood up; the commanding officer, Major Whistler, a few paces in advance of the centre of his line, facing him. After a pause of a minute, and a rapid survey of the troops, and a firm, composed observation of his people, the Red Bird said—looking at Major Whistler—"*I am ready.*" Then advancing a step or two, he paused, and added—"I do not wish to be put in irons. Let me be free. I have given my life, it is gone, (stooping down and taking some dust between his finger and thumb, and blowing it away,) like this—(eyeing the dust as it fell and vanished out of his sight). I would not have it back. It is gone." He then threw his hands behind him, to indicate that he was leaving all things behind him, and marched up to Major Whistler, breast to breast. A platoon was wheeled backwards from the centre of the line, when Major Whistler stepping aside, the Red Bird and We-kaw marched through the line in charge of a file of men, to a tent that had been provided in the rear, over which a guard was set. The comrades of the two captives then left the ground by the way they had come, taking with them our advice, and a supply of meat and flour.

I will now describe, as well as I can, *We-kaw*, the miserable, butcher-looking being who continued by Red Bird. He is, in all respects, the opposite of the Red Bird ; and you will make out the points of comparison by this rule : Never was there before, two human beings brought together for the same crime, who looked so totally unlike each other. Red Bird seemed a prince, and fit to command, and worthy to be obeyed ; but We-kaw looked as if he was born to be hanged. Meagre, cold, dirty in his dress and person, and crooked in form—like the starved wolf, gaunt, and hungry, and blood-thirsty—his whole appearance indicates the existence of a spirit, wary, cruel, and treacherous ; and there is no room left, after looking at him, for pity. This is the man who could scalp a child no more than *eleven months old,* and cut it across the back of its neck *to the bone,* and leave it, bearing off its fine locks, to suffer and die upon the floor, near its murdered father ! But his hands, and crooked and miserable looking fingers, had been wet, often, with blood before.

The *Red Bird* does not appear to be over thirty—yet he is said to be over forty. We-kaw looks to be forty-five, and is, perhaps, that old.

I shall see, on my arrival at the Prairie, the scene of these butcheries ; and as I may write you upon all the points of my tour that may have any interest, I will introduce you to that. The child, I forgot to say, by the latest accounts, yet lives, and promises to survive the wounds on its head and neck. The widow of *Gagnier* is also there, and I shall get the whole story from her own mouth, and then shall, doubtless, get it truly. You shall have it all, and a thousand things besides, that when I left home I never expected to realise—but once entered upon the scenes I have passed, there was no giving back. I see no danger, I confess, especially now ; but my way is onward, and I shall go.

I write in haste, and have only time to add the assurance of my friendship.

THOMAS L. McKENNEY.

The Red Bird and We-kaw were delivered over to General Atkinson, who commanded the expedition from Jefferson Barracks. He arrived with his command at the Portage, by way of the Ouisconsin, two days after the surrender. The prisoners were conveyed to Prairie du Chien. The Red Bird died in prison. We-kaw, and others who were taken as accomplices in the murder, were tried and convicted, but became the subjects of Executive clemency—the President, Mr Adams, extending a pardon to them.

hostilities with the Illinois tribes, and, associated with the Sauks and Foxes, they carried dismay even to the gates of Kaskaskias. In this long and active warfare the Illinois Indians were almost exterminated. Many of their bands have entirely disappeared, and those that remain are reduced to a few individuals. The Winnebagoes came out of this war a conquering and powerful people, but what their enemies could not accomplish, the elements did. Tradition says that six hundred of their warriors perished in canoes upon Lake Michigan during a violent storm.

The Winnebagoes are computed at five thousand eight hundred persons. It has been supposed by some, that latterly they have been increasing. There is, however, no good reason to believe this. The opinion has probably grown out of a comparison of different estimates of their population made by various persons, and under various circumstances. Such estimates are too loose and uncertain to furnish data for any calculations of this nature, more particularly when they contradict our uniform experience upon the subject of the aboriginal population. All the tribes with which we are acquainted are in a state of progressive and rapid diminution; and although those which are most remote are not within the sphere of the operation of the causes which result from their contact with a civilised people, yet a scanty and precarious subsistence, continued and active warfare, exposure to the elements and to the accidents of a hazardous life, are pressing with restless severity upon their spare population.

In manners and customs, the Winnebagoes resemble the other members of the aboriginal family. Like the Algonquin tribes they are divided into bands, each designated by the name of some animal, or of a supposed spirit, such as the bear, the Devil, or bad spirit, the thunder, etc. These divisions were originally an important feature in their polity, but they are now little more than nominal, having yielded, like many others of the peculiar traits, to the untoward circumstances which have for ages surrounded them.

Their village chiefs are hereditary in the lineal descent, and where the direct line fails, in the collateral descent. Female chiefs are not at present known among them, although Carver states, that when he visited this tribe, in 1767, a queen was at their head, and exercised her authority with much state, and without opposition. It is certainly a singular inconsistency in human nature, that rude and uncivilised people who hold women in contempt, and assign to them the performance of all those duties which are least honourable and most laborious, should yet admit them to the exercise of civil authority in supreme or subordinate situations.* The custom may have originated in another and more advanced state of society, and may have survived the wreck in which their early history has perished.

The southern Indians are consolidated into four great families, the Creeks, the Cherokees, the Choctaws, and Chickasaws. The Catawbas, and many other tribes, once scattered over the country from North Carolina to the Mississippi and the Gulf of Mexico, are now either extinct, or so nearly extinct, that any investigation into their condition would be inconsistent with the object we have in view—which is, an exhibition of the actual state of the Indian tribes at the present day. Nor is it easy to trace the history and progress of the declension and

---

* We remember, in 1826, to have seen admitted into council, at *Fond-du-lac Superior,* an aged woman, but she sat there as the representative of her husband, whose age and blindness prevented his attendance.

extinction of these Indians, or their incorporation into the other communities which yet survive so much of what has perished in our aboriginal memorials. The materials that have reached us are not satisfactory. The early French travellers and historians furnish us with the most valuable information on these subjects. If they did not examine them with more severity, they were more careful to record their observations, and by the facility of intercourse with the Indians, better enabled to collect them. With the southern tribes, however, their intercourse was not extensive, and the accounts which they have left us of their history and condition are meagre and unsatisfactory.

Adair, an English trader, published a book purporting to be a history of the four southern tribes, or rather it was published for him; and if human ingenuity had been taxed to compile a work, which, in a large compass, should contain the least possible information respecting the subject about which it treats, we might be well satisfied with Adair's quarto. He sees in the Indians the descendants of the Jews, and blind to the thousand physical and moral proofs adverse to this wild theory, he seizes upon one or two casual coincidences, and with an imagination which supplies everything else, he furnishes his reader with his speculations.

Over this region, and among the predecessors, or ancestors of some of these tribes, De Soto rambled with his followers in pursuit of gold, if the narrative of his expedition be not as fabulous as the El Dorado he was seeking. How precious would be a judicious and faithful account of the Indians written almost during the lifetime of Columbus, by a man of observation and candour, travelling, as is computed in the history of this expedition, more than five thousand miles in the country; and

PA-SHE-NINE
A Chippeway Chief

occupied in this journey nearly five years! And proceeding in a direction, eighteen hundred miles north of the point of debarkation—six hundred miles north of Lake Superior. For this is the grave calculation made from a reduction of the courses and distances given by De la Vega, the historian of the expedition.

It were a waste of time to indulge in speculations, as some sensible men have done, respecting the causes which have depopulated these regions, *"filled with great towns, always within view of each other!"* Of all the exaggerations to which the *auri sacra fames* of the Spaniards has given birth in the New World, this narrative is the grossest. It is utterly unworthy of a moment's serious consideration. All that it records is wholly inconsistent with the institutions and resources, and not less so with every authentic account which has come down to us.

The Creeks now occupy a tract of country in the eastern part of Alabama. Many of them, however, have already removed west of the Mississippi, and others are preparing to follow. From present appearances, it is probable they will all ere long follow the same route. Their whole numbers are estimated at twenty thousand.

The Seminoles, and the remains of other broken tribes, allies or confederates of the Creeks, and identified with them in manners and feelings, occupy a reservation in Florida, and number among their population about four thousand individuals.

The Creeks were so called by the English, because their country was watered and intersected by numerous small streams, along which these Indians were situated. They have long been known as a powerful and restless confederacy, and their sway formerly extended over much of Georgia, Alabama, and Florida. The principal and original band, the Muskogee, which in their own language

now gives name to the whole nation, claim to have
always inhabited the country now occupied by them.   As
other tribes became reduced in numbers and power, either
by the preponderance of the Muskogee, or by other
causes, they joined that band, and have in process of time
become, in some measure, though not altogether, a
homogeneous people.   The most extraordinary among
these, both as to their history, their institutions, and their
fate, were the Natchez.   Originally planted upon the
Mississippi, near the present town of that name, if the
accounts which have been given of their condition and
manners can be relied on, almost all the features they
present mark a striking difference between them and all
the other Indians who are known to us.   Some of these
we shall lay before our readers; and without giving full
credit to the whole account, there yet can be no doubt
that some peculiar characteristics prevailed among them.
It is a curious and interesting topic.   The Natchez are
said to have been numerous and powerful.   Their
principal chief was called the *Great Sun*, and the subordinate chiefs, *suns*.   Their government, unlike the pure
democracies, or rather the no-government of the other
tribes, was strong, and even despotic.   The Great Sun
was an object of reverence, and almost veneration, and
exercised unlimited power during his life; and in death
he was attended by a numerous band who had been
devoted to him from birth, and who were immolated on
his shrine.   The government was hereditary; but, as with
the Wyandots, and some of the other tribes, the succession was in the female line, from uncle to nephew.   The
members of the reigning family were not allowed to
intermarry with one another, but divorces were permitted
at will, and libertinism fully indulged.   The sun was the
great object of religious adoration, and in their temples a

perpetual fire was burning. Guardians were appointed for the preservation of this fire, and heavy penalties were prescribed for neglect. All this, and much more that is related of this people by respectable authors, some of them eye-witnesses, is so different from all around them, that if the leading facts are true, the Natchez must have been an insulated tribe upon the continent, deriving their origin from a different stock.

The final catastrophe, which closed their history and their independence, is indicative of their fierce and indomitable spirit. The tyrannical conduct of a French commandant of the port of Natchez led to a conspiracy for the destruction of their oppressors. The French were surprised, and almost the whole settlement, amounting to seven hundred persons, massacred. When the intelligence reached New Orleans, a formidable expedition was organised against these Indians, and all the warriors of the neighbouring tribes invited to accompany it. The Natchez defended themselves with desperate valour, but in the end were utterly overthrown. Their Great Sun, with many of their principal men, was transported to St Domingo, and sold into slavery, and the tribe itself disappeared from history.

There are among the Creeks the remains of a tribe known as the Uchees, the remnant of one of these dispersed, or conquered bands—tradition says they were conquered. Although forming part of the Creek tribe, and enjoying in common with it its honours and profits, such as they are, they speak a language entirely dissimilar, and wholly their own.

The Cherokees own a district of country, which extends into North Carolina, Georgia, Alabama, and Tennessee. That portion of the tribe that remains east of the Mississippi, contains about nine thousand persons.

Those who have emigrated to the west of that river, and are now situated west of Arkansas and Missouri, amount to about six thousand. The principal emigration has taken place since 1817.

This tribe, when first known to the French, resided in the country between Lake Erie and the Ohio. The causes which led to their emigration from that region can only be conjectured, but there is little doubt it was owing to the victorious career of the Iroquois; and that it occurred about the period when the Shawanese were driven to the same quarter.

After the settlement of the southern States, the Cherokees, instigated by the French, displayed for many years the most determined hostility, and kept the frontiers in a state of constant alarm and danger. Formidable exertions were required, from time to time, to check this spirit; nor was it fully accomplished until the near approach of the revolutionary troubles.

The language of the Cherokees, so far as we are acquainted with it, is radically different in its words from that of any other tribes. In its general structure, however, it closely resembles the dialects spoken by our whole aboriginal family.

The Choctaws reside in the State of Mississippi, and are computed at twenty thousand persons. They have recently ceded their entire country east of the Mississippi to the United States, and are removing to the west of that river.

The Chickasaws, numbering about three thousand six hundred, inhabit the northern part of Mississippi, and the north-western corner of Alabama.

These two tribes speak dialects of the same language, and are evidently branches of the same family. There is nothing in their condition or history which requires a

more particular notice, except that they, together with the
Cherokees, Creeks, and Seminoles, having outlived the
game, have ceased, from necessity, to be hunters. They
derive such subsistence as their manner of life, and
general abandonment of portions of these tribes to ardent
spirits will permit, from the soil.   There is a good deal of
individual comfort enjoyed, and an exception in such
cases from the common plague of drunkenness, particularly among the Cherokees and Chickasaws, which is
found also, though not to the same extent, among the
Choctaws.   There is nothing in the condition of individual
families, that could lead us to hope for any improvement
among the Creeks and Seminoles.   The annuities derived
from the Government under treaties with them for cessions
of their lands, are the main dependence of these latter
tribes ; and these it is found necessary sometimes to
pledge a year in advance, for corn to subsist upon.   We
merely observe, in regard to the Choctaws, that the custom
of flattening the heads of infants formerly prevailed
among them.

The Cherokees appear to be a homogeneous tribe,
originating in a different region from the one now occupied
by them.   The other three southern tribes have been
more or less formed by the admixture of dispersed or
conquered bands; and we have no evidence of their
migration from any other quarter.   They all, however,
in general characteristics resemble the other great
branches of their race.   Circumstances may occasionally
impress some peculiar feature upon different tribes, but
in the whole extent of their manners, customs, institutions,
and opinions, there is nothing which can preclude the idea
of their common origin.

Latterly the southern tribes have excited more than
common observation ; and the critical state of their

affairs has directed much of the public attention to them. Their reputed improvements in the elements of social life, and the attempt made by some of them to establish independent governments, have led to the belief with many, that the crisis of their fate is passed, and that a new era is before them. If they can be induced to pursue the course recommended by their best friends, and flee from the vicinity of the white settlements, and establish themselves permanently beyond the Mississippi, and the Government will accompany them with the means of protection and improvement, this hope may be realised— if not, they will but follow the fate of too many of the tribes that have gone before them.

Such is a general view of the past condition, and present situation of the various tribes of Indians who occupy any portion of the territory of the United States, east of the Mississippi, or who have passed that great barrier, and sought, in the immense plains of the West, a land of refuge and of safety. The great outlines of their character are easily delineated. In all their essential features, they are now what they were at the discovery. Indolent and improvident, they neither survey the wants of the future, nor provide for them. The men are free, and the women are slaves. They are restrained by no moral or religious obligations, but willingly yield themselves to the fiercest passions. Lost in the most degrading superstition, they look upon Nature with a vacant eye, never inquiring into the causes, or the consequences of the great revolutions of Nature, or into the structure or operations of their own minds. Their existence is essentially a physical one, limited to the gratification of their appetites, and the indulgence of their passions. Mental or moral improvement is not embraced by a single desire for the one or the other. As the only occupations of the men are war and hunting, their early discipline, and their habitual exertions, are directed to these pursuits; and as their faculties are confined within narrow limits, they acquire an ardour, intensity, and power, unknown in a different state of society. Marvellous tales are related of the sagacity with which the Indians penetrate the forest, pursuing their course with unerring skill and precision, and taking all their measures with a precaution which leaves little to accident. In this application of their powers they resemble many of the inferior animals, which by some mysterious process are enabled to return to places whence they have been taken, although every effort may have been made to deceive them. The Indians observe, accurately, the face of the country, the courses of the streams, the weather-beaten sides of the trees, and every other permanent landmark which can guide them through the world of the forest. And after all due allowance for exaggeration, enough of sober truth will remain to excite our surprise at the almost intuitive sagacity displayed by these rude hunters in the toils of the chase. The splendour of victory is in due proportion to the slaughter of their enemy, and in an inverse proportion to their own loss; and it is a point of honour with all the leaders of the war parties to bring back as many *braves*, or warriors, as possible. How terrible they are to a vanquished and prostrate foe, the whole history of our warfare with them but too mournfully tells. They neither expect mercy nor yield it. Their solicitude for the preservation of life too often degenerates into rank cowardice. But when escape is impossible, and the hour of trial comes, they meet their fate with a heroic fortitude, which would not dishonour the sternest martyr of civil or religious freedom, that ever went from the stake to his reward. Their conduct in this appalling extremity has been the theme of wonder and description, since they themselves have been known to us. All that is contemptuous in expression is poured upon their enemies; all that is elevated in feeling is given to their country; all that concerns life, its joys, or terrors, is cast behind them like a worthless thing. From infancy they have looked forward to this hour of suffering and triumph as a possible event. They have heard of it in the stories of the old, and in the songs of the young. They have seen it in the triumphant death of many a fierce captive enemy, whose song of defiance has been stimulated by the impulse of his own heart.

So far as natural affections depend upon natural instinct they participate with us, as well as with the brute creation, in their enjoyment. We do not, of course, speak now of those half, or entirely civilised families, upon whose minds and hearts education and social advantages have shed their influence, but of the Indian, as such; to him who owes nothing to culture, and but little to habit. It is idle to suppose that he feels and cherishes those kindly emotions of the heart which transport us beyond the magic circle of *self*, and give us the foretaste of another existence. Their hospitality is more the hospitality of improvidence than of feeling. The kettle of the Indian, while he has anything to put in it, is always on the fire, filled with victuals for his family, and for all who enter his wigwam.

AN ESSAY ON THE HISTORY OF THE NORTH AMERICAN INDIANS

By JAMES HALL

I.

THE North American Indians, when discovered by the Europeans, were a race of savages who had made no advances whatever towards civilisation. They dwelt in the wilderness, subsisted by hunting, and had no permanent dwellings. They were lodged, either in portable tents, or in huts made of bark or earth; and had no houses or other edifices constructed of durable materials, nor any towns, or stationary places of residence; their villages being mere encampments, at spots of occasional or habitual resort. They had no governments, or national organisation; being divided into families or tribes, who were independent of each other, and portions of whom occasionally united together for a season, to resist a common danger, or to join in the rites of a common superstition. They had no industry; produced nothing by labour, except a few vegetables for present use; possessed no trade nor commerce, and of course, no money, nor other medium of exchange. They kept no domestic animals, nor had they any property except in their arms and rude canoes. We have no evidence that they entertained any definite ideas of a future state, or of a Supreme Being; and although they had many vague notions of supernatural beings, and of another state of

83

existence, yet we are certain that they professed no
common faith, nor exercised any general form of religion.
Each tribe had some shadowy superstitions, scarcely
credited by themselves, and which we are inclined to
believe seldom outlived the generations in which they
were conceived. They made nothing, they erected
nothing, they established nothing, which might vindicate
to succeeding generations their character as rational
beings; and they seem to have been distinguished from
the brute creation by little else than the faculty of speech,
and the possession of reasoning powers, which appear
scarcely to have been exercised. Still they were human
beings, as much entitled to the sympathy of mankind, as
if their claims to respect had been greater; and their
condition and history present curious subjects of inquiry to
the philosopher and philanthropist.

Much curiosity has been excited in regard to the
origin of this people, and many ingenious attempts have
been made to trace their descent from some of the existing
nations of Europe and Asia. All these theories have
proved fallacious, and we speak the common sentiment of
all rational inquirers on this subject, when we assert, that
no fact has been discovered, which would lead to a just
inference, that the aborigines of North America have at
any time been more civilised than they are at present; or
which would render it even probable, that they are a
branch of any existing people more civilised than themselves. The more reasonable opinion is, that they are a
primitive people, a distinct branch of the human family,
separated from the common stock at some remote period,
in pursuance of the same inscrutable decree of Providence
which set apart the negro from the white man. How
they came to this continent cannot now be told; time has
effaced the footsteps of the progenitors of the race; and

it would be as impossible now to trace out their path, as it would be to unfold the still more mysterious act of the hand of God, which peopled the islands of the ocean.

In the course of these inquiries, much stress has been laid upon the discovery of certain works of art, which some have supposed to be the remains of a people more civilised than the present race of Indians, while others believe them to have been constructed by this race, in a higher state of cultivation, from which they have since receded. We think these theories equally defective, from the obvious consideration, that there is not evinced, in the construction of any of these works, a degree of skill beyond that of which the present Indian is capable. There is no mechanical skill whatever, no mathematical knowledge, nor any great display of ingenuity, evinced in any of them. They are for the most part composed of loose earth, heaped up in huge piles, more remarkable for their volume, than their form or structure. No wood nor metal has been found in them, and in the few instances where stone has been discovered, it has not borne the impress of any tool, while the remains of masonry have been so problematical, as not to afford the evidence upon which any hypothesis could be safely founded.

The mounds scattered profusely over the great central plain of the Mississippi, have attracted attention chiefly on account of their number and size; and it has been plausibly argued, that the present race of Indians, with their known indolence and aversion to labour, and their ignorance of all tools and machinery, would never have submitted to the toil requisite for so great a work. But this argument is insufficient. In order to appreciate the laboriousness of this work, it would be necessary to ascertain the numbers engaged in it, and the time employed in its completion. If we suppose that these mounds were burying places, that the bones of the dead were deposited on the ground, and earth brought in small parcels from the surrounding surface and heaped over them, and that successive layers were deposited from time to time, one above the other, it will be seen that the accumulation might eventually be great, though the labour would be gradually bestowed, and the toil almost imperceptible. When we consider the tendency of all communities to adhere tenaciously to burial places, consecrated by long use, it will not be thought strange that savages, however erratic their habits, should continue to bury their people, at the same spots, through many successive generations. Supposing this to have been the process, these mounds may have been growing through many successive ages, and neither their number, nor their bulk, would be matter of surprise. We have an example in our own times to justify the belief that such was their practice. *Blackbird*, a celebrated chief of the Mahas, was buried, by his own directions, on an eminence overlooking the Missouri River. He was seated on his favourite horse, dressed, painted and armed as if prepared for war, and the horse and man being placed on the surface of the ground, in the erect posture of life, the earth was heaped up around them until both were covered. A considerable mound would be made by this single interment; and is it improbable, that a spot thus signalised, would, in after generations, be sought by those who would desire to place the remains of their relatives under the guardianship of the spirit of a great warrior?

It is worthy of remark, that these mounds are usually found in places suitable for the sites of towns, and we think that the largest mounds, and the most numerous groups, always exist in the most fertile tracts of country, and on the borders of rivers. These are the points at which the productions of Nature, suitable for food, would be most abundant, and where savage hordes would naturally congregate, during the inclemency of the winter season. At some of these places the evidences of former habitation still remain, but many of them are on the open prairie, covered with long grass, and exhibiting no sign of recent population, while others are concealed in the tangled forest, in all its pristine luxuriance, and overgrown with great trees, whose ages may be computed by centuries. They are, therefore, of great antiquity; and while we believe, that among the present inhabitants of the wilderness, there are traces of the custom to which we have alluded as the probable cause of these remains, we also think that the practice has gone into disuse. It is not improbable, that the pressure of the white population during the last three centuries, the use of ardent spirits, and the introduction of foreign diseases, have modified their former habits, by rendering them more erratic, fomenting wars and dividing tribes, and greatly reducing their numbers.

Another class of remains, of a highly curious character, have recently been discovered in the Wisconsin Territory. These are mounds of earth, having the outlines and figures of animals, raised in relief, upon the surface of the plain. They are very numerous, and the original forms so well preserved, that the respective species of animals intended to be represented, are easily recognised. The figures are large, as much as thirty or forty feet in length, and raised several feet above the natural surface, and the bodies, heads, limbs, and in some instances the smaller members, such as the ears, are distinctly visible. They represent the buffalo, the bear, the deer, the eagle, the tortoise, the lizard, etc., drawn without much skill, and are precisely the figures which we find traced on the dressed buffalo skins of the present race of Indians, and displaying the same style in the grouping, and a similar degree of skill in the art of drawing. They are so peculiarly characteristic of the Indians, as to leave no doubt of their origin; nor do we question the fairness of the inference which would impute them to the same people, and the identical period, which produced the class of mounds supposed to have been sepulchres for the dead. We are indebted for our knowledge of these highly curious relics to Dr John Locke of Cincinnati, an eminent geologist, who carefully examined, measured, and delineated them, and whose very interesting description may be found in Silliman's *Journal*.

The remains of ancient fortifications are decidedly the most curious of all the relics of our Red population which have been handed down to us; and they have caused great doubt, in regard to their origin, in consequence of their magnitude, and the degree of skill evinced in their construction. That they were military defences, well adapted to the purpose for which they were intended, and exhibiting much ingenuity, are points which may be conceded; but some, whose opinions are entitled to great respect, have maintained further, that these works exhibit a knowledge of the science of engineering, as applied in modern warfare, far beyond the powers of combination and extent of knowledge, of any savage people, and which prove them to be the production of a more civilised people. We think these inferences are more plausible than just.

The discoverers of North America found the villages of the Indians surrounded by stockades, and there is scarcely a delineation of an Indian town to be found in any old book, in which there is not a representation of some form of exterior defence. This fact shows, that like their descendants, they lived on such terms with their neighbours, as made it necessary for them to be continually on their guard against surprise ; and, although their habits may have been those of a wandering people, and their towns then, as now, places of periodical resort, yet there may have been periods of a more protracted abode at one spot, and occasions when it became essential to make a stand against their enemies, and to take more than ordinary precautions against the assaults of a superior force.   If such was ever the case, one great difficulty is removed from this question.

The Indians are a military people.   They cultivate no art of social life, and the only road to distinction is the war-path.   The sole ambition of their leading men is to excel in war.   Whatever degree of wisdom, of cunning, or of any description of talent, may exist in the minds of the chiefs, or of aspiring men, must find its exercise in the battlefield, in plans to annoy others, or defend themselves. The intellect of such a people, while it would remain stationary and unproductive, in regard to every other kind of knowledge, and subject of reflection, would become sharpened, and to some extent cultivated, in relation to military affairs; like the trees of their native forests, the martial art would grow vigorously in the soil which gave nourishment to no other production.   It is true, that even this art could arrive at no high degree of perfection among a people who had no mechanical ingenuity, no knowledge of the use of metals, nor any of the implements or engines of war or of industry belonging to a cultivated people— without, in short, any of the kindred arts or sciences. With no weapons but the bow, the spear of wood, and the war-club, without magazines and the means of transporting provisions, the range of improvement in military tactics must have been confined to very narrow limits.

We only contend, that so far as the scope of their knowledge and experience in war extended, it gave employment to all the ingenuity of the people which was at all attempted to be exercised. Thus we have seen, that while the Indians have resisted every effort to introduce among them our social arts, they have eagerly adopted the use of the horse and of firearms; they listen with indifference or contempt to our explanations of the comforts of life, and of the advantages of agriculture and trade, and witness, without desire, the useful qualities of the ox, the axe, and the plough; but they grasp with avidity the knife and the tomahawk.

Among the various vicissitudes of a continual warfare, it must sometimes have become necessary, even for a people habitually wandering in their habits, to make a stand against their enemies. We know that wars for the conquest of territory have been common among the aborigines, and that tribes have often been dispossessed of their ancient hunting-grounds, and driven to seek other lands. There must have been occasions when pride, obstinacy, or a devoted attachment to a particular spot, impelled them to risk extermination rather than retreat before a superior force; or when a desperate remnant of a brave and fierce people, surrounded by foes, could only retreat from their own country into the lands of a hostile nation. In such emergencies they must have resorted to extraordinary means of defence; and necessity would suggest those artificial aids which, in all ages, and in every state of society, have been called to the support of valour and physical strength. They would be driven to the construction of fortifications; and though wholly unskilful at first, their warlike propensities, and martial habits, would render them fruitful of expedients, and lead to a rapid advancement in the art of improving the advantages

OCHE-FINCECO
A Half-Breed Creek

and covering the weaknesses of their position. The reader of American history will readily recall numerous instances in which the Indians have protected their armies, and surrounded their towns, by breastworks of logs, and the step from those to ramparts of earth, would be natural and easy.

The evidences of military science which have been detected in some of these works deserve attention. These have been found in the convenience of the positions in reference to supplies of water—in the existence of covered ways, of traverses protecting gateways, of angles, and even bastions. As these are parts of that combination which forms a regular system, they are supposed to be the results of science; but this may be a mistake, for it is not the existence of the parts, but their combination and harmony, which afford the proof of what we term science. The perfection of science often consists in the adaptation of the most simple elements to a desired purpose, and the discovery and proper arrangement of the laws by which causes are made to produce uniform effects. The savage may know nothing of the laws, but may adopt the principles ; because there are some elementary principles so inseparably connected with every mechanical operation, that it is impossible to conduct that operation conveniently without adopting those rudiments of the art. The economy of labour in connecting two points by a straight instead of a serpentine line of embankment, might readily occur even to the mind of a savage; and a military leader, however inexperienced, in planning a line of defence, would naturally consider and strengthen the points of attack. That an intelligent savage leader, watchful, crafty, and expert in devices, as we know them to be, and experienced in his own mode of warfare, should throw out a salient angle to overlook and command a line of defence, would not be surprising; and it would be still less remarkable, that he should pitch his camp near a supply of water, and construct a covered way by which the females could pass in safety to the reservoir of that indispensable element. If an opening must be left in a line of breastwork for egress, it would be natural to throw up a parapet behind it for the protection of the warriors engaged in its defence, in case of assault. All these are among the simple and obvious expedients which form the rudiments of the art of fortification : that all of them would be combined in a first attempt to fortify a savage camp, is not likely; but that some of them would be adopted on one occasion, and others be added subsequently, as necessity might suggest their expediency, does not seem improbable. It is true also, that some of the largest works, of which the remains are found, when delineated on paper, exhibit angles and bastions, and a general irregularity of outline, which appear to be the result of a plan adapted to some system of defence, when an examination of the ground would show them to be the mere effects of necessity. On tracing some of these lines upon the spot, it has been found that the position occupies an eminence or ground higher than that around it, and that the lines enclosing the table-land of the summit follow the sinuosities of the exterior lines of plane, and keeping along the edge of the declivity, form retiring angles in passing round the heads of ravines or gullies, and again shoot out into salient angles, to occupy protruding points, and in the latter case sometimes swell into a series of angles, developing the form of a bastion.

How far the habits of the Indians have been modified by their intercourse with the whites, cannot be ascertained with certainty, but we have data from which to draw conclusions. The earliest accounts of the Indians represent them as being, intellectually, what they now are. They had no art then which they have not now; nor has any trace been found of any art which they once possessed and have since lost. The pressure of the whites has driven them from the sea-coasts to the great plains of the West, and some change must have resulted from the difference in the character of the country, and modes of procuring food. The use of the horse, of firearms, and of other weapons of metal, has not been without effect. Mounted on this noble animal, they now overtake the buffalo, and procure abundant supplies of food—the gun has added wonderfully to the facility of hunting, and their military tactics must have been entirely changed. They are proud and fearless riders, delighting in the chase, in horse-racing, and in all exercises in which that animal is the instrument or companion of man. The introduction of ardent spirits has done much to deprave and enfeeble the Indian; and the prevalency of the small-pox and other diseases communicated by the whites, has thinned their numbers with fearful havoc. With these few exceptions, there seems to be little change in their character or condition since the discovery. The moral effects of their intercourse with the whites, we shall consider more fully in another place.

Of the two parties that were brought into contact by the discovery of North America, it may be remarked that they stood on the opposite extremes of refinement and barbarism; the North American savage not having advanced a single step in civilisation, while the European possessed all the learning, the cultivation, and the mechanical ingenuity of the age; the one was a heathen, the other enjoyed the Christian faith in the purest form in which it then existed. It may not be uninteresting to trace out the beginning of an intercourse between races thus opposed in character; because, in the examination which we propose to make of the relations since established, it is important to observe the foundation which was laid, and to notice the prejudices and antipathies which have pervaded and perverted that intercourse.

We do not assume to have made any new discovery, when we assert, that there are more popular errors in existence in respect to the Indians, than in regard to almost any other matter which has been so much and so frequently discussed. These have arisen partly out of national antipathies, partly out of the misrepresentations of interested persons, and to some extent are inseparable from the nature of the subject, which is intricate in itself and delicate in many of its bearings. The usual mode of disposing of the question, by asserting that the Indians are savages, not capable of civilisation, nor to be dealt with as rational beings, is unchristian and unphilosophical. We cannot assent to such a conclusion, without discarding the light of revelation, the philosophy of the human mind, and the results of a vast deal of experimental knowledge. The activity of body and mind displayed by the Indian in all his enterprises, the propriety and closeness of reasoning and the occasional flashes of dignity and pathos in some of their speeches, sufficiently establish the claims of this race to a respectable station in point of intellect; and we have no reason to believe that they have worse hearts, or more violent passions, than the rest of the human family, except so far as their natures have been perverted by outward circumstances. Why is it then that they are savages? Why have they not ascended in the great scale of civil subordination? Why are they ferocious, ignorant, and brutal, while we their neighbours are civilised and polished? Why is it that, while our intercourse with every other people is humane, enlightened, just—having its foundations fastened upon the broad basis of reciprocity, we shrink with horror from the Indian, spurn him from

our firesides and altars, and will not suffer the ermine of
our judges to be tarnished by his presence? Why is it
that while nearly all the world is united, as it were, in one
great and concentrated effort to spread the light of knowledge, to burst the shackles of superstition, to encourage
industry, and to cultivate the gentle and domestic virtues,
one little remnant of the human family stands unaffected
by the general amelioration, a dark and lonely monument
of irretrievable ignorance and incorrigible ferocity?

It is in the hope of answering some of these questions
that this discussion is attempted; and in order to arrive
at a successful result, it is necessary to go back beyond
our own times, and to examine events in which *we* are not
immediately concerned as a people.

If we refer to the earliest intercourse between the
existing Christian nations and the barbarous tribes, in
different quarters of the world, we find the disposition and
conduct of the latter to have been at first timid and
pacific, and that the first breaches of harmony arose out
of the aggressions committed by the former. When,
therefore, we speak of our present relations with them, as
growing out of necessity, and as resulting from the faith-
lessness and ferocity of the savage character, we assume
a position which is not supported by the facts. That a
great allowance is to be made for the disparity between
civilised and savage nations, is true; and it is equally true,
that the same degree of confidence and cordiality cannot
exist between them as between nations who acknowledge
a common religious, moral, and international code, which
operates equally upon both parties. But this does not
preclude all confidence, nor prove the Indian destitute of
moral virtue and mental capacity. On the contrary, it
must be admitted, that the Indians in their primitive state
possessed a higher moral character than now belongs to

them, and that they have been degraded in some degree by their intercourse with civilised men; and we ought, in all our dealings with them, to endeavour to atone for the injury done to them and to human nature by our departure from Christian principles, and to bring them back to a state of happiness and respectability at least equal to that in which we found them. In establishing these positions, we do not design to cast any imputation upon our own Government, nor will it be necessary. The great mistakes in policy, and the monstrous crimes committed against the savage races, to which we propose to allude, were perpetrated by almost all civilised nations before our own had any existence: and no criminality can attach to us for a state of things in the creation of which we had no agency. We know of no deliberate act of cruelty or injustice towards the tribes with which we are chargeable as a people. On the contrary, our policy has been moderate and just, and distinguished, as we shall show, by a spirit of benevolence. It is true, however, that this spirit has been misdirected, and that with the very best intentions we have done great wrong to the aborigines, to ourselves, and to humanity.

We shall first show how other nations have acted towards the savage tribes, what have been the examples set to us, and how far those examples have influenced our conduct.

The first discoverers were the Portuguese. Under Don Henry, a prince in point of knowledge and liberal feeling a century in advance of the age in which he lived, this people pushed their discoveries into the Canary Islands, the continent of Africa, and the East Indies. They were received with uniform kindness by the natives, who regarded them as a superior race of beings, and were willing to submit implicitly to their authority.   Had the Europeans of that day, and their descendants, cultivated an amicable understanding with these simple heathens, and rigidly adhered to a system of good faith and Christian forbearance, there is no calculating the advantages that might have ensued ; nor is it to be doubted that those ignorant and confiding tribes would have yielded themselves, with hardly a struggle, to the teaching of their more intelligent and powerful neighbours.   But so far from making the slightest effort to establish friendly relations with the savages, the very earliest discoverers exhibited a propensity for wanton mischief towards them, more characteristic of demons than of men, and which rendered them, and the religion they professed, so odious, that the benevolent exertions of statesmen and Christians since that time have wholly failed to eradicate the deeply rooted prejudices so injudiciously and wickedly excited.   Among a simple race, who viewed their visitors with superstitious reverence as creatures more than human, there must have been a mortifying revulsion of feeling, when they discovered in those admired strangers all the vices and wantonness which disgraced the rudest barbarians, joined to powers which they imagined were possessed only by the gods.   "Their dread and amazement was raised to the highest pitch," says Lafiteau, "when the Europeans fired their cannons and guns among them, and they saw their companions fall dead at their feet without any enemy at hand or any visible cause of their destruction."

Alluding to these transactions, Dr Johnson remarks— "On what occasion, or for what purpose muskets were discharged among a people harmless and secure, by strangers, who, without any right, visited their coast, it is not thought necessary to inform us.   The Portuguese could fear nothing from them, and had, therefore, no adequate provocation ; nor is there any reason to believe but that they murdered the Negroes in wanton merriment, perhaps only to try how many a volley would destroy, or what would be the consternation of those that should escape. We are openly told, that they had the less scruple concerning their treatment of the savage people, because *they scarcely considered them as distinct from brutes;* and indeed the practice of all European nations, and among others of the English barbarians that cultivate the southern islands of America, proves that this opinion, however absurd and foolish, however wicked and injurious, *still continues to prevail."*

"By these practices the first discoverers alienated the natives from them ; and whenever a ship appeared, every one that could fly betook himself to the mountains and the woods, so that nothing was to be got more than they could steal; they sometimes surprised a few fishers and made them slaves, and *did what they could to offend the natives and enrich themselves."*—(Introduction to *The World Displayed.*)

These events commenced about the year 1392, which is the date of the discovery of the Cape of Good Hope by the Portuguese. Chivalry was at its zenith about the same time. It was an age of moral darkness and military violence. Tamerlane, the Tartar, was reigning in Persia, and Margaret, the Semiramis of the North, in Denmark. It was the age of Gower and Chaucer, the fathers of English poetry, and of Harry Percy, the celebrated Hotspur. About the same time Wickliffe, the "morning star" of the Reformation, had made the first English translation of the Bible, and Huss and Jerome of Prague began to publish their doctrines. By keeping these facts in mind, we shall be at no loss to account for a course of conduct on the part of the Portuguese towards the

Africans, differing but little from the intolerance, the deception, and the wanton barbarity which distinguished the intercourse of European nations with each other.

In 1492 Columbus gave a new world to European curiosity, avarice and despotism. It would be vain to attempt to follow the Spanish conquerors in their desolating progress through the islands and continent of America. Like the Portuguese, they were kindly received; like them, they repaid kindness with cruelty. Their footsteps were dyed with blood—violence and lust marked all their actions. Men seemed to be transformed into ministers of darkness, and acted such deeds in real life as the boldest and darkest imagination has never ventured to suggest in fiction, or even in poetic phrensy. Bearing the cross in one hand, and the sword in the other, combining bigotry with military rapine, and the thirst for gold with the lust for power, they united in one vast scheme all the most terrible engines and worst incentives of crime. We do not know that there is to be found in history a recital more touching than the account of the conquest of Mexico by Cortes, or than that of Peru by Pizarro. In each of these instances the conquerors were at first received with hospitality by their confiding victims. They each found an amiable people, possessing many of the social arts, living happily under a government of their own choice, and practising fewer of the unnatural rites of superstition than commonly prevailed among the heathen.

The discovery and invasion of Mexico by the Spaniards under Hernan Cortes, occurred in the sixteenth century, and the Europeans were not a little surprised at the greatness of the population and the splendour of the cities. The city of Mexico, exclusive of its suburbs, is said to have measured ten miles in circumference, and contained, according to the Spanish writers, 60,000 houses. Dr

Robertson thinks it did not contain more than that number of inhabitants; but that point cannot now be settled, nor is it important. Enough is known to satisfy us that the people had passed from the savage state, in which the subsistence of man is chiefly derived from fishing and hunting, and had congregated in large towns. They had a regular government and a system of laws. The king lived in great state. "He had," says Cortes, "in this city of Mexico, such houses for his habitation, so deserving of admiration, that I cannot sufficiently express their grandeur and excellence; I shall therefore only say, *there are none equal to them in Spain.*" One of the Spanish leaders, who is styled the "Anonymous Conqueror," writes thus: "There were beautiful houses belonging to the nobles, so grand and numerous in their apartments, with such admirable gardens to them, that the sight of them filled us with astonishment and delight. I entered from curiosity four times into a palace belonging to Montezuma, and having pervaded it until I was weary, I came away at last without having seen it all. Around a large court they used to build sumptuous halls and chambers, but there was one above all so large that it was capable of containing upwards of three thousand persons without the least inconvenience: it was such that in the gallery of it alone a little square was formed where thirty men on horseback might exercise." It is certain, from the affirmation of all the historians of Mexico, that the army under Cortes, consisting of 6400 men and upwards, including the allies, were all lodged in the palace formerly possessed by King Axajacath; and there remained still sufficient lodging for Montezuma and his attendants.

"There were," says Gomara, "many temples in the city of Mexico, scattered through the different districts, that had their towers, in which were the chapels and altars for the repositories of the idols." "All these temples had houses belonging to them, their priests and gods, together with everything necessary for their worship and service." Cortes says that he counted more than four hundred temples in the city of Cholula alone. They differed, however, in size ; some were mere terraces, of little height, upon which there was a small chapel for the tutelary idol—others were of stupendous dimensions. In speaking of one of these, Cortes declares that "it is difficult to describe its parts, its grandeur, and the things contained in it."

It is certain that the Mexicans defended their cities by fortifications, which indicated some advance in the military art; they had walls, bastions, palisades, ditches, and entrenchments. They were very inferior indeed to those of Europe, because their knowledge of military architecture was imperfect; nor had they occasion to cover themselves from artillery, but they afforded sufficient proof of the industry and ingenuity of the people.

Taking them altogether, the Mexicans had many high and estimable traits in their national character, and they probably enjoyed in social life as much happiness as is usually allotted to man. Speaking of Lascalteca, a city of Mexico, Cortes says : "I was surprised at its size and magnificence. It is larger and stronger than Grenada, contains as many and as handsome buildings, and is much more populous than that city was at the time of its conquest. It is also much better supplied with corn, poultry, game, fresh water, fish, pulse, and excellent vegetables. There are in the market each day thirty thousand persons, including buyers and sellers, without mentioning the merchants and petty dealers dispersed over the city. In this market may be bought every necessary of life, clothes, shoes, feathers of all kinds, ornaments of gold and silver, as well wrought as in any part of the world; various kinds of earthenware, of a superior quality to that of Spain; wood, coal, herbs, and medicinal plants. Here are houses for baths, and places for washing and shearing goats; in short, this city exhibits great regularity and has a good police; the inhabitants are peculiarly neat, and far superior to the most industrious of the Africans." The city of Cholula is described by Bernal Diaz as "resembling Valladolid," and containing 20,000 inhabitants. Both of these cities were of course vastly inferior to the city of Mexico; but it is not necessary to swell our pages by a laboured attempt to prove the civilisation of the Mexicans. If we except the single article of the Christian faith and the Bible, in which the Spaniards had the advantage of them, we question whether they were not, immediately previous to their subjugation, in a higher state of civilisation than their oppressors; whether they had not better practical views of civil liberty, more just notions of private right, and more of the amiable propensities and softer virtues of life.

Their laws were superior to those of the Greeks and Romans, and their magistrates more just. They punished with death their judges who passed a sentence that was unjust or contrary to law, or who made an incorrect statement of any cause to the king, or to a superior magistrate, or who accepted a bribe. Any person who altered the measures established in their markets, met with the same punishment. Guardians who wasted the estates of their wards were punished capitally. Drunkenness in their youth was punished with death; in persons more advanced in life, it was punished with severity, though not capitally. A nobleman who was guilty of this vice, was stripped of his dignity, and rendered infamous; a plebeian was shaved and had his house demolished. Their

maxim was that he who could voluntarily deprive himself
of his senses, was unworthy of a habitation among men;
but this law did not extend to the aged, who were
allowed to drink as much as they pleased on their own
responsibility.

They had a good police and excellent internal regulations. Couriers were maintained, by whom intelligence
was regularly and rapidly transmitted. Their highways
were repaired annually; in the mountains and uninhabited
places there were houses erected for the accommodation
of travellers; and they had bridges and boats for crossing
rivers. The land was divided by appropriate boundaries,
and owned by individuals, and the right of property in
real, as well as personal estate, was thoroughly understood and respected.

Such is the character given to the Mexicans by those
who assumed the right to plunder and oppress them,
under the plea that they were savages and heathens.
After making due allowance for the exaggerations incident
to such questionable testimony, enough remains to show
that this singular people were advanced far beyond mere
barbarism; and the recent discoveries by Mr Stevens and
others, place that question beyond all cavil. The subject
is curious and highly interesting. Few are aware of the
degree of civilisation which existed among the Mexicans
and South American nations previous to their conquest
by the Spaniards—the intelligence, the kindness, the
hospitality and respectable virtues of the natives, and the
atrocious character of the marauders by whom they were
despoiled and enslaved.

One instance, in proof of these assertions, may be found
in the fascinating work of a distinguished American writer,
so affecting, and strongly in point, that I cannot forbear
alluding to it. Vasco Nunez, one of the most celebrated

of the conquerors of New Spain, had been hospitably received by one of the native princes. With the usual perfidy of his time and country, he made captives of the Cacique, his wives and children, and many of his people. He also discovered their store of provisions, and returned with his captives and his booty to Darien. When the unfortunate Cacique beheld his family in chains, and in the hands of strangers, his heart was wrung with despair: "What have I done to thee," said he to Vasco Nunez, "that thou shouldest treat me thus cruelly? None of thy people ever came to my land, that were not fed and sheltered, and treated with kindness. When thou camest to my dwelling, did I meet thee with a javelin in my hand? Did I not set meat and drink before thee, and welcome thee as a brother? Set me free, therefore, with my people and family, and we will remain thy friends. We will supply thee with provisions, and reveal to thee the riches of the land. Dost thou doubt my faith? Behold my daughter, I give her to thee as a pledge of my friendship. Take her for thy wife, and be assured of the fidelity of her family and people!"

Vasco Nunez felt the power of these words, and knew the importance of forming a strong alliance among the natives. The captive maid also, as she stood trembling and dejected before him, found great favour in his eyes, for she was young and beautiful. He granted, therefore, the prayer of the Cacique, and accepted his daughter, engaging, moreover, to aid the father against his enemies, on condition of his furnishing provisions to the colony.

"Careta (the Indian prince) remained three days at Darien, during which time he was treated with the utmost kindness. Vasco Nunez took him on board his ships and showed him every part of them. He displayed before him also the war-horses, with their armour and rich caparisons, and astonished him with the thunder of artillery. Lest he should be too much daunted by these warlike spectacles, he caused the musicians to perform an harmonious concert on their instruments, at which the Cacique was lost in admiration. Thus having impressed him with a wonderful idea of the power and endowments of his new allies, he loaded him with presents and permitted him to depart.

"Careta returned joyfully to his territories, and his daughter remained with Vasco Nunez, *willingly*, for HIS SAKE, giving up her family and her native home. They were never married, but she considered herself as his wife, as she really was, according to the usages of her own country, and he treated her with fondness, allowing her gradually to acquire a great influence over him."—*Irving*.

I envy not the man who can read this affecting passage without mingled emotions of admiration and pity. Who, in this case, displayed the vices of barbarians? Was it the daring marauder, who violated the rules of hospitality? Was it the generous chief, who opened his heart and his house with confiding hospitality to the military stranger— who, when betrayed, appealed to his treacherous guest with all the manly simplicity of an honest heart, mingled with the deep emotion of a bereaved parent and an insulted sovereign—and who, with magnanimous patriotism, gave up his child, a young and beautiful maiden, to purchase the liberty of his people? Or was it the Indian maid, adorned with graces that could win the heart of that ruthless soldier, "willingly, for his sake, giving up her family and native home," discharging with devoted fidelity the duty of the most sacred relation in life, and achieving by her talents and feminine attractions a complete conquest over her country's conqueror? Shame on the abuse of language that would call such a people savage, or their oppressors Christians!

At a much later period, and when the Christian world was far more enlightened than in the days of Cortes, the British commenced their conquests in India; yet we do not find the superior light they possessed, both religious and political, had any other effect than to make them more refined in their cruelties. They acted over again in the East Indies, all the atrocities which had been perpetrated in New Spain, with this only difference, that they did not pretend to plead the apology of religious fanaticism. The Spaniards attempted to impose on others, and may possibly, in some instances, have imposed on themselves the belief, that they served God in oppressing the heathen; for their conquests were made in an age when such opinions were prevalent. But the "English barbarians," as Dr Johnson calls them, had no such notions; for some of their best patriots and soundest divines had lived previous to the conquest of India, and the intellectual character of the nation was deeply imbued with the principles of civil and religious liberty before that period. The love of money and of dominion were their only incentives; and they pillaged, tortured, murdered, and enslaved a people as civilised and as gentle as the Mexicans, without the shadow of an excuse. Millions of wealth have been poured into England, to enrich and adorn the land, to support the magnificence of the Court, and to minister to the pleasures of a proud aristocracy, which were wrung from an unoffending people by acts of violence and extortion no better than piracy. The disclosures made before the British Parliament at the trial of Warren Hastings justify these assertions; and subsequent events in India, China, and other parts of the East, exhibit the same grasping and ruthless injustice on the part of that nation.

Need we pursue the navigators of these and other

PO-CA-HON-TAS

The Princess who rescued Captain Smith

(*For Notes on the Portrait, see pp. ix-xii*)

nations to the different quarters of the globe into which scientific curiosity, mercantile enterprise, and naval skill have penetrated? Such an investigation would but add new facts in support of the positions we have taken.

We pause here, then, to inquire how it has happened, that wherever the civilised European has placed his foot upon heathen soil, he seems at once to have been transformed into a barbarian. All the refinements of civilised life have been forgotten. His benevolence, his sensibility, his high sense of honour, his nice perception of justice, his guarded deportment, his long habits of punctuality and integrity, are all thrown aside; and not only has he been less honest than the savage in his private dealings, but has far outstripped him in the worst propensities of human nature—in avarice, revenge, rapine, blood-thirstiness, and wanton cruelty. To the caprice of the savage, and that prodigality of life which distinguishes men unaccustomed to the restraints of law, and the ties of society, he has added the ingenuity of art, and the insolence of power. The lust of empire, and the lust of money, have given him incentives to crime which do not stimulate the savage; and his intellectual cultivation has furnished him with weapons of war and engines of oppression, which have been wielded with a fearful energy of purpose and a monstrous depravity of motive.

Nor were the desperate adventurers, who led the van of discovery and conquest in heathen lands, alone implicated in the guilt of these transactions. They were sanctioned by the Throne and the Church. The Pope formally delivered over the heathen into the hands of the secular power; Kings abandoned them to the military leaders; and the nobles, the merchants, the wealthy and reputable of all ranks, became partners in those nefarious enterprises—sharers in the pillage, and accessories in the

murder of inoffensive nations. We are struck with
astonishment, when we see the people of countries professing the Christian faith, having social regulations, and
respecting a code of international law among themselves,
thus turned into ruthless depredators, and trampling under
foot every maxim of justice, human and divine.

In searching out the moving causes of this apparently
anomalous operation of the human mind, we remark, in
the first place, that the age of discovery was an age of
ignorance. Few of the great fountains of light had been
opened to pour out the flood of knowledge which has since
penetrated into every quarter of the globe, and to
disseminate the principles of conduct which now regulate
the intercourse of men and of nations. In Europe the
great mass of the people—all of those whose united
opinions make up what is called public sentiment, were
alike destitute of moral culture ; the ruler and the subject,
the noble and the plebeian, the martial leader and the
wretched peasant, were equally deficient in literature and
science. All knowledge was in the hands of the priests,
and was by them perverted to the forwarding of their own
selfish purposes. The great secret of their influence
consisted in an ingenious concealment of all the sources of
knowledge. The Bible, the only elevated, pure, and
consistent code of ethics the world has ever known, was a
sealed book to the people. The ancient classics were
carefully withheld from the public eye ; and the few
sciences which were at all cultivated, were enveloped in
the darkness of the dead languages. No system could
have been more ingenious or more successful, than thus to
clothe the treasures of knowledge in languages difficult of
attainment, and accessible only to the high-born and
wealthy—for as the latter seldom undergo the labour of
unlocking the stores of learning, and still less frequently

teach to others what they have acquired, such a system amounted in practice to a monopoly of learning in the hands of the priesthood.

Not only were the people of that day destitute of education, but the intercourse of nations with each other, previous to the discovery of the mariner's compass, was extremely limited ; and the wonderful facilities for gaining and diffusing intelligence, afforded by the art of navigation, had just begun to operate in the days of Columbus and Cortes.

The little knowledge that existed was perverted and misapplied. Where there was little freedom of thought, and no general spirit of inquiry, precedents were indiscriminately adopted, however inconsistent, and examples blindly followed, however wicked or absurd. The scholar found authority for every crime in the classics of heathen Greeks and Romans, who have left nothing behind them worthy of admiration, except a few splendid specimens of useful luxury and worthless refinement, and some rare fragments of magnanimity and virtue; while their literature abounds in incentives to ambition, rapine, and oppression. The few who read the Scriptures wrested the precepts of revelation and the history of the primitive nations into authority for their own high-handed aggressions; and because distinctions were made between the Jews and the heathen by whom they were surrounded, ignorantly believed, or perversely maintained, that the same relation continued to exist between the true believer and the heretic, and that the latter " were given to them for an inheritance."

The era now under contemplation was a martial age. Ambition expended all its energies in the pursuit of military glory; the fervours of genius were all conducted into this channel; and, confined in every other direction, burst forth like a volcano, in the flame and violence of military achievement. The only road to fame or to preferment led across the battle-field; the hero waded to power through seas of blood, or strode to affluence over the carcasses of the slain; and they who sat in high places, were accustomed to look upon carnage as a necessary agent, or an unavoidable incident to greatness. The people everywhere were accustomed to scenes of violence. The right of conquest was universally acknowledged, and success was the criterion of merit. Private rights, whether of person or property, were little understood, and generally disregarded; and national justice, in any enlarged sense, was neither practised nor professed. Certain chivalrous courtesies there were, practised among the military and the high-born, and gleams of magnanimity occasionally flashed out amid the gloom of anarchy, but they afforded no steady light. They were the grim civilities of warriors, or the formal politeness of the great, which did not pervade the mass of the people, and tended not to refine the age, nor to soften the asperities of oppression.

It was an age of intolerance, bigotry, superstition, and ecclesiastical despotism; when those who regulated the minds and consciences of men, were persons of perverted taste, intellect, and morals; men who lived estranged from society, aliens from its business, strangers to its domestic relations, its noblest virtues, and its kindest affections. It was, in short, the age of the inquisition and the rack, when opinions were regulated by law, and enforced by the stake and the sword, and when departures from established dogmas were punished by torture, disfranchisement, and death.

Under such auspices commenced the intercourse between civilised and savage men, and unfortunately the pioneers, who led the way in the discovery and colonisation of new countries, were, with a few bright exceptions, the worst men of their time—the soldier, the mariner, the desperate seeker after gold—men inured to cruelty and rapine, and from whose codes of religion, morality, and law, imperfect as they were, the poor heathen was entirely excluded.

We shall not dwell in detail on the facts to which we have briefly alluded. It would require volumes to record the unprovoked cruelties perpetrated by civilised upon savage men. The lawless invasion of Mexico by Cortes; the horrid atrocities of the ruffian Pizarro, acted in Peru; the long series of robberies and bloodshed perpetrated by the British in India; the dreadful scenes of the slave trade; the track of carnage, and the maledictions of the heathen, which have marked the discoveries of the European in every quarter of the globe, are but too familiar to every reader of history. It is obvious that the first aggression was almost invariably committed by the whites, who have continued to be, for the most part, the offending party; yet history does not afford the slightest evidence, that any public disapprobation was manifested, either by the Governments or the people of those countries, whose adventurers were overrunning the uncivilised parts of the world, in search of plunder, and in the perpetration of every species of enormity. A classic hatred of barbarians, a holy zeal against unbelievers, animated all classes of society, and sanctioned every outrage which was inflicted, in the name of religion or civilisation, by commissioned freebooters, upon the unoffending inhabitants of newly discovered regions.

In the discovery and settlement of North America, the conduct of the whites was far less blameable than in the instances to which we have alluded; still it was aggressive, and productive of the most unhappy conse-

quences. We propose to touch on some of the prominent
points of this history, and to present a few instances
illustrative of its spirit, and in support of our general
views.

Captain John Smith informs us, that "The most
famous, renowned, and ever worthy of all memorie, for
her courage, learning, judgement, and virtue, Queen
Elizabeth, granted her letters patent to Sir Walter
Raleigh, for the discovering and planting new lands and
countries not actually possessed by any Christians. This
patantee got to be his assistants, Sir Richard Grenville the
valiant, Mr William Sanderson a great friend to all such
noble and worthy actions, and divers other gentlemen
and marchants, who with all speede provided two small
barkes well furnished with necessaries, under the command
of Captaine Philip Amidas and Captain Barlow. The
27th of Aprill they set sayle from the Thames, the 10th of
May passed the Canaries, and the 10th of June the West
Indies," etc. "The second of July they fell in with the
coast of Florida, in shoule water, where they felt a most
delicate sweete smell, though they saw no land, which ere
long they espied," etc.

Here we find, that the power delegated by the Crown
to those lovers of worthy and noble actions, was simply
for the discovering and planting of new lands, not actually
possessed by other Christians; but although the rights of
other Christians, who had no rights, were thus carefully
reserved, no regard seems to have been paid to those
of the aboriginal possessors of the countries to be discovered. With respect to them, the adventurers were at
full liberty to act as their own judgment or caprice might
dictate.

The inhabitants received them with confidence. In
the *History* of Smith we read : "Till the third day we saw

not any of the people, then in a little boat three of them appeared, one of them went on shore to whom we rowed, and he attended us without any sign of feare, after he had spoken much, though we understood not a word, of his own accorde he came boldly aboord us ; we gave him a shirt, a hat, wine, and meate, which he liked well, and after he had well viewed the barkes and vs, he went away in his own boat, and within a quarter of a mile of vs, in half an hour, he loaded his boat with fish, with which he came againe to the point of land, and there divided it in two parts, pointing one part to the ship, and the other to the pinace, and so departed."

" The next day came diuers boats, and in one of them the King's brother, with forty or fifty men, proper people, and in their behaviour very ciuil." "Though we came to him well armed, he made signs to vs to sit downe without any sign of feare, stroking his head and brest, and also ours, to expresse his loue. After he had made a long speech to vs, we presented him with diuers toyes, which he kindly accepted."

" A day or two after, shewing them what we had, Grangranæmeo taking most liking to a pewter dish, made a hole in it, and hung it about his neck for a brestplate, for which he gaue vs twenty deere skins, worth twenty crownes ; and for a copper kettle, fiftie skins, worth fiftie crownes. Much other trucke we had, and after two dayes he came aboord, and did eat and drinke with vs very merrily. Not long after he brought his wife and children," etc.

" After that these women had been here with vs, there came doune from all parts great store of people, with leather, corrall, and diuers kinde of dyes, but when Grangranæmeo was present, none durst trade but himself, and them that wore red copper on their heads as he did. Whenever he came he would signifie by so many fires he came with so many boats, that we might knowe his force. Their boats but one great tree, which is burnt in the form of a trough with gins and fire, till it be as they would haue it. For an armour he would haue engaged vs a bagge of pearle, but we refused, as not regarding it, that wee might the better learne where it grew. He was very iust of his promise, for oft we trusted him, and would come within his day to keepe his word. He sent vs commonly every day a brace of bucks, conies, hares, and fish, sometimes mellons, walnuts, cucumbers, peas, and diuers roots. This author sayeth their corne groweth three times in fiue months; in May they sow, in Iuly reape; in Iune they sow, in August reape."

It is difficult to separate the truth from the fiction in these early histories. There seems to be an inherent propensity for exaggeration in English travellers, which has pervaded their works, and cast a shade upon their character from the earliest time to the present. We know that our own corn does not grow "three times in five months, and that it cannot be planted in May and reaped in July in any part of our country; the story of the "bagge of pearle" is very questionable; nor do we put much faith in the "corrall" or the "red copper," which the natives are said to have possessed. These were flourishes of the imagination, thrown in by the writers, for purposes best known to themselves. But we may believe the evidence of the voyagers, as to the hospitality with which they were received by the natives, because in these statements they all agree, and we have ample reason to believe that such was usually the deportment of the aborigines towards the Europeans who first visited our shores. The historian of this voyage sums up the whole in the expression, "a more kind loving people cannot be," and adds, "this discovery was so welcome into England,

LEDAGIE
A Creek Chief

ON-GE-WAE
A Chippeway Chief

that it pleased her majestie to call this country of Wingandacoa, *Virginia*, by which name you are now to understand how it was planted, dissolued, reuned, and enlarged."

In 1585 Sir Richard Grenville departed from Plymouth with seven sail for Virginia. On his first arrival we are told, "the Indians stole a silver cup, wherefore we burned their town and spoiled their corn, and so returned to our fleet." Here we see how hostilities between the whites and Indians commenced. All the hospitality of those who were lauded as "a kind loving people," was effaced by a single depredation, committed most probably by a lawless individual, whose act would have been disavowed by the tribe; and in revenge for the stealing of a cup, a town was burned, and the cornfields of an unoffending community destroyed. Dr Williamson, the historian of North Carolina, remarks: "The passionate and rash conduct of Sir Richard Grenville cost the nation many a life. The fair beginning of a hopeful colony was obscured, it was nearly defeated, by resenting the loss of a silver cup."

Another voyager, John Brierton, who accompanied Captain Gesnall in 1690 to Virginia, speaks of the "many signs of loue and friendship," displayed by the Indians, "that did helpe us to dig and carry saxafras, and doe any thing they could." "Some of the baser sort would steale; but the better sort," he continues, "we found very civill and iust." He considers the women as fat and well favoured; and concludes, "the wholesomeness and temperature of this climate doth not onely argue the people to be answerable to this description, but also of a perfect constitution of body, active, strong, healthful, and very witty, as the sundry toyes by them so cunningly wrought may well testifie."

Captain Smith, in a subsequent visit to Virginia, found the people "most civill to giue entertainment." He declares that "such great and well proportioned men are seldome seene, for they seemed like giants to the English, yea, and to the neighbours, yet seemed of an honest and simple disposition; with much adoe we restrained them from adoring us as gods." In another place he says, "They are very strong, of an able body, and full of agilitie, able to endure to lie in the woods vnder a tree by a fire in the worst of winter, or in the weeds and grasse, in ambuscade, in the sommer. They are inconstant in every thing but what feare constraineth them to keepe. Craftie, timourous, quicke of apprehension, and very ingenious. Some are of a disposition fearful, some bold, most cautelous and savage." "Although the country people be very barbarous, yet have they among them such government, as that their magistrates for good commanding, and their people for due subjection and obeying, excell many places that would be accounted very civill."—*Smith's Hist.*, vol. i. p. 142.

Another early writer on the settlement of Virginia, William Timons, "doctour of divinitie," remarks, "it might well be thought, a countrie so faire (as Virginia is) and a people so tractable, would long ere this have been quietly possessed, to the satisfaction of the adventurers, and the eternising of the memory of those that effected it." We need not multiply these proofs. History abounds in facts to prove the positions we have taken, and to convict the white man of being almost invariably the aggressor in that unnatural war which has now been raging for centuries between the civilised and savage races.

Several fruitless attempts were made to plant a colony in Virginia before that enterprise succeeded. "The emigrants, notwithstanding the orders they had received, had never been solicitous to cultivate the good will of the natives, and *had neither asked permission when they occupied* their country, nor *given a price for their valuable property*, which was violently taken away. The miseries of famine were soon superadded to the horrors of massacre." (See Chalmer's *Political Annals*, under the head Virginia.) Under all the disasters suffered by that colony, and with repeated examples and admonitions to warn them, they could never bring themselves to entertain sufficient respect for the Indians to treat them with civility, or negotiate with them in good faith. Their great error was, that they did not consider themselves, in their intercourse with savages, bound by the same moral obligations which would have governed their dealings with civilised men. They were loose and careless in their deportment; they threw off the ordinary restraints of social life; the decent and sober virtues were laid aside; and while as individuals they forfeited confidence by their irregularities, they lost it as a body politic by weak councils and bad faith. It is to be recollected that the colonists were intruders in a strange land; they had to establish a character. Their very coming was suspicious. There was no reason why the natives should think them better than they seemed, but many, why, they might suspect them to be worse. The Indians having few virtues in their simple code, practise those which they do profess with great punctuality; and they could not but lightly esteem those who made great professions of superior virtue, while they openly indulged in every vice and set all moral obligations at defiance.

The romantic story of Pocahontas forms a beautiful episode in the history of this period. Though born and reared in savage life, she was a creature of exquisite loveliness and refinement. The gracefulness of her person, the gentleness of her nature—her benevolence, her courage, her noble self-devotion in the discharge of duty, elevate this lovely woman to an equality with the most illustrious and most attractive of her sex; and yet those winning graces and noble qualities were not the most remarkable features of her character, which was even more distinguished by the wonderful tact, and the delicate sense of propriety, which marked all the scenes of her brief, but eventful history. The mingled tenderness and heroism of her successful intercession for the adventurous Smith, presents a scene which for dramatic effect and moral beauty, is not excelled either in the records of history or the most splendid creations of inventive genius. Had she been a Christian, had the generous spark of love, which is inbred in the heart of woman, been cherished by the refinements of education, or fanned by the strong impulse of devoted piety, it could not have burned with a purer or a brighter flame. The motive of that noble action was benevolence, the purest and most lofty principle of human action. It was not the caprice of a thoughtless girl, it was not the momentary passion for the condemned stranger, pleading at a susceptible heart, for her affections were reserved for another, and the purity as well as the dignity of her after life, showed that they were truly and cautiously bestowed. By her intervention, her courage, and her talent, the colony of Virginia was several times saved from famine and extermination; and when perfidiously taken prisoner by those who owed everything to her noble devotion to their cause, she displayed in her captivity a patience, a sweetness of disposition, and a propriety of conduct that won universal admiration. As the wife of Rolfe, she was equally exemplary; and when at the British Court she stood in the presence of royalty, surrounded by the beauty and refinement of the proudest aristocracy in the world, she was still a lovely and admired woman, unsurpassed in the appropriate graces of her sex. Yet this woman was a savage! A daughter of a race doomed to eternal barbarism by the decree of a philosophy which pronounces the soil of their minds too sterile to germinate the seeds of civilisation!

An authentic portrait of this lovely and excellent woman, copied from a picture in the possession of her descendants in Virginia, forms the chief attraction of this number of our work. Her original name was Matoaka, which signifies literally the *Snow feather*, or the snow flake, which was also the name of her mother; and both were represented as being remarkably graceful and swift of foot. She was afterwards called Pocahontas, *A rivulet between two hills*, a name supposed by some to be prophetic, as she was a bond of peace and union between two nations.

Her intercession for Smith is thus described by the ancient historians : " The captive, bound hand and foot, was laid upon the stones, and Powhattan, to whom the honour was respectfully assigned, was about to put him to death. Something like pity beamed from the eyes of the savage crowd, but none dared to speak. The fatal club was uplifted ; the captive was without a friend to succour him, alone among hostile savages. The breasts of the multitude already anticipated the dreadful crash that world deprive him of life, when the young and beautiful Pocahontas, the King's darling daughter, with a shriek of terror and agony, threw herself on the body of the victim ! Her dark hair unbound, her eyes streaming with tears, and her whole manner bespoke the agony of her bosom. She cast the most beseeching looks at her angry and astonished father, imploring his pity, and the life of the captive, with all the eloquence of mute but impassioned sorrow."—*Smith*.

"The remainder of this scene," says Burk, "is highly honourable to Powhattan, and remains a lasting monument that, though different principles of action, and the influence of custom, had given to the manners of this people an appearance neither amiable nor virtuous in general, yet they still retained the noblest property of the human character—the touch of sympathy and the feelings of humanity. The club of the Emperor was still uplifted ; but gentle feelings had overcome him, and his eye was every moment losing its fierceness. He looked round to find an excuse for his weakness, and saw pity in every face. The generous savage no longer hesitated. The compassion of the rude state is neither ostentatious nor dilatory, nor does it insult its object by the exaction of impossibilities. Powhattan lifted his grateful and delighted daughter from the earth, but lately ready to receive the blood of the victim, and commanded the stranger captive to rise."

Pocahontas was born about the year 1594, and was therefore about twelve or thirteen years old when she saved the life of Smith in 1607. She afterwards, on several occasions, rendered essential services to the English colonists. From the year 1609 to 1611, about two years, it is said that she was never seen at Jamestown, and it is supposed that her father, jealous of her kindness towards the whites, had taken means to interrupt the intercourse. "About this time," says Stith, "or perhaps earlier, the Princess was not seen for some time. Rumour said she was banished to her father's remote possessions."

It was probably during this absence from home, that she was perfidiously captured by Captain Argall, who, being on a trading expedition up the Potowmac, discovered that Pocahontas was on a visit to that neighbourhood. "He immediately conceived the project," says Burk, "of getting her into his power, concluding that the possession of so valuable a hostage would operate as a check on the hostile dispositions of her father, the Emperor, and might be made the means of reconciliation." Having decoyed her on board of his vessel, he seized, and carried her to Jamestown. Here she became acquainted with Mr John Rolfe, a gentleman of great respectability, who soon afterwards led her to the altar. She was converted to Christianity and baptised, about the time of her marriage. The name given her in baptism was Rebecca. Shortly after her marriage, and when under twenty years of age, she accompanied her husband to England, where she was well received and greatly admired. All accounts unite in ascribing to her the gentler and more attractive virtues of her sex ; she was graceful, modest, and retiring ; yet had sufficient strength of character to sustain herself well in the station in which she was placed. She died at Gravesend, whither she went to embark to her native land, in **1616**, after residing in England two years. She left one son, of whom the historian Stith says, " at the death of Pocahontas, Sir Lewis Steukley of Plymouth took the child ; but he soon fell into disrepute, in consequence of his treacherously betraying Sir Walter Raleigh to execution. The boy, Thomas Rolfe, was sent to his uncle, Henry Rolfe, who educated him. He afterwards returned to Virginia, where he became a man of great eminence ; and marrying, left an only daughter, from whom are descended many of the first families in the State."

The founders of New England were a pious race, who brought with them a political creed far more enlightened, and a much purer system of moral action, than any portion of Europe had then learned to tolerate. They were disposed to act conscientiously in their public as well as in their private concerns, and their relations with the Indians

were commenced in amity and good faith. Their great
fault was their religious intolerance. Theirs was an
intolerant age, and they were a bigoted race ; and it is not
surprising that a people who persecuted each other on
account of sectarian differences of opinion, should have
little charity for unbelievers. They who burned old women
for indulging in the innocent pastime of riding on broom-
sticks, fined Quakers for wearing broad brimmed hats, and
enacted all the other extravagances of the blue laws, may
well have fancied themselves privileged to oppress the
uncivilised Indian. They could not brook the idea of
associating with heathens as with equals. They looked
upon them with scorn, and negotiated with them as
with inferiors. However a sense of duty might restrain
them from open insult or injury, they could not conceal
their abhorrence for the persons and principles of their new
allies. That a free, untamed race, accustomed to no
superiors, should long remain in amiable intercourse with
a precise sectarian people, who held them in utter aversion,
was not to be expected ; and accordingly we find that the
hollow friendship of these parties was soon interrupted.
Wars ensued, and no lasting peace was ever restored until
the Indian tribes were extinguished or driven from the
country.

We consider this the fairest instance that could be
quoted in proof of the universal prevalence of that public
sentiment in relation to savages, to which we have alluded.
"The settlement of New England," says one of the most
respectable of their historians, "purely for the purpose of
religion, and the propagation of civil and religious liberty, is
an event which has no parallel in the history of modern
ages. The piety, self-denial, patience, perseverance, and
magnanimity of the first settlers, are without a rival. The
happy and extensive consequences of the settlements which

NAH-ET-LUC-HOPIE
A Muskogee Chief

they made, and the sentiments which they were careful to propagate to their posterity, to the Church, and to the world admit of no descripton." If there is any truth in this description—and we do not dispute it, extravagant as it seems—a strange discrepancy is evinced in the practice and professions of a people of such pretensions. The perversion of public opinion, which could induce such men, themselves the subjects of oppression and the propagators of civil and religious liberty, to treat the savages as brutes, must have been wide spread and deeply seated ; but such was certainly their conduct.

When we remark the weakness of the first settlements in New England, and observe that their infant villages were on several occasions almost depopulated by famine and sickness, it is obvious that the Indians must have been peaceably disposed towards them, as there were several periods at which they could with ease have exterminated all the colonists. We have on this subject positive evidence. In Baylie's *Memoir of Plymouth*, we are told that the Mohawks, the most powerful nation of New England, " were never known to molest the English." " They were never known to injure an Englishman either in person or property. The English frequently met them in the woods when they were defenceless, and the Indians armed, but never received from them the slightest insult." " Unbounded hospitality to strangers " is one of the qualities ascribed by this historian to the Indians generally, of that region, and his work abounds in anecdotes of their kindness to the first settlers.

Trumbull, the historian of Connecticut, who has collected all the oldest authorities with great care, remarks that, "the English lived in tolerable peace with all the Indians in Connecticut and New England, except the Pequots, for about forty years." " The Indians at their first settlement performed many acts of kindness towards them.   They instructed them in the manner of planting and dressing Indian corn.   They carried them upon their backs through the rivers and waters; and, as occasion required, served them instead of boats and bridges.   They gave them much useful information respecting the country; and when the English or their children were lost in the woods, and were in danger of perishing with cold or hunger, they conducted them to their wigwams, fed them, and restored them to their families and parents.   By selling them corn when pinched with famine, they relieved their distresses and prevented them from perishing in a strange land and uncultivated wilderness."—(Vol. i. p. 57.)

How did the Puritans repay this kindness, or what had they done to deserve it ?   They settled in the country without the permission of the inhabitants, and evinced by all their movements a determination to extend their dominion over it.   One of their earliest acts was of a character to create disgust and awaken jealousy.   William Holmes of Plymouth carried a colony into Connecticut and settled at Windsor, where he built the first house that ever was erected in that state.   A number of Sachems, "who were the original owners of the soil, had been driven from this part of the country by the Pequots, and were now carried home on board Holmes' vessel. *Of them* the Plymouth people *purchased the land* on which they erected their house."   Intruders themselves, in a strange country, they came accompanied by persons towards whom the inhabitants were hostile, undertook to decide who were the rightful owners of the soil, and purchased from the party which was not in possession.   And what was the consequence ?   "The Indians were offended at their bringing home the original proprietors and lords of the country, and the Dutch"—who had settled there before them—"that they had settled there, and were about to rival them in trade, and in the possession of those excellent lands upon the river; they were obliged, therefore, to combat both, and to keep a constant watch upon them."

Notwithstanding the unhappy impression which some of the early acts of the Puritans were calculated to produce upon the minds of the Indians, the latter continued to be their friends. In the winter of 1635, the settlements on Connecticut river were afflicted by famine. Some of the settlers, driven by hunger, attempted to find their way, in this severe season, through the wilderness from Connecticut to Massachusetts. Of thirteen in one company who made this attempt, one, in passing a river, fell through the ice, and was drowned. The other twelve were ten days on their journey, and would all have perished, had it not been for the assistance of the Indians. "The people who kept their stations on the river, suffered in an extreme degree. After all the help they were able to obtain by hunting, and from the Indians, they were obliged to subsist on acorns, malt, and grain." "Numbers of cattle, which could not be got over the river before winter, lived through without anything but what they found in the woods and meadows. They wintered as well, or better, than those that were brought over."—Winthrop's *Journal*, p. 88.

"It is difficult to describe, or even conceive, the apprehensions and distresses of a people in the circumstances of our venerable ancestors, during this doleful winter. All the horrors of a dreary wilderness spread themselves around them. They were encompassed with numerous fierce and cruel tribes of wild and savage men, who could have swallowed up parents and children at pleasure, in their feeble and distressed condition. They had neither bread for themselves nor children; neither

habitations nor clothing convenient for them. Whatever
emergency might happen, they were cut off, both by land
and water, from any succour or retreat. What self-denial,
firmness, and magnanimity are necessary for such enterprises? How distressful, in the commencement, was the
beginning of these now fair and opulent towns on
Connecticut river!"—*Trumbull*, vol. i. p. 63.

Yet those "wild and savage men, who could have
swallowed up parents and children," did not avail themselves
of this tempting opportunity to rid their country of the
intruding whites. On the contrary, they proved their best
friends—aided those who fled, sustained those who
remained, and suffered the cattle of the strangers to roam
unmolested through the woods, while they themselves
were procuring a precarious subsistence by the chase. If
ever kindness, honesty, and forbearance were practised with
scrupulous fidelity, in the face of strong temptation inciting
to an opposite course of conduct, these virtues were
displayed by the Indians on this occasion.

This humane deportment on the part of the aborigines
seems to have been considered by the Puritans as mere
matter of course, and as not imposing upon them any
special obligation of gratitude ; for no sooner did a state
of war occur, than all sense of indebtedness to the Indians
appears to have been obliterated, and the whites vied with
their enemies in the perpetration of wanton cruelty.
Within two years after the famine alluded to, we are
informed by Trumbull that a party under Captain
Stoughton "surrounded a large body of Pequots in a
swamp. They took eighty captives. Thirty were men,
the rest were women and children. The men, except two
Sachems, *were killed*, but the women and children were
saved. The Sachems promised to conduct the English to
Sassacus, and for *that purpose* were spared *for the present*."

The reader will doubtless feel some curiosity to know what was done with the women and children who were saved by those who had massacred in cold blood thirty men, save two, taken prisoners in battle. The same historian thus details the sequel. " The Pequot women and children who had been captivated, were divided among the troops. Some were carried to Connecticut, others to Massachusetts. The people of Massachusetts sent a number of the women and boys to the West Indies, and *sold them as slaves*. It was supposed that about seven hundred Pequots were destroyed."

"This happy event," concludes the historian, alluding to the conclusion of the war, by the extermination and captivity of so many human beings, "gave great joy to the colonies. A day of public thanksgiving was appointed ; and in all the churches of New England devout and animated praises were addressed to Him who giveth His people the victory, and causeth them to dwell in safety !"

In an old and curious work, Gookin's *History of the Praying Indians*, the author consoles himself on account of the atrocities practised against the Indians, by the comfortable reflection that, "doubtless one great end God aimed at, was the punishment and destruction of many of the wicked heathen, whose iniquities were now full."

In the instructions given to Major Gibbons, who was sent from Massachusetts in 1645, against the Narragansets, are these words : "You are to have due regard to the distance which is to be observed, betwixt Christians and barbarians, as well in wars as in other negotiations."

On this passage Governor Hutchinson remarks, "It seems strange that men, who professed to believe that God hath made of one blood all nations of men, for to dwell on the face of the earth, should so early, and upon every occasion, take care to preserve this distinction.

Perhaps nothing has more effectually defeated the endeavours for christianising the Indians." This is exactly the proposition we are endeavouring to establish.

We have not forgotten the Elliots, the Brainerds, and other good men who devoted themselves with zeal and fidelity to the work of Christianising the savages. Their memories will live in history, and be cherished by every friend of humanity. In every nation, and in all ages, there have existed noble spirits, imbued with a love for their species, and acting upon the highest impulses of a generous nature, or humble Christians who were content to tread in the path of duty. We would not even pass them by, without the tribute of our approbation ; but their deeds form no part of the history on which we are commenting, and are but slightly connected with it. Our purpose is not to treat of the good or evil conduct of individuals, whose influence was but temporary and local ; —it is to show the general current of the impressions made upon the minds of the aborigines, by the actions of communities and public functionaries.

We have not selected these instances invidiously, but only because they are prominent and clearly attested. The same feelings and code of morals, the same disregard of the rights of the Indians, and of the obligations of justice and Christian benevolence, were general. They pervaded the public sentiment of the age, and marked the conduct of all the colonists, with a few honourable exceptions, which we shall proceed to notice.

In order to make out the case which I propose to establish, it is necessary to show, not only that the whites have abused the hospitality, trampled on the rights, and exasperated the feelings of the Indians, without any just provocation, but that a contrary course would have been practicable as well as expedient.

We are aware that it may be suggested, that in some instances the Indians were the first aggressors, that they were treacherous and fickle, and when hostilities were once provoked, their implacable dispositions, and cruel mode of warfare, rendered conciliation impossible, and gave necessarily a harsh character to the warfare. All this may be admitted without affording any extenuation of the conduct of the whites. They were intruders in a strange land; their coming was voluntary and uninvited; they had to establish a character. They were Christians, professing an elevated code of morals, in which forbearance and the forgiveness of injuries form conspicuous points, while the Indians were wholly ignorant of those virtues. Among the Indians revenge is a point of duty, in the Christian code it is a crime. What was right, or at least innocent, in the one party, was highly criminal in the other.

If the Indians are constitutionally inaccessible to kindness—if they are wholly intractable—if they can form no just appreciation of the conduct of other men, and are incapable of gratitude—the question is at rest. But we apprehend that they might have been conciliated by kindness, just as easily as they were provoked by violence; and that the foundations of mutual esteem and confidence might have been laid as deep and as broad as those of that stupendous fabric of revenge, hatred, and deception, which has grown up, and is now witnessed with sorrow by all good men.

To establish this position we shall refer to two instances in which the Indians were treated with uniform kindness, and in both which the results were such as to prove the correctness of our reasoning.

The first is that of William Penn, whose great wisdom and benevolence have never been esteemed as highly as they deserve, and who has never yet received the applause

which is his due as a statesman and philanthropist. In
uniting these characters, and acting practically upon the
broad principles of justice, he was in advance of the age
in which he lived, and was neither understood nor imitated.
It was in Pennsylvania that the true principles of liberty
were first planted on this continent.   Others, with greater
pretensions, saw but dimly the dawn of that glorious day
which was destined to burst upon our land.   Liberty was
to them an abstraction; they understood the theory, and
discussed it ably in all its bearings, but followed out its
precepts with little success.   The founder of Pennsylvania
lived up to the principles that he professed.   In his public
conduct he consulted his conscience, his sense of right and
wrong, and his knowledge of human nature.   He believed
that the Indians had souls.   He treated them individually
as human beings, as men, as friends; and negotiated with
their tribes as with independent and responsible public
bodies, trusting implicitly in their honour, and pledging in
sincerity his own.   He was a man of enlarged views,
whose mind was above the petty artifices of diplomacy.
"His great mind was uniformly influenced, in his intercourse with the aborigines, by those immutable principles
of justice, which everywhere, and for all purposes, must
be regarded as fundamental, if human exertions are to be
crowned with noble and permanent results."   In the 13th,
14th, and 15th sections of the Constitution of his Colony,
it was provided as follows :

"No man shall, by any ways or means, in word or
deed, affront or wrong an Indian, but he shall incur *the
same penalty* of the law as if he had committed it against
his fellow planter ; and if any Indian shall abuse, in word
or deed, any planter of the province, *he shall not be his own
judge* upon the Indian, but he shall make his complaint to
the Governor, or some inferior magistrate near him, who

shall, to the utmost of his power, take care with the King of the said Indian, that all reasonable satisfaction be made to the injured planter. All differences between the planters and the natives shall also be ended by *twelve men*, that is, *six planters* and *six natives*, so that we may live friendly together, as much as in us lieth, preventing *all occasions* of heart-burnings and mischief."

In these simple articles we find the very essence of all good government—*equality of rights*. The golden rule of the Christian code was the fundamental maxim of his political edifice. Instead of making one rule of action for the white man, and another for the Indian, the same mode and measure of justice was prescribed to both; and while his strict adherence to the great principles of civil and religious freedom entitle the virtuous Penn to the highest place as a lawgiver and benefactor of mankind, it justly earned for him from the Indians the affectionate title by which they always spoke of him, "their great and good Onas." The result was, that so long as Pennsylvania remained under the immediate government of its founder, the most amicable relations were maintained with the natives. His scheme of government embraced no military arm; neither troops, forts, nor an armed peasantry. The doctrine of keeping peace by being prepared for war, entered not into his system; his maxim was to avoid "*all occasions of* heart-burnings and mischief," and to retain the friendship of his neighbours by never doubting nor abusing it. He put on righteousness and it clothed him. The great Christian law of love was the vital principle of his administration, and was all-potent as an armour of defence, and as a strong bulwark against every foe.

The Indians, savage as they are, were awed and won by a policy so just and pacific; and the Quakers had no Indian wars. The horrors of the firebrand and the tomahawk, of which other colonists had such dreadful experience, were unknown to them; and they cultivated their farms in peace, for nearly sixty years, with no other armour than the powerful name of Penn, and the inoffensiveness of their own lives.

In Watson's *Account of Buckingham and Solebury*, in Pennsylvania, published in the *Memoirs of the Historical Society of Pennsylvania*, we find the following striking remarks : " In 1690, there were many settlements of Indians in these townships. Tradition reports that they were kind neighbours, supplying the white people with meat, and sometimes with beans and other vegetables, which they did *in perfect charity*, bringing presents to their houses, and *refusing pay*. A harmony arose out of their mutual intercourse and dependence. The difference between the families of the white man and the Indian was not great—when to live was the greatest hope, and to enjoy a bare sufficiency, the greatest luxury." This passage requires no comment ; so strongly does it contrast with the accounts of other new settlements, and so fully does it display the fruits of a prudent and equitable system of civil administration.

There are many facts connected with the settlements upon the Delaware which are extremely interesting. The Swedes, who were the first occupants, date back as far as the year 1631, and remained scattered at several places for something like forty years, previous to the arrival of Penn. They were few in number, and were neither a military nor a trading people ; neither the love of gold, nor the lust of carnage, tempted them into acts of insult and oppression, and they lived in uninterrupted harmony with the Indians. Had their intercourse with the savages been interrupted by hostilities, Penn would not have been received with the cordiality and confidence which marked his first interviews with the tribes, and characterised all his relations with them.   But he found the Indians friendly notwithstanding their long intercourse with the Swedes.

It is a singular circumstance that the Quakers had so much confidence in their own system of peace and forbearance, that they did not erect a fort, nor organise any militia for their defence, nor provide themselves with any of the engines or munitions of war, but went quietly about their business, clearing land, farming, building, and trading, without any molestation from the Indians, and without any apprehension of danger.   In the fragments of history handed down to us from those times, we read affecting accounts of suffering from sickness, hunger, poverty, exposure—from all the causes which ordinarily afflict an infant colony, except war—but we read of no wars nor rumours of war.   Of the Indians, but little is said.   They are only mentioned incidentally, and then always with kindness.   "In those times," says one of their historians, "the Indians and Swedes were kind and active to bring in, and vend at moderate prices proper articles of subsistence."   An instance is told of a lady, Mrs Chandler, who arrived at Philadelphia with eight or nine children, having lost her husband on the voyage out.   She was lodged in a cave, on the bank of the river, and being perfectly destitute, was a subject of general compassion. The people were kind to them, and none more so than the Indians, who frequently brought them food.   "In future years," says our authority, "when the children grew up, they always remembered the kind Indians, and took many opportunities of befriending them and their families in return."

An old lady, whose recollections have been recorded by one of her descendants, was present at one of Penn's first interviews with the "Indians and Swedes"—for she names them together, as if they acted in concert, or at least in harmony. "They met him at or near the present Philadelphia. The Indians, as well as the whites, had severally prepared the best entertainment the place and circumstances could admit. William Penn made himself endeared to the Indians by his marked condescension and acquiescence in their wishes. He walked with them, sat with them on the ground, and ate with them of their roasted acorns and homany. At this they expressed great delight, and some began to show how they could hop and jump; at which exhibition, William Penn, to cap the climax, sprang up and beat them all!"

The date of Penn's patent was in 1681, and he governed Pennsylvania until 1712. It is the boast of his people, a boast of which they may well be proud, that no Quaker blood was shed by the natives. They employed neither fraud nor force in gaining a foothold upon the soil of Pennsylvania; and there is neither record nor tradition which accuses them of injustice or intolerance towards the ignorant and confiding tribes by whom they were kindly received. His government was founded upon the principles of the Bible, and such was their efficacy, that not only during the continuance of his government, but for some years after he ceased to rule, the white and red men lived in peace. In 1744, a petition was addressed to the King, by the City Council of Philadelphia, "setting forth the defenceless state of said city, and requesting his Majesty to take the defenceless condition of the inhabitants into consideration, and afford them such relief as his Majesty shall think fit." This is the first record that we find, in which allusion is made to military defences in that colony, and this was fifty-three years after the date of Penn's patent, during all which time they had maintained peace by their good conduct, not by their defensive armaments.

The other instance we shall adduce is deemed particularly apposite, as it occurred at the same period, under similar circumstances, and among a people the very reverse of the Quakers in character, and who had not the slightest communication or connection with them. The French settled at Kaskaskia previous to the year 1700. We cannot fix the precise date; but there are deeds now on record, in the public offices at that place, which bear date in 1712, and it is probable that several years must have elapsed from the first settling of the colony, before regular transfers of real estate could take place, and before there could have been officers authorised to authenticate such proceedings. It is the general understanding of the old French settlers, that Philadelphia, Detroit, and Kaskaskia were settled about the same time. The French in Illinois lived upon the most amicable terms with the Indians. Like the Quakers, they kept up an interchange of friendly offices, treating them with kindness and equity, and dealing with them upon terms of perfect equality. They even intermarried with them—which the Quakers could not do without being turned out of meeting—entertained them at their houses, and showed them in various ways that they considered them as fellow creatures, having a parity of interests, principles, and feelings with themselves. Their nearest neighbours were the English, on the shores of the Atlantic, distant a thousand miles, from whom they were separated by interminable forests, and a barrier of mountains then deemed insurmountable, and with whom they had no more intercourse than with the Chinese. A mere handful, in the heart of a vast wilderness, and cut off from all the civilised world, they could not have existed a day but by permission of the numerous savages by whom they were surrounded.

The French were allured to Illinois in search of gold.

The leaders of the colony were adventurers of some intelligence, but the mass of the people were peasants from an interior part of France, who brought with them the careless gaiety, the rustic simplicity, the unsophisticated ignorance, which distinguished the peasantry of that country before the Revolution. Contented and unambitious, the disappointment of not finding mines of the precious metal did not affect them deeply, and they sat down quietly in the satisfied enjoyment of such pleasures and comforts as the country afforded.   Having no land speculations in view, nor any commercial monopolies in prospect, they were under no temptation to debase the Indian mind, and all their dealings with the savages were conducted with fairness.   They had five villages on the Mississippi : Kaskaskia, Prairie du Rocher, Saint Phillippe, Fort Chartres, and Cahokia.   Fort Chartres was a very strong fortification, and might have protected the village of the same name, adjacent to it.   There was a fort at Kaskaskia, but it was small, and being on the opposite side of the river from the town, could have afforded little protection to the latter from an attack of Indians.   The only other fortress was at Cahokia, and is described by an early writer as "no way distinguished, except by being the meanest log house in the town."   The villages of Prairie du Rocher and Saint Phillippe had no military defences. Yet we do not hear of burnings and scalpings among the early settlers of that region.   Now and then an affray occurred between a Frenchman and an Indian, and occasionally a life was lost; but these were precisely the kind of exceptions which prove the truth of a general rule ; for such accidents must have been the result of departures by individuals from those principles of amity which were observed by their respective communities.   The French were expert in the use of fire-arms ; they roamed far and wide into the Indian country, and it would have been a strange anomaly in the history of warriors and hunters, had no personal conflicts ensued. But these affrays did not disturb the general harmony, which is a conclusive evidence that no latent jealousy, no suppressed resentment for past injuries, rankled in the bosom of either party. The Indians even suffered themselves to be baptized; and at one time a large portion of the Kaskaskia tribe professed the Roman Catholic faith.

Such was the confidence inspired by the pacific conduct of the French settlers here and in Canada, that their traders ascended the St Lawrence and the Mississippi, traversed the Northern lakes, and penetrated to every part of the Western wilderness without molestation. They engrossed the fur trade, and became so fascinated with this mode of life, that numbers of them devoted themselves to the business of conducting the canoe, and formed that class of *voyageurs* who continue to this day to be the chief carriers of that trade. They pass between the white men and Indians, partaking the habits of both, and living happily with either. While the Englishman dared not venture beyond the frontier of his settlements, the Frenchman roamed over the whole of this vast region, and was everywhere a welcome visitor. The travellers La Salle, Hennepin, Marquette, and others, traversed the entire West, and were received with cordiality by all the tribes.

Here then we perceive the contrast, which affords an explanation to some of the apparent difficulties of this subject. Those who came among the aborigines with sincerely pacific intentions, who conducted themselves with frankness, practising the law of love, and observing the obligations of good faith, found the natives accessible to kindness, and were enabled by their superior knowledge to exert over them a beneficial influence. But those who came with peace on their lips, with arms in their hands, with plunder in their hearts, and persecution and scorn of the heathen in their creeds, soon became the objects of that never dying spirit of revenge which is the master passion of the savage bosom.

No sooner did Penn cease to rule in Pennsylvania, than those humane precepts, which exalted his government above that of every other colony, and which establish for him the highest claim to the honour of having planted the true principles of civic liberty on this continent, began to be neglected. His memory, and the grateful odour of his good deeds, for a while threw an armour of defence over those who succeeded him; but in a short time Pennsylvania began to be desolated by Indian wars. With him ceased all good faith with the tribes. His successors had neither his talents, his honesty, nor his firmness; they followed none of his precepts, nor kept any of his engagements. Fire-arms, gunpowder, and that insidious drug which the Indians call the *firewater of the white man*, were freely used in the colony, and sold to the natives. The planters began to arm in self-defence. *Occasions of offence* were frequent, and no effort was made to prevent them. "The great and good Onas" was no longer there to pour out his kind spirit, like oil, upon the waves of human passion. Hostilities ensued; the frontiers of Pennsylvania suffered all the horrors of border warfare, and the sentiment expressed by Penn in 1682 proved prophetic : "If my heirs do not keep to God, in justice, mercy, equity, and fear of the Lord, they will lose all, and desolation will follow."

The same result occurred in Illinois. The amiable French lived in peace with the Indians for a whole century; but when the "Long Knives" began to emigrate

AMISKQUEW
A Menominie Warrior

to the country, greedy for gain, eager to possess the lands of the natives, and full of novel speculations, hostilities commenced, and continued until the whites gained the complete mastery.

In order to give full weight to these facts, and to perceive clearly their application to our subject, it must be recollected that national prejudices are most deeply rooted, and most lasting, among an unenlightened people. The ignorant have narrow views because they can judge only from what they see. Those simple and unlettered tribes, whose only occupations are war and hunting, preserve the few events that interrupt the dull monotony of their national existence, by traditions, which are handed down with singular tenacity from generation to generation. The only mental culture which the children receive, consists in repeating to them the adventures of their fathers, and the infant mind is thus indelibly impressed with all the predilections and antipathies of the parent. To these early impressions there is no counter-influence; no philosophy to enlarge the boundaries of thought, to examine evidence, and to detect error; no religion to suggest the exercise of charity, or impose the duty of forgiveness. The traditions of each tribe are widely spread by the practice of repeating them at the great councils, at which the warriors of various tribes are assembled; and thus the wrongs which they suffered from the white men, became generally known, and perhaps greatly exaggerated. Among them, too, revenge is a noble principle, imbibed with their mother's milk, justified by their code of honour, and recognised by their customs. It is as much a duty with them to revenge a wrong, as it is with us to discharge a debt or fulfil a contract; and the injury inflicted upon the father rankles in the bosom of the child, until recompense is made, or retaliation inflicted. We infer then, that we owe much of the unhappy state of feeling which exists between the Indians and ourselves, to the injuries inflicted on their race, and the prejudices excited by the discoverers and colonists, and to the want of sincere, judicious, and patient exertions for reconciliation on our part.

We have now passed hastily over a period during which no settled policy seems to have been adopted by the British or French Governments in regard to their intercourse with the aborigines. Every colony, every band of adventurers, was left free and unshackled, to pursue the dictates of whim or of conscience, of grasping avarice or enlightened liberality—to gain a landing upon the continent at their proper peril, and upon their own terms—to negotiate, to fight, to plunder—to convert the heathen, or to exterminate them, as seemed good in their own eyes. They were only restrained from intruding upon "other Christians," who were similarly engaged, in order that each community might carry on its own larcenies and homicides, according to its own standard of taste and morals, without jostling its next neighbour. Their intercourse with the natives was the result of accident or caprice, or was dictated by the master-mind of some distinguished philanthropist or conqueror, by a persecuted sectarian refugee, an exiled cavalier, a gold-hunting adventurer, or a soldier of fortune—by a Penn or a Pizarro, a Howard or a Dugald Dalgetty.

It is unhappily true, as true as gospel, that the heart of man is "deceitful and desperately wicked," and that whenever men are left to pursue their own inclinations unrestrained by law, and by a wholesome public sentiment, there will be corruption and violence. In the settlement of America there *were* corruption, and violence, and wrong, perpetrated upon the native occupiers of the soil, from one end of the continent to the other; and although brilliant exceptions occurred, they were like the electric flashes in the storm, which deepen the gloom of the darkness by comparison, while they afford the light which discloses the havoc of the tempest.

Our object has been to show the *first* impression that was made upon the savage mind—to show that it was deep and lasting—and that it was adverse to civilisation. These impressions are now hardened into prejudice and conviction; they prevail wherever the Red man exists, or the white man is heard of, from the frozen wilds of Canada, where the wretched savage shivers half the year in penury and famine, to the sunny plains of the South, where the painted warrior, decked in gaudy plumage, and mounted on the wild steed of the prairie, exhibits all the magnificence of barbarian pomp. They form his creed, and are interwoven with his nature; and though few can express them so well, they all feel, what was said by the eloquent *Red Jacket* to a Missionary, who explained to him the pure and beautiful code of the Redeemer, and asked permission to teach it to his people: "Go," said he, "and teach those doctrines to the white men,—make *them* sober and honest—teach *them* to love one another— persuade *them* to do to others as they would have others do to them, and then bring your religion to the red men— *but not until then!*"

II.

In our preceding remarks, we have endeavoured to show the *first impressions* made upon the Indian mind by the conduct of the discoverers and colonists, acting without concert with each other, in pursuit of their own purposes, which were selfish and mercenary.

We now propose to point out the policy of the European Governments when the colonies became of sufficient importance to claim their attention, and the commerce of the new countries held out a prospect of gain which excited their cupidity. The unscrupulous conduct of Great Britain in the prosecution of her vast schemes of commercial aggrandisement, is too well understood to require comment. Bold, ruthless, and unprincipled in her mercantile policy, it was she who planted slavery upon the soil of North America, who fattened upon the blood and sweat of the slave in the West Indies, who wrung countless millions of treasure from the timid and semi-civilised inhabitants of India, by the most audacious system of oppression; who is now, in China, murdering an inoffensive and ingenious people for refusing to purchase from them, upon compulsion, a poisonous drug, and whose armies are desolating the mountains of Afghanistan.

The new lands of America, which had been freely given to every adventurer who asked for them, no sooner began to develop resources for commerce, than the greedy appetite of the mother country became whetted for spoil. The boundaries of the colonies began to be enlarged, forts were established in the wilderness to awe the natives, who saw their ancient hunting grounds narrowed continually, and their dwelling-places occupied by a rapacious people, and an insolent soldiery; until, driven from boundary to boundary, they realised, while in life, the beautiful description of death, by the sacred poet, "the places that knew them once, knew them no more for ever."

The intercourse with the natives was conducted through forts and trading posts, by officers and agents, whose aim was to secure the fur trade, and to obtain grants of land; and for the valuable property thus obtained, they gave them fire-arms, ammunition, trinkets, gaudy clothing, and spirituous liquors. No effort was made to introduce among them useful articles, which would have promoted their comfort, and tended to their civilisation. No thought was taken to inculcate accurate notions of property and value, by giving them fair equivalents for the articles received, and by inducing them to take the more useful and the least perishable of our fabrics. The contrary policy was artfully adopted; tinsel ornaments and toys were given to amuse the savage mind, drink to destroy his reason and stimulate his passions, and instruments of war to encourage his love of carnage. We can readily believe, that had the Europeans, in their earliest intercourse with the natives, shown a desire for their welfare by withholding from them the means of dissipation and the engines of destruction, and had furnished them with articles of substantial comfort, many of them would have been allured to the sedentary habits of civilisation, and all of them induced to confide in the sincerity of the white man.

At a very early period, the English and French colonists were engaged in wars with each other, and both parties endeavoured to conciliate the natives, and engage them as auxiliaries. With a full knowledge of their mode of warfare, which destroys without respect to age, sex, or condition, they were regularly hired, and sent forth upon their bloody mission. Furnished with arms, and ammunition, clothing, and provisions, they acquired additional powers of mischief, and learned to feel the importance of their friendship and their enmity.

Both parties sought to secure their co-operation by making them presents, and it soon became the custom at all solemn councils, to make valuable donations to the chiefs and influential men, before proceeding to business. We have no evidence, that previous to our negotiations with the tribes, they were in the habit of making valuable presents to each other upon such occasions. The North American Indians were poor, and we suspect that among them, if presents were made at all, they were of little value, and given only in token of sincerity. We intend this observation to apply, of course, to cases where the parties treated upon terms of perfect equality, for among all nations, civilised as well as savage, a subdued party is compelled to purchase peace.

It is also true, that treaties have always been least faithfully observed among those nations whose customs require the weaker party to purchase the friendship of the stronger by bribes; one party is governed by fear, the other by rapacity, and while the one is always seeking pretences to make new exactions, the other is ever watching to obtain revenge or indemnity. It has been somewhat thus with our predecessors, and their Indian allies. The presents, which at first were voluntarily given, and were received with gratitude, soon became periodical, and began at last to be demanded as of right. The Indians acted precisely as the pirates of the Barbary states have always done under similar circumstances. They saw that their situation enabled them to harass the whites, and that the latter were always willing to avert their hostility by the payment of a valuable consideration. War led to negotiations, and treaties—and treaties always brought presents. Implements of war, and articles of dress and luxury, had been introduced among them, to which they had previously been strangers; new wants were created, without the simultaneous creation of any means to supply them; every treaty with their wealthy neighbours brought in fresh stores of these foreign products, which their own country did not afford, and which they could not procure in sufficient abundance, either by traffic or by plunder; and it became clearly their interest to multiply the occasions of such profitable diplomacy. They made war, therefore, whenever they needed supplies; whenever cupidity or famine goaded the nation, or ambition stimulated a ruling chief; and they made peace whenever a sufficient inducement was tendered to their acceptance. If war existed between the whites, they fought on the side on which they were employed; if not, they assailed either side for the sake of a profitable treaty.

They no longer fought for fame or conquest, to retrieve honour, or redress wrong; and the military virtues that usually attend these noble impulses entirely forsook them; we had made them banditti; and they made war to get money, rum, guns, and gunpowder. The pernicious system of giving them regular supplies of arms, ammunition, clothing, and provisions, became firmly established, and drew after it a train of evil consequences; injury to the whites, and misery to the wretched objects of their misplaced bounty. They became the regular followers of the camp; the periodical visitants and beggars at the gates of forts and trading houses. The alms, or the stipends, that were given them, wretched as they were, were sufficient to destroy their

K

self-dependence. Furnished with arms and clothing, they became less provident; supplied with munitions of war, their propensity for mischief was quickened by the increased means of its gratification; the passion of avarice was awakened, and habits of extortion were cherished, by the continual experience of their power to enforce the payment of tribute.

The system of making presents to the tribes, and enlisting them in our quarrels, bad as it was, was innocent in comparison with the abuses that unavoidably grew out of it. The employment of agents necessarily attended these negotiations, and the persons so engaged were exposed to continual temptations to act corruptly, while they were exempt from the ordinary restraints, and the usual motives, which ensure the fidelity of public functionaries. They acted at distant points, beyond the reach of the observation of their superiors, where neither instruction nor reproof could often reach them, and where much was necessarily left to their discretion. They were sent to an illiterate people, who had no channel through which to report their misconduct, for they were themselves the only medium of communication between the principals, and could easily deceive both parties; and the eye of detection could not penetrate into the distant wilderness that formed the scene of their operations. If faithful, they had little hope of being rewarded for that which their own Government did not know, and their own people did not care for; and they had, therefore, strong temptation to make their emolument out of the power and the money which they were entrusted to wield. The office was one which took them from the social circle, from the refinements of life, from the restraints of law, from the sound of the church-going bell, and which offered no inducement to the cultivated and moral man, and was too often filled by men of the coarsest mould. In the backwoods they could peculate or intrigue, oppress and extort, with impunity; and it is known only to the All-seeing Eye how often the tomahawk has been raised to gratify the bad passions of an agent, to feed his avarice, to revenge his quarrel, or to raise his importance by enabling him to become the mediator of a peace.

The trade with the Indians has always been conducted within their own borders, as well under the British Government as under that of the United States. Instead of permitting and inducing them to trade in our markets, where they would reap the advantages of competition, would acquire just notions of value, would learn the use of money, would have a choice of the articles they might desire to purchase, would be under the protection of our laws and our public opinion, and would imbibe necessarily some knowledge of our language, institutions, and arts; they have been compelled to deal with licensed traders, at obscure points in the wilderness. Under the British Government, the trade for furs and peltries is in the hands of two great companies; and within our limits it is conducted by licensed companies and individuals, who have monopolies of this valuable branch of commerce, which they carry on without competition and without any restraint. The intercourse is held in the aboriginal languages, by means of interpreters, and every art is used to keep the Indians in their original state of ignorance, and to encourage them to persevere in their improvident and erratic habits. The abuses perpetrated under this system are almost incredibly enormous. The Indians assemble at the trading post, in the autumn, to exchange the skins taken in the past season for the arms and ammunition required for the ensuing year, and for the blankets and other articles necessary for their support during the winter.   For several hundred dollars worth of peltry, the product of a whole year's hunting, and of immense danger, exposure, and fatigue, the hunter gets a gun, a few pounds of powder, a knife, a blanket, and some trinkets, and then as a gracious present some tin ornaments for the arms and nose, and a little scarlet cloth and cheap calico, to make a dress for his wife—the whole not worth a tenth, perhaps not a twentieth part, of the articles extorted from the wretched savage.   And there are numerous well authenticated instances in which the hunter has been robbed, while in a state of intoxication, of the whole produce of his year's labour, and turned out bare and destitute, to suffer during the rigours of the winter the extreme of famine, or to perish miserably in the wilderness.

To these national injuries have been added wrongs of a private and personal, but not less aggravating character. Too often have our citizens perpetrated, in the deep recesses of the forest, crimes from which, had they been suggested to the same persons when living in civilised society, surrounded by the strong restraints of law, and by the full blaze of a pure public opinion, they would have shrunk with horror.   Too often has the trader been seen, led on by the overmastering lust for money, violating every principle of honour, trampling on the rites of hospitality, rending asunder the most sacred ties, and breaking down every barrier of good faith, to accomplish the sordid purpose of a nefarious traffic.   The affecting story of Inkle and Yarico is no fiction.   It has been acted over and over again in our forests, with every variation of ingenious cruelty.

It is no unfrequent occurrence for the most beautiful, the highest born maid of a powerful tribe to give her hand in marriage to some attractive stranger ; yielding up her affections with that implicit confidence, that all-absorbing self-devotion, which is everywhere the attribute of woman. Impelled by the purest and most disinterested of human passions, she sacrifices, for that nameless and houseless stranger, everything that nature and custom had rendered most dear. To please his taste she throws aside the graceful ornaments of her tribe, and assumes the apparel of a foreign and detested people. Her raven locks are no longer braided upon her shoulders; she no longer chases the deer, or guides her light canoe over the wave; and her dark eye flashes no more with the pride of conscious beauty as the warriors of her nation pass before her; for in their eyes she is, if not a degraded, an alienated being. But still she is supremely happy, in the possession of that one object, around whom all her affections are entwined. In the seclusion of her cottage, in the cheerful performance of every domestic duty, in advancing the interests of her husband by conciliating in his favour all the influence of her kindred, and the lingering affection of her people, and in protecting him from danger at every hazard, her days exhibit a continual scene of self-devotion. Her dream of happiness is soon and fatally dissolved. Her husband has accomplished his commercial purposes, and she is abandoned to disgrace and poverty. Although the whole story of her affection has exhibited that loveliness of character, that purity and nobleness of mind, which in civilised society raises a superior woman above her species, and gives her an almost unlimited influence within the sphere of her attractions—yet, *she* is a savage—a poor, untaught, deluded Indian—and she is abandoned by her *civilised* husband with the same apathy with which a worn-out domestic animal is turned loose to perish on the common.

As an example of the class of wrongs to which we

now refer, we shall relate a well-authenticated incident, the particulars of which may be found in the interesting account of Long's first expedition to the Rocky Mountains. An enterprising young trader, who had established himself, at a remote Indian village, on the Missouri, married a beautiful girl, the daughter of a powerful chief. *He* considered the marriage a matter of business, his sole object being to secure the protection of the chief, and to advance his own interests by gaining the confidence of the tribe. *She* entered into the engagement in good faith, and proved herself a most devoted wife, assiduous in promoting the happiness of her husband, and in contributing to his prosperity—faithful and self-sacrificing as woman ever is where her affections are interested. They lived together in harmony for several years, when the trader, about to proceed on his annual visit to St Louis, announced, on the eve of his departure, his intention to carry with him their only child, a boy of two years old. She remonstrated against this proceeding —but he, promising to return and to bring back the child, effected his nefarious purpose. She had reason to believe that the separation would be final, but with the implicit obedience of an Indian wife, she submitted, until the moment of parting, when her grief became over-whelming—she gazed after the boat which was rapidly carrying away all that was dear to her, with frantic sorrow —then rushing madly along the shore, followed it for miles, uttering the most piercing lamentations; and when it was no longer visible, and the sound of the oar died upon her ear, she sank upon the ground in a state bordering upon insanity. In this condition she was found, and carried home by her friends. For days and weeks she remained inconsolable, and only recovered a tolerable degree of composure as the time approached when her husband had promised to return, and then, hope springing up in her bosom, persuaded her that he would be faithful to his engagement. But the time arrived, and passed away, and the perjured white man came not.

In the meanwhile the trader hastened to St Louis, to fulfil a matrimonial engagement with a lady who was to enjoy the wealth acquired chiefly through the influence, the labours, and the economy of his Indian wife. He was residing near that city, with his beautiful bride, in an elegant residence, when the deserted wife and heart-broken mother made her appearance at his door, and solicited a private interview. Alone, and on foot, she had traversed the trackless wilderness, for several hundred miles, subsisting on the products of the forest, and lodging without any shelter but the canopy of Heaven, and she stood before her husband, worn out and almost famished, a wretched wreck of her former self. She asked, not to be restored to favour, not to share the wealth she had assisted in earning, nor even for a morsel of bread to revive her fainting frame—but only for her child; and was sternly refused. She begged to be admitted into the house as a servant, or to be allowed to live in the neighbourhood—to be suffered on any terms to remain near the sole remaining object of her love; but this was refused, and she was coldly and brutally repulsed from the door of her husband, and the roof that sheltered her only child. She was the offspring of a high-spirited people—she was a *woman*, all whose rights had been outraged, whose holiest affections had been violated—and the submissiveness which as a wife she had practised with becoming meekness, ceased to be a virtue in her estimation. She retired for the present, concealed herself in the neighbouring coverts, and watching her opportunity, entered the mansion by stealth, and bore away her offspring. Evading pursuit with all the artifice and all the courage of her race, she resumed her lonely journey, towards the hunting grounds of her nation. Long, and painful, and perilous was that journey; bearing her precious burthen on her shoulders, subsisting on roots, on wild fruit, and on such of the smaller animals as she could entrap, and creeping at night to a pallet of leaves, in any thicket that chance might offer, the wretched mother pursued her weary pilgrimage, with undaunted perseverance, and had nearly reached her destination when she sunk under the effects of hunger and fatigue. Some of the officers of our army, passing through the wilderness, found the squalid and famished woman, with her starving child, unable to proceed further, coiled in the lair in which she had thrown herself to die; and relieving her present necessities, carried her to her native village, where she probably still resides, a living witness of the ameliorating effects of Christianity and Civilisation upon the human heart, and especially upon the domestic virtues.

During the revolutionary war, Great Britain adopted the sanguinary policy of inciting the Indian tribes to take up the hatchet against the Colonies—a policy the more criminal on her part, as we refused to employ the savages, and used our influence to induce them to remain neutral, until we were compelled in self-defence to engage some of the tribes in our service. They now made war as the mercenary auxiliaries of a powerful nation; and while their native ferocity was increased by the hope of reward, the antipathies of the Americans against them were greatly enhanced, as they who are hired to fight in the quarrel of another always excite more aversion than the principal party who makes battle in his own cause. Emissaries were now planted along the whole frontier, the chiefs strutted in scarlet coats, and British gold and military titles were lavished among the tribes. The few restraints that prudence and decency had heretofore suggested, were now forgotten; rum was dealt out without stint; the desolating work of the tomahawk and the firebrand went forward with renewed vigour under the patronage of the Defender of the Faith, and new laurels were added to the British wreath by the midnight incendiary, by the plunder of an unarmed peasantry, and the murder of women and children. It was no longer thought necessary to inculcate the observance of humanity, or any Christian virtue, and the laws of war were suspended for the occasion. The savage appetite for blood was sharpened by artful devices; and there are instances on record in which English emissaries presided at the torturing of prisoners, and rivalled their red allies in the demoniac arts of vengeance. The Indians were now literally turned loose, and systematic exertions were used to awaken their jealousy and hatred against the colonists. The success of these intrigues is written in characters of blood in the history of our struggle for independence.

An affecting and conclusive illustration of the truth of these remarks may be found in the life of Joseph Brant, the celebrated Mohawk chief, recently published. Possessed of strong natural abilities, and sent in early life to a school in New England, he profited by these advantages so far as to obtain a tolerable English education, and to embrace, with much outward zeal, the Christian religion. The Mohawks, who then resided in the western part of New York, had always lived in amity with the settlers, and on the breaking out of the American revolution, their most natural policy would have been to take part with the colonists who had been their friends and neighbours, or to have remained neutral. The latter was the course strongly urged upon them by the colonists, who deprecated the horrors of Indian warfare, and were unwilling to inflict, even on their enemies, the dreadful evils attendant upon a sanguinary code of hostility. Their humane counsels were alike disregarded by the British and the Indians, and the Mohawks, with the rest of the Six Nations, became the allies of the Crown. Brant was the war chief of that noted confederacy, and was employed chiefly in harassing our frontier settlements—in burning the dwellings, and desolating the farms, of his former neighbours—in pillaging and murdering a defenceless people, with whom his own followers had been living on friendly terms, and with whom they had now no quarrel. In scarcely an instance do we find him leading his warriors against the American armies, or engaged in that legitimate warfare which is alone considered justifiable between civilised nations or honourable to those engaged in it. He seems not to have coveted the glory which is won on the battle-field. He ravaged the fields and burned the dwellings of our people; he stole upon them in the defence-less hour of the night, and slaughtered men, women, and children, or carried them into a captivity worse than death. Those helpless beings, who in civilised warfare are never considered the proper subjects of hostility, were marched in mid-winter, through the snow, day after day, to be delivered over as prisoners of war at a British garrison. He carried the horrors of war to the fireside and the altar, burned churches and granaries, and practised all the cruelties of savage warfare.

We are aware that the biographer of Brant, while he details these atrocities with a painful minuteness, endeavours to exonerate that leader from the charge of personal cruelty. We have nothing to do with these nice distinctions: the leader is accountable for the deeds of his followers,

ITCHO-TUSTENNUGGEE
A Seminole Chief

especially for such as are transacted under his immediate notice, and within the sphere of his personal command. Humanity shudders at the recital of the enormities practised throughout a series of years, upon the frontiers of New York, by the Indians and Tories, led by Sir Guy Johnston, the Butlers, and Brant ; and the odium of those deeds of blood will rest, not upon the wretched incendiaries and murderers, whose hands were imbrued in the blood of a peaceable and unoffending peasantry, but upon those who planned and conducted these nefarious expeditions. The apology attempted to be set up for the marauding chiefs— that they could not restrain their followers—proves too much ; for it points out in the strongest light the wicked-ness of employing such instruments, and leading them upon such enterprises. Those who are acquainted with the military habits of the Indians, the caution with which their expeditions are planned, the exact discipline which is observed by a war party, and the implicit obedience of the warriors, will know how to estimate this excuse. The truth is, that while the country suffered indescribably from these inhuman and impolitic incursions, the Indian mind was excited, exasperated, and debased by them, and the unhappy breach between the two races was greatly widened.

We have seen that, from the first settling of the whites in America, there have been, from one cause or another, continual disputes between them and the savage tribes, which have given rise to frequent and destructive wars. All the border settlements of our country have been exposed to predatory incursions and an unsparing warfare, and a peculiar class of our population has been raised up, who have occupied a prominent position in regard to the intercourse with the Indians, and done much to modify its character. We allude to the *backwoodsmen*, who have occupied the frontiers of most of the states, although they have been most numerous and conspicuous in the West. Dwelling from generation to generation on the frontier, far from the marts of commerce, and from the more enlightened portions of society, they acquired a distinct and strongly marked character. They were nominally farmers, but were rather a pastoral than an agricultural people, depending for food more upon their cattle and hogs, that ran at large in the woods, than upon the produce of the soil. They were hunters and warriors, relying on the chase for a large portion of their subsistence, and bearing arms continually, to protect their roaming herds from the marauding Indian, their dwellings and barns from conflagration, and their wives and children from the tomahawk. Having no commerce, and scarcely any intercourse with strangers, destitute of all the luxuries, and of many of what we esteem the necessaries of life, their wants were few and their habits simple. They dwelt in log cabins constructed by themselves, with scarcely any other tools than the axe and the auger; and their furniture was, for the most part, of their own fabrication. Their mode of life induced independence of thought, and habits of self-reliance; for as there was but one class, and one occupation, all were equal, and each was thrown upon his own resources. They had none of the helps that we enjoy in refined societies, from the variety of professions and trades, which administer to all our wants, and relieve us from the necessity of exerting our own ingenuity and physical strength, except in the single direction in which we choose to employ them.

They were a social and hospitable people; brave, generous, and patriotic; poor, but not sordid; laborious, but not frugal. From early infancy, they were accustomed to the baying of the wolf and the yell of the Indian; and associating these sounds as fraught alike with treachery and danger, they learned to distinguish in each the voice of a foe. The tales that first awakened the attention of childhood, were of the painted savage, creeping with the stealthy tread of the panther, upon the sleeping inmates of the cabin—of the midnight conflagration lighting up with its horrid glare the gloom of the surrounding forest—of bleeding scalps torn from the heads of gray-haired old men, of infants, and of women—of mothers and children carried away into captivity—and of the dreadful scenes of torture at the stake. The tales of the veteran warrior— the adventures that almost every venerable matron could relate from her own experience—the escapes of the hunter from the savage ambuscade—the stirring incidents of the battle—the strategy of border warfare—the sudden return of long-lost friends—and the recital of the prisoner delivered from captivity—these formed the legendary topics of the border, and moulded the minds and the prejudices of the people. They grew up in dread and loathing of the wolf, the panther, the rattlesnake, and the Indian; regarding them as foes alike ruthless and insidious, who waylaid their path, and stole upon them in the hour of sleep. So extensive and successful had been the incursions of the Indians, that there was scarcely a neighbourhood that had not its battle-field, or its rude sepulchre of departed valour, nor a family which had not its tale of sorrow, relating to some peculiar and melancholy bereave- ment by the hand of the savage. Yet so enamoured were these people of their sylvan life, environed as it was with inquietude and danger, that, as the natives receded farther and farther to the West, they pursued their footsteps, eager to possess the new lands and the fresh pastures they had forsaken, and regardless of dangers to which they were accustomed. Bred from generation to generation in the forest, they were as expert as the Indian, in all the arts of the hunter and all the devices of savage life. Like him they could steer their way with unerring skill through the trackless forest, could find and prepare their own food, and defend themselves against the vicissitudes of the weather. Compelled at first by their necessities to derive a subsistence from the spontaneous wealth of Nature, they learned to seek with skill and assiduity all the products of the wilderness, the flesh of the buffalo and the deer, the skin of the beaver, and the nutritious hoard of the bee, and became so addicted to these pursuits as to prefer them to the labours of husbandry. Acquiring hardihood and courage by these manly exercises, they became a martial people, enterprising and fearless, careless of exposure, expert in horsemanship, and trained to the use of arms. In their long hunting expeditions they penetrated into the Indian country, and made reprisals for the depredations of the savages ; and in retaliation for the hostilities of the red men, they organised parties, and pursued them by laborious marches to their distant villages. It will be readily seen that the hatred between these parties, handed down from father to son, and inflamed by continual aggressions, would be mutual, deadly, and irreconcilable.

Between parties thus mutually hostile, there would arise, unavoidably, many occasions of offence, which no prudence nor foresight on the part of the Government could prevent. Kind and forbearing as our Government were in overlooking past aggressions, and liberal as they were in all the dealings with the tribes, it was impossible to soothe the spirit of revenge implanted in the savage breast by a long series of war and encroachments. Restless and warlike in their habits, the inducements to peace could never be strongly impressed on their minds, and when the prospect of plunder was added to the lust for revenge, the temptation was so strong as to overcome all prudential motives. Even when the tribes as bodies were friendly, and their leaders disposed to maintain peace, there were loose and vicious individuals, who, strolling off under the pretence of hunting, would form small bands, and annoy the settlements by stealing horses, or killing the cattle and hogs that roamed in the woods. Sometimes these private wars, if we may make the distinction, were carried further: a house would be burned, a family murdered, and a whole neighbourhood alarmed. The borderers were not slow to retaliate. Upon the perpetration of such an outrage, a party would be collected with wonderful celerity, and the depredators being pursued, were often overtaken, and a part, if not all, of them slain. Passion is never just, and revenge is not scrupulous as to the measure of the retribution it exacts. Parties engaged in pursuing marauders were not always satisfied with punishing the guilty, but in the heat of passion attacked other Indians whom they accidentally met, or destroyed the villages of unoffending tribes. Unfortunately, it was difficult to discriminate in cases of this kind, for the Indians were so fickle, and their violations of their engagements so frequent and sudden, that the whites, living in continual apprehension, and in the constant experience of the irritable and hostile state of the Indian mind, were in most cases unable to decide whether an aggression committed was the act of a lawless few, or the assault of a war party, and the forerunner of a bloody war.

The Indians, on the other hand, were subject to a very serious grievance. Subsisting entirely by hunting, the game in their forests is as valuable to them as our cattle are to us, and they consider themselves as possessing a property in their hunting grounds, which they regard with great jealousy. Severe laws were passed by Congress, to protect them in these rights, and forbidding our people from trespassing upon the Indian hunting grounds; yet our hunters would often pass into the Indian country and destroy vast quantities of game. The practice of hunting upon their lands grew into a monstrous abuse; thousands of wild animals, from which they derived their sole subsistence, were annually destroyed by the whites. Many parts of the country which abounded in game, at the conclusion of the general peace in 1795, soon became totally destitute. The settlers on the neighbouring frontier were in the habit of passing into the Indian territory every autumn, to kill bear, deer, and buffaloes, merely for the skins, by which means these animals, particularly the latter, were in some places become almost extinct.

It is gratifying to observe, in the very first operations of our own Government, a spirit of moderation towards our savage neighbours. When we came to take possession of our national heritage for which we had fought, we found it encompassed with enemies. The southern and western tribes were generally hostile. On the borders of Pennsylvania, Virginia, and North Carolina, the tomahawk was busy, and the forests of Kentucky and Tennessee presented a vast scene of carnage. Had our rulers been animated by the same grasping and unscrupulous policy, which seems to have been pursued by all other nations in their dealings with the heathen, a fair opportunity was offered for its exercise. The pioneers were already sustaining themselves with credit on our western borders, and with a little encouragement from the Government, would have extirpated all the tribes who opposed their progress. Employment might have been given to the troops, which Congress found it necessary to disband; and the veterans who had fought for independence, might have been rewarded with the lands of our enemies. But the great men who then swayed our councils disdained the paltry spirit of revenge, and were too upright to commit an act which would have been morally wrong. They knew that the Indians had been abused and misled, by the same power which had trampled on our own rights, and had adulterated our best institutions by an admixture of foreign and pernicious principles; and they determined to forget all the aggressions of that unhappy race, to win them to friendship by kindness, and to extend to them the moral and civil blessings which had been purchased by our own emancipation. President Washington recommended the Indians to the paternal care of Congress, and all his successors have been governed by the same enlarged and humane views.

The wars which succeeded that of the revolution were neither sought by us, nor were they prosecuted for one moment longer than was necessary for the defence of the frontiers. So foreign from the views of our Government were all ideas of conquest, that the troops sent out under Harmer and St Clair were not sufficiently numerous to maintain a stand in the wilderness, nor provided with supplies for even one campaign; and the army of Wayne was victorious only through the exertion of singular skill and gallantry.

The Treaty of Greenville, made in 1795, by General Wayne, at the head of a victorious army, with the chiefs of the tribes who had just been vanquished in battle, affords the strongest evidence of the pacific views of our Government. Nothing is claimed in that treaty by right of conquest. The parties agree to establish a perpetual peace, the Indians acknowledge themselves to be under the protection of the United States, and not of any foreign power; they promise to sell their land to the United

States only, the latter agrees to protect them, and a few regulations are adopted to govern the intercourse between the parties; a boundary line is established, by which the Indians confirm to us large tracts of land, nearly all of which had been ceded to us by former treaties; and the United States agrees to pay them goods to the value of $20,000, and to make them a further payment of $9500 annually. Thus in negotiating a peace, at the headquarters of our army, after a signal victory, when we might have dictated, and probably did dictate, the terms, we require nothing of the other parties, but the performance of their previous voluntary engagements, and we purchase their friendship by an annual tribute. I advert to this treaty as one of the most important, and as forming the model and basis of almost all the Indian treaties which have succeeded it.

From this time forward, our Government continued to pursue a conciliatory and humane conduct towards the Indians. In a letter from the Secretary of War to General Harrison, Governor of the Indiana Territory, dated February 23, 1802, the following language is used:—"It is the ardent wish of the President of the United States, as well from a principle of humanity as from duty and sound policy, that all prudent means in our power shall be unremittingly pursued, for carrying into effect the benevolent views of Congress, relative to the Indian nations within the bounds of the United States. The provisions made by Congress, under the heads of intercourse with the Indian nations, and for establishing trading houses among them, etc., have for their object not only the cultivation and establishment of harmony and friendship between the United States and the different nations of Indians, but the introduction of civilisation by encouraging and gradually introducing the arts of husbandry and domestic manufactures among them."

President Jefferson himself wrote thus to the same Governor:—"Our system is to live in perpetual peace with the Indians, to cultivate an affectionate attachment from them by everything just and liberal we can do for them within the bounds of reason, and by giving them effectual protection against wrongs from our people."   Again: "In this way our settlements will circumscribe and approach the Indians, and they will either incorporate with us as citizens of the United States, or remove beyond the Mississippi.   The former is certainly the termination of their history most happy for themselves; but in the whole course of this, it is most essential to cultivate their love; as to their fear, we presume that our strength and their weakness are now so visible, that they must see we have only to shut our hand to crush them, and all our liberality to them proceeds from motives of humanity only."

Under the date of December 22, 1808, President Jefferson wrote thus:—"In a letter to you of February 27, 1802, I mentioned that I had heard there was still one Peoria man living, and that a compensation making him easy for life should be given him, and his conveyance of the country by regular deed obtained.   If there be such a man living, I think this should still be done."   Here was an instance in which, a tribe being supposed to be extinct, the Government had taken possession of the country which had been owned by them; but the President of the United States afterwards hearing that one individual of that tribe was in existence, proposed to pay him for the soil and get a conveyance from him.   We doubt whether, in the annals of any other nation than our own, so scrupulous an act of justice can be shown; and we suppose that Mr Jefferson had regard not merely to the rights of the survivor of the almost extinct tribe, but to the salutary and important principle to which he wished to give publicity, and which has always been recognised by our Government, namely, that we claim no right to take the lands of the Indians from them except by purchase.

From the close of the revolution the agents of the British Government continued to exercise all the incendiary arts of their despicable diplomacy, in perpetuating the animosity of the Indians against our country and people. It is probable that until the conclusion of the war of 1812, the mother country never entirely abandoned the hope of reducing her lost Colonies to their former state of subjection. Alarmed at the rapidity with which our settlements were spreading to the West, they attempted to oppose barriers to our advance in that direction, by inciting the savages to war; and equally alarmed at our efforts to civilise the tribes, and fearful that they might be induced to sit down under the protection of our republican institutions, and thus bring an immense accession to our strength, they insidiously endeavoured to countervail all our benevolent exertions of that description. If I had not the proof at hand, I would not venture to expose to the Christian world the extent, the wickedness, the unhappy tendency of these intrigues. The United States were engaged in an experiment which was approved by every virtuous man, and ought to have been supported by every enlightened nation. They were earnestly endeavouring to reclaim the savage—to induce the tribes to abandon their cruelties, their superstitions, their comfortless and perilous wanderings, and to sit down in the enjoyment of law, religion, peace, industry, and the arts. They wished to send the Cross of the Redeemer, the blessings of civil liberty, and the light of science, abroad throughout this vast continent; and to establish peace and goodwill in those boundless forests which had heretofore been the gloomy abodes of ferocious ignorance, vindictive passion, and sanguinary conflict.   Had they been successful in this beneficent design, they would have achieved a revolution as glorious as that which gave us independence.   The English Cabinet, nursing their resentment, and brooding over their gigantic but sordid schemes of commercial aggrandisement, saw the possibility of such a result, and trembled at the consequences.   They could not consent that the United States should reap the honour of so proud a triumph, or that their own means of access to our Western settlements, for annoyance or conquest, should be cut off.   Even the paltry boon of the fur trade was a sufficient inducement in their eyes for withholding from the Red men the Bible and the arts of peace.   Their emissaries therefore were multiplied, and stimulated to renewed activity; and while the agents of our Government, the Christian missionaries, and hundreds of benevolent individuals, laboured assiduously to enlighten the savage mind, and allure it to peace and industry, the unhallowed ambassadors of corruption toiled as industriously to perpetuate the darkness of heathenism, the gloom of ignorance, and the atrocities of war.   They represented our Government as having interests inimical to those of the Red men; and endeavoured to fasten upon us, as a people, those enormities which had been practised under the sanction of their own Government, and of which we had been the sufferers, in common with the aborigines. They characterised our missionaries as political agents; and appealed successfully to the ambition of the chiefs, and the prejudices and national pride of the tribes, by insinuating that our efforts to extend to them our customs, arts, faith, and language, were intended to destroy their integrity and independence, to efface their traditions, and blot out their names from the list of nations.   They were told that they were to be reduced to slavery, and made to labour with the negro.   Stronger and more direct arts than even these were resorted to : while we inculcated the virtue of temperance, and showed the Indian that intemperance was rapidly destroying his name and kindred, the British agent secretly distributed brandy with lavish hand ; while we invited the warrior to peace, he gave him arms and ammunition, and incited him to war and plunder ; while we offered the tribes our gospel, and our arts, he lavished among their chiefs military titles, red coats, epaulets, and trinkets, thus administering aliment to every savage propensity, and neutralising the effect of every wise precept and virtuous example.   Such miscreants as McKee and Girty—the latter a vulgar renegade from our own country, and the former a British officer of high rank—while in the daily perpetration of those odious crimes, received from the British Government the honours and rewards which are only due to virtuous and patriotic services.

The facts that support these assertions are found scattered abundantly throughout our history.   President Washington complained to the British Government of the tampering with the Indians within our limits by Lord Dorchester, Governor of Canada.   Mr Jefferson, in a speech to certain chiefs of the Miami, Pottowatomie, Delaware, and Chippeway tribes who visited our seat of Government, said :—

" General Washington, our first President, began a line of just and friendly conduct towards you.   Mr Adams, the second, continued it ; and from the moment I came into the Administration, I have looked upon you with the same good-will as my own fellow-citizens, have considered your interests as our interests, and peace and friendship as a blessing to us all.   Seeing with sincere regret that your people were wasting away ; believing that this proceeded from your frequent wars, the destructive use of spirituous

liquors, and the scanty supplies of food, I have inculcated
peace with all your neighbours, have endeavoured to prevent the introduction of spirituous liquors, and have pressed
it upon you to rely for food on the culture of the earth more
than on hunting.   On the contrary, my children, the English
persuade you to hunt.   They supply you with spirituous
liquors, and are now endeavouring to persuade you to join
them in a war against us, should a war take place.

"You possess reason, my children, as we do, and you
will judge for yourselves which of us advise you as friends.
The course they advise has worn you down to your
present numbers; but temperance, peace, and agriculture
will raise you up to what your forefathers were, will
prepare you to possess property, to wish to live under
regular laws, to join us in our government, to mix with
us in society, and your blood and ours united will spread
over the great island."

Contrast these sentiments, so honourable to our
country and to humanity, with the following talk from
Colonel McKee, the British Superintendent of Indian
Affairs, delivered to the Pottowatomie chiefs, at the River
St Joseph of Lake Michigan, in November 1804 :—

"My children, it is true that the Americans do not
wish you to drink any spirituous liquors, therefore they
have told *their* traders that they should not carry any
liquor into your country; but, my children, they have no
right to say that one of *your father's* traders among you
should carry no liquor among his children.

"My children, your father, King George, loves his Red
children, and wishes his Red children to be supplied with
everything they want.   He is not like the Americans, who
are continually blinding your eyes, and stopping your ears
with good words, that taste sweet as sugar, and getting
all your lands from you.

"My children, I am told that Wells has told you, that it was your interest to suffer no liquor to come into the country; you all know that he is a bad man," etc.

On another occasion he said : " My children, there is a powerful enemy of yours to the East, now on his feet, and looks mad at you, therefore you must be on your guard; keep your weapons of war in your hands, and have a look out for him."

This language was addressed, by the authorised agent of a nation at peace with us, to the Indians living south of the Lakes and within our acknowledged limits, at a council held in their country and within our jurisdiction, at which he could not be present for any purpose inimical to our interests except as a spy and an incendiary. It was the language which, for years, the emissaries of that nation continued to address to our Indians.

To enable herself to carry on these intrigues, the British Government had, in violation of the existing treaty of peace, kept possession of several military posts, south of the Lakes, and within our admitted boundaries, which she retained for twelve years after the close of the revolutionary war, and until the victory of Wayne blasted all her hopes in this quarter. This was the period during which the most distressing hostilities were carried on, against the settlers along the whole line of the Ohio River, and the most brutal outrages were committed—when the scalpings, the burnings, and the torture at the stake were most frequent, and attended with the most atrocious cruelties. Yet during that whole time the Indians on this frontier were supplied from these British posts with arms and ammunition, and urged on to the work of blood. They were assembled periodically to receive presents, and to listen to inflammatory harangues against the American Government and people—a Government on which they were dependent, and a people with whom they could not make war, but to their own utter destruction. During all that period, Brant, an able and most active partisan of the British, was passing frequently along the whole of our North-Western frontier, holding councils, advising the tribes to an uncompromising warfare with the United States. He was a secret and unacknowledged emissary, but in Mr Stone's *Life* of him recently published, these transactions are avowed and established; and in that work are exhibited letters, which passed between this noted savage and the British officers, and public documents recently obtained from the British archives, which develop all these facts. And this conspiracy was rendered the more criminal by the circumstance, that General Knox, as Secretary of War, was at that very time corresponding with Brant, who was an educated man, and a professing Christian, inviting his mediation between us and those deluded tribes who were still hostile, and representing to him the advantages to them, and the honour to himself, which would result from a pacification of the frontier, through his instrumentality. Brant had affected to listen to these overtures, and had visited Philadelphia, upon the urgent invitation of General Knox, for the ostensible purpose of consulting with the Cabinet in regard to this philanthropic plan, but really, as it turned out, to blind the eyes of the American Government. Several distinguished American philanthropists were also, about this period, exchanging letters with this forest Talleyrand on the same subject, and he contrived to delude them also, with the expectation that all the western tribes might be conciliated through his mediation.

It is now known, as a part of the well authenticated history of our country, that in the savage army opposed to our forces under General Wayne, there were more than one hundred Canadians, British subjects, who were engaged in the battle which concluded that decisive campaign ; that the British officers from the neighbouring fort assisted in the council of chiefs who arranged the plan of that engagement ; and that the vanquished savages took shelter in the British fort.

The conduct of Great Britain, in tampering with the American Indians, was so inexcusable, was fraught with such cruel mockery to the Indians who were the ignorant dupes of that policy, and exercised so powerful an influence upon the fate and character of that unfortunate people, that it will not, we trust, be considered inappropriate to exhibit some of the proofs of this interference. These proofs are numerous, but we shall only select a few at random.

Colonel Gordon, a British officer in Canada, in a letter to Captain Brant, dated June 11, 1791, in allusion to the attempts of the American Government to make peace with the Indians, remarks :—" It must strike you very forcibly, that in all the proceedings of the different commissioners from the American States, they have cautiously avoided applying for our interference, as a measure they affect to think perfectly unnecessary ; wishing to impress the Indians with ideas of their own consequence, and of the little influence, they would willingly believe, we are possessed of. This, my good friend, is not the way to proceed. Had they, before matters were pushed to extremity, requested the assistance of the British to bring about a peace upon equitable terms, I am convinced the measure would have been fully accomplished before this time."—Stone's *Life of Brant*, vol. ii. p. 301.

The cool arrogance with which the Americans are sneered at, for not inviting the interference of a foreign Government, in a quarrel with savages, living within our

DAVID VANN
A Cherokee Chief

limits, is only exceeded by the art evinced in the assertion that such a mediation would have been successful. The writer knew that the existing dissatisfaction was caused chiefly by the intrigues of his own Government, and he hazarded little in saying that with the assistance of the British, peace might have been established.

On the 1st of May 1792, Brant was addressed by Mr Joseph Chew, an officer under Sir John Johnson, expressing much satisfaction at the refusal of Captain Brant to accept an invitation, from the Secretary of War, to visit Philadelphia, on a mission of peace, and advising the chief of the preparations the Americans were making for an Indian campaign. The following passage occurs in this letter :—" I see they expect to have an army of about five thousand men, besides three troops of horse. By the advertisements for supplies of provisions, etc., it seems that this army will not be able to move before the last of July. What attempts Wilkinson and Hamtramck may make with the militia is uncertain. *Our friends ought to be on their guard.* I long to know what they think in England of the victory gained over St Clair's army."—Stone's *Life of Brant*, vol. ii. p. 327.

The Government of the United States, in its anxiety to make peace with the North-Western tribes, in February 1793, appointed General Benjamin Lincoln, Mr Beverly Randolph, and Colonel Timothy Pickering, commissioners, to hold a treaty at the Miamis with such of the tribes as might choose to be represented. The arrangement for this meeting had been made with the Indians the preceding autumn, and it is a curious fact, that they requested that some individuals of the Society of Friends should be attached to the mission—so widely had the fame of Penn and his people extended, and such was the confidence of the tribes in the integrity of that pacific sect. At the same time, some Quaker gentlemen, without concert with the Indians, and instigated only by the purest impulse of benevolence, had voluntarily offered their aid and mediation, which was accepted. The commissioners therefore were accompanied by John Parish, William Savery, and John Elliot, of Philadelphia; Jacob Lindlay, of Chester County; and Joseph Moore and William Hartshorne, of New Jersey, members of the Society of Friends.

On the arrival of the commissioners at Queenston, on the Niagara, on the 17th of May, they found that Brant and some of his Indians, with Colonel Butler, the British Superintendent of Indian Affairs, had proceeded to the place of meeting—but the commissioners were detained here, under various pretences, by Governor Simcoe, until the 26th of June. On their arrival at the mouth of Detroit River, they were obliged to land, by the British authorities at Detroit, who forbade their further approach, for the present, towards the place of meeting. Here they were met by a deputation from the Indian nations already assembled in council, who, among other things, asked them if they were fully authorised by the United States to fix firmly on the Ohio River as the boundary line between the white and red men. From the 1st to the 14th of August, the commissioners were detained at this place by the intrigues of the British officers; in the meanwhile the Indians decided in the great council that they would not treat upon any other terms than the settlement of the Ohio River as the boundary. To this the commissioners could not consent, the more especially as large purchases of land had been made, from the Indians, north of that river, upon which settlements had been made; and they returned without having been permitted even to meet the tribes in council.

If any doubt existed as to the duplicity of the Canadian

authorities in regard to this transaction, it would be removed by the testimony of Captain Brant, who played a conspicuous part in those councils. His biographer, Mr Stone, among the many valuable documents, brought to light by his research, has published the following extract from a speech, which he found among the papers of Brant, in the handwriting of the chief :—

" For several years " (after the peace of 1783,) " we were engaged in getting a confederacy formed, and the unanimity occasioned by these endeavours, among our Western brethren, *enabled them to defeat two American armies.* The war continued, without our brothers the English giving any assistance, excepting *a little ammunition;* and they seeming to desire that a peace might be concluded, we tried to bring it about at a time that the United States desired it very much, so that they sent commissioners from among their first people, to endeavour to make peace with the hostile Indians. We assembled also, for that purpose, at the Miami River, in the summer of 1793, intending to act as mediators in bringing about an honourable peace ; and if that could not be obtained, we resolved to join our Western brethren in trying the fortune of war. But to our surprise, when on the point of entering upon a treaty with the commissioners, *we found that it was opposed by those acting under the British Government, and hopes of further assistance were given to our Western brethren,* to encourage them to insist on the Ohio as a boundary between them and the United States."—Stone's *Life of Brant,* vol. ii. p. 358.

In all the intrigues of Canadian authorities with the Indians, Brant was the agent most frequently employed, and it was after a thorough investigation of the papers of that chief, and of a mass of documentary evidence furnished by his family, that Mr Stone came to the conclusion, "that during the whole controversy between the Indians and the United States, from 1786 to the defeat of St Clair, the former had been countenanced and encouraged by English agents, and repeatedly incited to actual hostilities, there was no doubt."

In the year 1794, Lord Dorchester, who is better known in American history by his former title of Sir Guy Carleton, delivered a speech to a number of Indian deputies, from the tribes within the United States, among whom was the celebrated "Little Turtle," in which he held the following language :—

"Children :—I was in expectation of hearing from the people of the United States, what was required by them ; I hoped that I should have been able to bring you together, and make you friends.

"Children :—I have waited long and listened with great attention, but I have not heard a word from them.

"Children :—I flattered myself with the hope that the line proposed in the year eighty-three, to separate us from the United States, *which was immediately broken by themselves as soon as the peace was signed*, would have been mended, or a new line drawn in an amicable manner. Here, also, I have been disappointed.

"Children :—Since my return, I find no appearance of a line remains ; and from the manner in which the people of the United States rush on, and act, and talk, on this side ; and from what I learn of their conduct toward the sea, I shall not be surprised if we are at war with them in the course of the present year ; and if so, a line must then be drawn by the warriors.

"Children :—You talk of selling your lands to the State of New York : I have told you that there is no line between them and us. I shall acknowledge no lands to be theirs which have been encroached on by them since the year

1783.   They then broke the peace, and as they kept it not on their part, it doth not bind on ours.

"Children :—They then destroyed their right of pre-emption.   Therefore, all their approaches towards us since that time, and all the purchases made by them, I consider an infringement on the King's rights.   And when a line is drawn between us, be it in peace or war, they must lose all their improvements and houses on our side of it.   Those people must all be gone who do not obtain leave to become the King's subjects.   What belongs to the Indians will of course be secured and confirmed to them.

"Children :—What further can I say to you ? you are witnesses that on our parts we have acted in the most peaceable manner, and borne the language and conduct of the people of the United States with patience.   But I believe our patience is almost exhausted."

The authenticity of this remarkable speech was denied when it was first made public ; but General Washington, then President of the United States, believed it to be genuine, and the Secretary of State remonstrated strongly with Mr Hammond, the British Minister, against it, and against the conduct of Governor Simcoe, who was engaged in hostile measures.   The inquiry was evaded, and the authenticity of the speech remained somewhat doubtful. All doubt has been now removed by the successful research of Mr Stone, who in collecting materials for the life of Brant, found a certified copy among the papers of that chief.

In 1794, Governor Simcoe, on hearing of the prepara-tions for the campaign of the American army, under General Wayne, hastened to the West, as did also Brant, attended by one hundred and fifty of his best warriors— " evidently for the purpose of continuing in the exercise of an unfriendly influence upon the minds of the Indians

against the United States.   The Governor was at the Fort
near the battle-field on the 30th of September, as also were
Captain Brant and Colonel McKee.   The Indians had
already made some advances to General Wayne toward a
negotiation for peace; but their attention was diverted by
Simcoe and Brant, who invited a council of the hostile
nations to assemble at the mouth of the Detroit River, on
the 10th of October.   The invitation was accepted, as also
was an invitation from General Wayne, who was met by a
few of their chiefs; so that the wily savages were in fact
sitting in two councils at once, balancing chances, and
preparing to make peace only in the event of finding little
further encouragement to fight."—Stone's *Brant*, vol. ii.
p. 392.

In the council of the 10th of October, Simcoe said to
these ignorant and deluded creatures :—"I am still of
opinion that the Ohio is your right and title.   I have given
orders to the commandant of Fort Miami to fire on the
Americans whenever they make their appearance again.
I will go down to Quebec and lay your grievances before
the great man.   From thence they will be forwarded to
the King your father.   Next spring you will know
the result of everything, what you and I will do."

Nor did these unfortunate and criminal intrigues end
here.   The correspondence of the Territorial Governors,
Harrison of Indiana, Edwards of Illinois, and Howard of
Missouri, with the War Department, during several years
immediately preceding the war of 1812, are replete with
conclusive evidence of this inhuman and discreditable
tampering with the savages.   They give the circumstances,
the names of some of the emissaries, and the details of
their intrigues.   Of the many causes of discontent, which
have arisen between Great Britain and the United
States, no one has contributed more to embitter the

minds of the American people than this—especially in the Western States, where citizens suffered severely from savage hostilities, caused chiefly, as they confidently maintain, by this malign influence.

Thus while our Government endeavoured to throw the veil of oblivion over past irritations, and to establish with its Red neighbours those friendly relations by which the best interests of both parties would have been promoted, the design was frustrated by the imprudence of a few of our citizens, and the unjustifiable intrigues of a foreign Government. The consequence was, that our frontiers continued to be desolated by petty wars, of the most distressing character—wars, the miseries of which fell solely upon individuals who were robbed, and tortured and murdered by those who professed to be the allies, and who were, in fact, the dependents and beneficiaries of our own Government.

Towards the year 1812, the Indians became more and more audacious. The expectation of a war between this country and Great Britain, the increased bribes and redoubled intrigues of that nation, and the prospect of gaining in her a powerful ally, gave new fuel to their hatred, and new vigour to their courage. At this period, the celebrated Tecumseh appeared upon the scene. He was called the Napoleon of the West; and so far as that title could be earned by genius, courage, perseverance, boldness of conception, and promptitude of action, it was fairly bestowed upon that distinguished savage.

Tecumseh was a remarkable man. He rose from obscurity to the command of a tribe, of which some of his family were distinguished members, but in which he had no hereditary claims to power or authority. He was by turns the orator, the warrior, and the politician; and in each of these capacities gave evidence of a high order of intellect, and an elevated tone of thought.   As is often the case with superior minds, one master passion filled his heart, and gave to his whole life its character.   This was hatred to the whites; and, like Hannibal, he had sworn that it should be perpetual.   He entertained the vast project of inducing the Indian tribes to unite in one great confederacy, to bury their feuds with each other, and to make common cause against the white men.   He wished to extinguish all distinctions of tribe and language, and to combine the power and prejudices of all, in defence of the rights and possessions of the whole, as the aboriginal occupants of the country.   He maintained that the Great Spirit, in establishing between the white and red races the distinction of colour, intended to ordain a perpetual separation between them.   He insisted that this country had been given to the Indian race; and while he recognised the right of each nation or tribe to the exclusive use of their hunting grounds, so long as they chose to possess them, he indignantly denied the power of any to sell them. When the occupants of any tract of country removed from it, he considered it as reverting to the common stock, and free to any other Indians who might choose to settle upon it.   The idea of selling land, he scouted as an absurdity. "Sell land!" he exclaimed on one occasion; "as well might you pretend to sell the air, and the water.   The Great Spirit gave them all alike to us, the air for us to breathe, the water to drink, and the earth to live and to hunt upon—you may as well sell the one as the other!" He contended, therefore, that as the Indians had no right to cede any portion of their territory, all the cessions that had been made were void.   In these views he was strengthened by the British officers, who found in him an able and apt coadjutor, and by their joint machinations the whole frontier was thrown into commotion.   By their advice he insisted upon the Ohio River as the line of separation between the United States and the Indians, and refused to make peace upon any other terms than the solemn recognition of this as a *perpetual boundary*.

It was a part of the policy of this chief, to destroy entirely the influence of the whites, by discouraging their intercourse with the Indians. He deprecated the civilisation of the latter, as a means of betraying them into the power of the white people, and he considered every kind of trade and intercourse between these parties as fraught with danger to the independence of the Red men. He wished the latter to discard everything, even the weapons, which had been introduced among them by the whites, and to subsist, as their ancestors had done, upon the products of their plains and forests, so that the inducement to traffic with the whites should be destroyed. He set the example, by abstaining entirely from the use of ardent spirits, and many other articles sold by the traders; he refused to speak the English language, and adhered as strictly as possible to the customs of his people.

It was with Tecumseh himself that General Proctor, the commander of the British forces, made the disgraceful compact, at the commencement of the campaign of 1813, by which it was stipulated, that General Harrison, and all who had fought with him at Tippecanoe, should, if taken, be delivered up to the Indians, to be dealt with according to their usages. He was the terror and scourge of his foes, the uncompromising opposer of all attempts at civilising the Indians, the brave, implacable, untiring enemy of our people. But he was a generous enemy. Previous to his time, the Shawanese had been in the practice of torturing prisoners taken in battle. At the commencement of his career, probably after the first engagement in which he commanded, he rescued a prisoner from torture by his personal interference, and declared that he would never, upon any occasion, permit a captive to be cruelly treated. In this manly resolution he persevered, and greatly ameliorated the horrors of war, wherever he was present.

The character of Tecumseh was so marked and peculiar that it deserves from us at least a passing notice. He was remarkable for temperance and integrity, was hospitable, generous, and humane. One who knew him, said of him, "I know of no peculiarity about him that gained him popularity. His talents, rectitude of deportment, and friendly disposition, commanded the respect and regard of all about him. I consider him a very great, as well as a very good man, who, had he enjoyed the advantages of a liberal education, would have done honour to any age or nation."

In the *Life of Tecumseh*, by the late amiable and lamented Benjamin Drake, of Cincinnati, we find the following highly interesting anecdote. "The next action in which Tecumseh participated, and in which he manifested signal prowess, was an attack made by the Indians, upon some flat boats, descending the Ohio, above Limestone, now Maysville. The year in which it occurred is not stated, but Tecumseh was probably not more than sixteen or seventeen years of age. The boats were captured, and all the persons belonging to them killed, except one, who was taken prisoner, and afterwards burnt. Tecumseh was a silent spectator of the scene, having never witnessed the burning of a prisoner before. After it was over he expressed, in strong terms, his abhorrence of the act, and it was finally concluded by the party that they would never burn any more prisoners; and to this resolution, he himself, and the party also, it is believed, ever after scrupulously adhered. It is not less creditable to the humanity than to the genius of Tecumseh, that he should

have taken this noble stand, and by the force and eloquence
of his appeal, have brought his companions to the same
resolution.   He was then but a boy, yet he had the
independence to attack a cherished custom of his tribe,
and the power of argument to convince them, against all
their preconceived notions of right, and the rules of their
warfare, that the custom should be abolished.   That his
effort to put a stop to this cruel and revolting rite, was not
prompted by a temporary expediency, but was the result
of a humane disposition, and a right sense of justice, is
abundantly shown by his conduct towards prisoners in
after life."   We may add, that not only did the friends of
Tecumseh and his nation abandon the practice of burning
prisoners, but the Indians generally ceased from about this
period to perpetrate this outrage, and it is reasonable to
infer that he was the principal cause of the revolution.

The noble and magnanimous conduct of this chief
towards some Americans who were taken prisoners, at the
sortie from Fort Meigs, in 1813, is worthy of record.
These prisoners were taken to the headquarters of General
Proctor, the British commander, and confined in Fort
Miami, "where the Indians were permitted to amuse
themselves by firing at the crowd, or at any particular
individual.   Those whose taste led them to inflict a more
cruel and savage death, led their victims to the gateway,
where, under the eye of General Proctor and his officers,
they were coolly tomahawked and scalped.   Upwards of
twenty prisoners were thus, in the course of two hours,
massacred in cold blood, by those to whom they had
voluntarily surrendered."

"Whilst this bloodthirsty carnage was raging, a
thundering voice was heard in the rear, in the Indian
tongue, and Tecumseh was seen coming with all the
rapidity with which his horse could carry him, until he

drew near to where two Indians had an American, and were in the act of killing him. He sprang from his horse, caught one by the throat and the other by the breast, and threw them to the ground; drawing his tomahawk and scalping knife, he ran in between the Americans and Indians, brandishing his arms, and daring anyone of the hundreds that surrounded him to attempt to murder another American. They all appeared confounded, and immediately desisted. His mind appeared rent with passion, and he exclaimed almost with tears in his eyes, "Oh! what will become of my Indians." He then demanded in an authoritative tone where Proctor was; but casting his eye upon him at a short distance, sternly inquired why he had not put a stop to the inhuman massacre. "Sir," said Proctor, "your Indians cannot be commanded." "Begone!" returned Tecumseh, with the greatest disdain, "you are unfit to command; go and put on petticoats!"—Drake's *Life of Tecumseh*, p. 182.

"When Burns, the poet, was suddenly transferred from his plough in Ayrshire, to the polished circles of Edinburgh, his ease of manner, and nice observance of the rules of good breeding, excited much surprise, and became the theme of frequent conversation. The same thing has been remarked of Tecumseh; whether seated at the tables of General McArthur and Worthington, as he was during the council at Chillicothe, in 1807, or brought in contact with British officers of the highest grade, his manners were entirely free from vulgarity and coarseness : he was uniformly self-possessed, and with the tact and ease of deportment which marked the poet of the heart, and which are falsely supposed to be the result of civilisation and refinement only, he readily accommodated himself to the novelties of his new position, and seemed more amused than annoyed by them."

"Rising above the prejudices and customs of his people, even when those prejudices and customs were tacitly sanctioned by the officers and agents of Great Britain, Tecumseh was never known to offer violence to prisoners, nor to permit it in others. So strong was his sense of honour, and so sensitive his feelings of humanity, on this point, that even frontier women and children, throughout the wide space in which his character was known, felt secure from the tomahawk of the hostile Indians, if Tecumseh was in the camp. A striking instance of this confidence is presented in the following anecdote. The British and Indians were encamped near the River Raisin; and while holding a talk within eighty or a hundred yards of Mrs Ruland's house, some Sauks and Winnebagoes entered her dwelling and began to plunder it. She immediately sent her little daughter, eight or nine years old, requesting Tecumseh to come to her assistance. The child ran to the council house, and pulling Tecumseh, who was then speaking, by the skirt of his hunting shirt, said to him, 'come to our house—there are bad Indians there.' Without waiting to close his speech, the chief started for the house. On entering he was met by two or three Indians, dragging a trunk towards the door. He seized his tomahawk, and levelled one of them at a blow: they prepared for resistance, but no sooner did they hear the cry, 'Dogs! I am Tecumseh!' than, under the flash of his indignant eye, they fled from the house. 'And you,' said Tecumseh, turning to some British officers, 'are *worse* than dogs, to break your faith with prisoners.'"—Drake's *Life of Tecumseh*.

We have noticed these events, for the purpose of showing the obstacles which have embarrassed our Government in all their schemes for extending the mild and moralising influence of our Christian and republican principles throughout the Western forests. With the conclusion of the war in 1815 our wars with the Indians ceased. The brilliant exploits of our navy, and the signal victories gained by our armies at New Orleans, at the River Thames, on the Niagara, and at Plattsburgh, convinced the British of the futility of their hopes of conquest on this continent, and spread an universal panic among the tribes. The eyes of the latter were opened to our power, as they had been to our forbearance. They saw that they had nothing to hope from our weakness, or our fears, and much to gain from our friendship. Their foreign confederates had made peace for themselves, leaving them no alternative but to follow the example. They had either to submit, or, by contending single-handed against the victorious troops who had defeated their martial allies, draw down inevitable destruction on their own heads. At this juncture, the American Government again held out the olive branch. The enlightened Madison, ever pacific in his public character, as he was amiable and philanthropic in private life, spared no pains to heal the unhappy wounds which had been inflicted upon the mutual peace; and his successors, by pursuing the same policy, have given permanence to a system of amicable relations between us and our misguided neighbours.

Although we believe our system of relations with the Indian tribes to be radically wrong, and to be productive of great wrong to them, we have been careful to state distinctly that the intentions of our Government, and the feeling of the American people towards that unfortunate race, have been always benevolent, forbearing, and magnanimous. We deem this position sufficiently important to be deserving of proof, and in evidence of the professions and intentions of our Government, from its commencement, we quote extracts from the communications of the respective Presidents to Congress. (*See* pages 202-219, this Vol.).

We come now to consider briefly the precise character of the relations of the American Government and people with the Indian tribes. We have shown that those relations were shaped by the mother country, and modified, first by the colonial policy, and afterwards by the intrigues of foreign nations. It became necessary, therefore, for our Government to soothe past irritations, and remove long settled prejudices, before a system of amicable intercourse could be established ; and to this beneficent work has her attention been steadily directed. But we shall show, that with the very best intentions towards the aborigines, our Government has not only failed to accomplish its benevolent purposes towards them, but has in fact done much positive wrong to them, and to ourselves ; and reflecting men cannot but perceive the ruinous tendency of the policy now pursued, and the absolute necessity of a speedy and radical change.

The existence, within our territorial limits, of tribes acknowledged to be independent, involves in itself a paradox ; while the details of our negotiations with them, and of our legislation with respect to them, are full of the strangest contradictions. We acknowledge them to be sovereign nations, yet we forbid them to make war with each other ; we admit their title to their lands, their unlimited power over them while they remain theirs, and their full possession of the rights of self-government within them ; yet we restrain them from selling those lands to any but ourselves ; we treat with them as with free states, yet we plant our agents and our military posts among them, and make laws which operate within their territory. In our numerous treaties with them, we acknowledge them to be free, both as nations and as individuals; yet we claim the power to punish in our courts, aggressions committed within their boundaries, denying to them a concurrent jurisdiction, and forbidding them from adjudicating in their councils and according to their customs, upon the rights of our citizens, and from vindicating the privileges of their own. We make distinctions, not merely in effect, but in terms, between the white man and the Indian, of the most degrading character; and at the moment when our commissioners are negotiating solemn leagues with their chiefs, involving the most important interests, pledging to them the faith of our Government, and accepting from them similar pledges, we reject those same chiefs if offered as witnesses in our courts, as persons destitute of truth—as creatures too ignorant to understand, or too degraded to practise, the ordinary rules of rectitude. In many of the states, negroes, mulattoes and, Indians are by law declared to be incompetent witnesses against a white man. Whatever necessity the institution of slavery may impose as regards the negro and mulatto, there is no reason for this stigma upon the Indian, and we apprehend that a case could hardly occur in which the ends of justice would not be advanced by submitting the credibility of such a witness to the jury.

This simple exposition of a few of the leading features of our intercourse with the Indians, must satisfy every rational mind that so unnatural a state of things cannot be lasting; that any system of relations founded upon such principles, must be unjust, unprofitable, and temporary; and that although in the infancy of our Government it might have been excusable in us to adopt such a policy towards our savage neighbours, as their barbarities or our weakness might have forced upon us, it becomes us now, as a great and enlightened people, to

JULCEE MATHLA
A Seminole Chief

devise a system more consistent with our national dignity, and better adapted to advance the interests of the respective parties.

To ascertain the exact position of the parties in respect to each other, we shall call the attention of the reader to a few of the treaties and laws which regulate the subject-matter, confining ourselves chiefly to those which have been made most recently. Our present system of Indian relations, although commenced under the Administration of General Washington, has been chiefly built up since the last war between the United States and Great Britain. The treaties have been so numerous, that it is impossible, in a work like this, to enter into their details, or to do more than to refer in a compendious manner to their leading features. We shall adopt this plan as sufficient for our purpose. The following propositions, then, will be found to contain the leading principles of this anomalous diplomacy, and to have obtained admission into our treaties with nearly all the tribes :—

1. The United States have almost invariably given presents, in money, arms, clothing, farming implements, and trinkets, upon the negotiation of a treaty; and in treaties for the purchase of territory, we pay an equivalent for the lands, in money or merchandise, or both, which payment is generally made in the form of annuities, limited or perpetual.

2. When a tribe cedes the territory on which they reside, other territory is specified for their future occupancy, and the United States guarantee to them the title and peaceable possession thereof.

3. The Indians acknowledge themselves to be under the protection of the American Government, and of no other power whatsoever.

4. They engage not to make war with each other, or

with any foreign power, without the consent of the United States.

5. They agree to sell their lands only to the United States. Our citizens are prohibited by law from taking grants of land from the Indians ; and any transfer or cession made by them, except to our Government, would be considered void.

6. White men found hunting on the Indian lands, may be apprehended by them, and delivered up to the nearest agent of the United States.

7. White men are not to trade with the Indians, nor reside in their country without licence from our authorities.

8. An Indian who commits a murder upon a white man, is to be delivered up to be tried and punished under our laws ; stolen property is to be returned, or the tribe to be accountable for its value.

9. The United States *claims the right* of navigation, on all navigable rivers which pass through an Indian territory.

10. The tribes agree that they will at all times allow to traders, and other persons travelling through their country, under the authority of the United States, a free and safe passage for themselves and their property ; and that for such passage, they shall at no time, and on no account whatever, be subject to any toll or exaction.

11. Should any tribe of Indians, or other power, meditate a war against the United States, or threaten any hostile act, and the same shall come to the knowledge of a tribe in amity with the United States, the latter shall give notice thereof to the nearest Governor of a State, or officer commanding the troops of the United States.

12. No tribe in amity with the United States shall supply arms or ammunition, or any warlike aid, implements, or munition, to a tribe not in amity with us.

The following special Articles have been assented to by particular tribes, and have been inserted in treaties with some other tribes, so as to prevail to a considerable extent :—

"The United States *demand an acknowledgment* of the right to establish military posts and trading houses, and to open roads within the territory guaranteed to the Creek nation in the second Article, and the right to the navigation of all its waters."—*Treaty of 9th August* 1814.

"The Shawanoe nation do acknowledge the United States to be sole and absolute sovereigns of all the territory ceded to them by a treaty of peace made between them and the King of Great Britain, on the 14th January 1786."

"It is agreed on the part of the Cherokees, that the United States shall have the sole and absolute right to regulate their trade."—*Treaty of 2nd July* 1791.

"Fifty-four tracts of one mile square each, of the land ceded by this treaty, shall be laid off under the direction of the President of the United States, and sold, for the purpose of raising a fund, to be applied for the support of schools for the education of the Osage children."—*Treaty of 2nd June* 1825.

"The United States agree to furnish at Clarke, for the use of the Osage nation, a blacksmith and tools to mend their arms, and utensils of husbandry, and engage to build them a horsemill or watermill ; also to furnish them with ploughs," etc.—*Ibid.*

"The United States, immediately after the ratification of this convention, shall cause to be furnished to the Kansas nation, 300 head of cattle, 300 hogs, 500 domestic fowls, three yoke of oxen and two carts, with such implements of husbandry as the Superintendent of Indian Affairs may think necessary ; and shall employ such persons to aid and instruct them in agriculture as the President of the United States may deem expedient; and shall provide and support a blacksmith."—*Treaty of 3rd June* 1825.

"Thirty-six sections of good land on Big Blue River, shall be laid out under the direction of the President of the United States, and sold for the purpose of raising a fund to be applied, under the direction of the President, to the education of the Kansas children within their nation."—*Ibid.*

"The Tetons, Yanctons, and Yanctonies, and bands of the Sioux, admit the right of the United States to regulate their trade."—*Treaty of 2nd June* 1825.

If we turn to the Statute Books, for the purpose of showing the spirit of our legislation in regard to the Indian tribes, it will be seen that the leading *intention* of those laws, as expressed on their face, is just and benevolent. Whatever mistakes our Government may have committed, and however their beneficence may have been misdirected, it could never have been their purpose to oppress a people towards whom they have used language, such as we find in the several acts of Congress, relating to the Indians, and of which the following expressions are specimens:—"For the purpose of *providing against the further decline, and final extinction* of the Indian tribes, adjoining the frontier settlements of the United States, and for introducing among them *the habits and arts of civilisation,*" etc. "In order *to promote the civilisation* of the friendly Indians, and to secure the continuance of their friendship," etc. The third Article of an Ordinance for the government of the territory of the United States, north-west of the River Ohio, passed in 1787, runs as follows:—"Religion, morality, and knowledge, being necessary to good government and the happiness of mankind, schools and the means of education shall for ever be encouraged. The utmost good faith shall always be observed towards the Indians ; their lands and property shall never be taken from them without their consent ; and in their property, rights, and liberty, they shall never be invaded or disturbed unless in just and lawful wars authorised by Congress ; but *laws founded in justice and humanity* shall from time to time be made for preventing wrongs being done to them, and for preserving peace and friendship with them."

These are noble sentiments ; and they represent truly the feelings of the great body of the American people towards the aborigines, and the principles by which the intercourse with the Indian tribes was intended to be governed. We shall, when we come to inquire what have been the *results* of our intercourse with those tribes, and whether those results have realised the wishes of the American people, and the intentions of the Government, refer to these extracts as expressing those wishes and intentions.

We shall not detail at large the statutory provisions to which we intend to refer, but will content ourselves with such a synopsis as will answer our purpose. Our Indian affairs are conducted by several superintendents, and a number of agents and sub-agents, who are required to reside within their respective agencies, and through whom the Government conducts all its negotiations with the tribes, except when special trusts are committed to military officers, or to commissioners appointed for the occasion. We regulate the trade with them by statute, rigorously prohibiting all ingress into their country by our citizens, or by foreigners, and all traffic, except by special licence from our authorities. An Indian who kills a white man, or a white man who slays an Indian, are alike tried by our laws, and in our courts, even though the offence may have been committed in the Indian Territory.

Larceny, robbery, trespass, or other offence, committed by
white men against the Indians, in the country of the latter,
is punishable in our courts, and where the offender is
unable to make restitution, the just value of the property
taken or destroyed is paid by our Government; if a similar
aggression is committed by an Indian against a white man,
the tribe is held responsible. The President is authorised
to furnish to the tribes, schoolmasters, artisans, teachers of
husbandry and the mechanic arts, tools, implements of
agriculture, domestic animals ; and generally to exert his
influence to introduce the habits and arts of social life
among them.

Although we have omitted a great many provisions
similar to those which we have quoted, we believe that we
have not passed over anything that is necessary to a fair
exposition of the principles of our negotiations with the
Indians, and our legislation over them. It will be seen
that we have never claimed the right, nor avowed the
intention to extirpate this unhappy race, to strip them of
their property, or to deprive them of those natural rights
which we have, in our Declaration of Independence,
emphatically termed *indefeasible.* On the contrary, our
declared purpose, repeatedly and solemnly avowed, has
been to secure their friendship—to civilise them—to give
them the habits and arts of social life—to elevate their
character, and increase their happiness.

If it be asked, to what extent these objects have been
attained, the answer must be appalling to every friend of
humanity. It is so seldom that the energies of a powerful
Government have been steadily directed to the accomplishment of a benevolent design, that we cannot, without deep
regret, behold the exertion of such rare beneficence defeated
of its purpose. Yet it is most certainly true, that notwithstanding all our professions, and our great expenditure of

labour and money, the Indians, so far from advancing one step in civilisation and happiness, so far from improving in their condition, or rising in the scale of moral being, are every day sinking lower in misery and barbarism. The virtues which they cherished in their aboriginal state, have been blunted by their intercourse with the whites, and they have acquired vices which were unknown to their simple progenitors. We take no account here of the Creeks, Cherokees, Choctaws, and Chickasaws, a portion of whom present an exception to the great body of the Indians. We speak of the wandering tribes—of the Indians at large, who continue to reject the arts and habits of social life, who fear and despise the white man, and tenaciously adhere to all the ferocious customs and miserable expedients of savage life. If we have failed to soften their rude natures, to enlighten their under-standings, or to imbue their minds with any of our principles of moral action, equally have we failed to secure their friendship. We have tamed them into submission by displays of our power, or brought them into subservience with our money, but we have not gained their love or their confidence.

Nor is this all. Our system is not only inefficient, but it is positively mischievous. Its direct tendency is to retard the civilisation of the Indian. We have stripped their nations of freedom, sovereignty, and independence. We claim the right to regulate their trade, to navigate their rivers, to have ingress into their country; we forbid all intercourse with them, except by special licence from our authorities; we try them in our courts for offences committed in their country, and we do not acknowledge the existence of any tribunal among them, having authority to inflict a penalty on one of our citizens. They are subjected to the restraints, without enjoying the privileges, the protection, or the moral influence, of our laws. Theirs is, therefore, a state of subjection—of mere vassalage—precisely that state which has always been found to destroy the energies, and degrade the character, of a people.

But, as if by a refinement of cruelty, similar to that which decks a victim in costly robes, and surrounds him with pleasing objects of sense, at the moment of execution, we leave them in the *nominal* possession of independence, and in the possession of all their long-cherished and idolised customs, prejudices, and superstitions. They are kept separate from us, and their own national pride naturally co-operates with our injudicious policy, to keep them for ever a distinct, an alien, and a hostile people. They gain nothing by the example of our industry, the precepts of our religion, the influence of our laws, our arts, our institutions, for they see or feel nothing of the salutary operation of all these, and only know them in their terrors or their restraints. They are a subjected people, governed by laws in the making of which they have no voice, and enjoying none of the privileges pertaining to the citizens of the nation which rules them. They obey their own laws and customs, so far as these do not conflict with our convenience; and are left without law, so far as our interference is concerned, except where our interest induces us to stretch over them the arm of authority. By giving them presents and annuities, we support them in idleness, and cherish their wandering and unsettled habits. We bribe them into discontent, by teaching them that every public convention held for the settlement of misunderstandings, is to bring them valuable tributes; while the same cause trains them to duplicity, and induces them to exercise all their ingenuity in seeking out causes of offence, and in compounding their grievances to the best advantage.

These are the accidental, and unintentional, but unavoidable effects of a system, which is radically wrong, though devised and maintained in the spirit of benevolence.

If all this is faulty in principle, it is still worse in practice. The Indian Department has already become one of the most expensive branches of our Government. Our foreign relations are scarcely more costly than our negotiations with the tribes. If the vast sums which are annually laid out in this manner were productive of any permanent good to the Indians, no patriot or Christian would regret the expenditure. But when we see our treasure squandered with a lavish hand, not only without any good effect, but with great positive injury to the miserable race, whom we have reduced to the state of dependence upon our bounty, it is time to pause. When we examine further, and see how large a portion of these vast sums are intercepted before they reach the hand of the Red man—how much is expended in sustaining military posts, paying agents, transporting merchandise, holding treaties, and keeping in operation, in various ways, a vast, complicated, and useless machinery—when we reflect how much is unavoidably lost, squandered, and misapplied, the question assumes a fearful importance.

The British Government, when attempting to subdue the ferocious spirit of the Scottish Highlanders, and to allure them to the arts of peace, prohibited them from wearing the national dress, and from carrying arms, and used its influence to destroy the power of the chieftains, and to eradicate the use of the Gaelic language; because all these things tended to foster the pride of descent, to cherish ancient recollections, and to keep the clans separate from the rest of the nation, and from each other.

Our Government has pursued a policy directly the reverse. We are continually administering nourishment to the prejudices of the Indians, and keeping alive the distinctions that separate them from us. They are constantly reminded of their nominal independence by the embassies which are sent to them, and by the ridiculous mock pageantry exhibited on such occasions; when our commissioners, instead of exerting the moral influence of example, comply with all their customs, imitate the style of their eloquence, and even flatter them for the possession of the very propensities which distinguish them as savages. So far from endeavouring to abolish the distinction of dress, we furnish them annually with immense quantities of trinkets, cloths, and blankets, made expressly for their use, and differing essentially from anything that is worn, or even sold, in our country. Waggon loads of the most childish trinkets, and the most ridiculous toys, are annually sent as presents from this great and benevolent nation, to its Red allies, as assurances of the very profound respect, and tender affection, with which they are regarded by the American people. Immense sums of money are also given them as annuities—money which to the savage is perfectly valueless, and which is immediately transferred to the trader, in exchange for whisky, tobacco, gunpowder, looking-glasses, tin bracelets, and ornaments for the nose.

The idea of elevating the character of the Indian and softening down his asperities, by pampering his indolence, and administering to his vanity, is supremely ridiculous. The march of mind will never penetrate into our forests by the beat of the drum, nor will civilisation be transmitted in bales of scarlet cloth and glass beads. This, however, is the natural effect of treating with the Indians in their own country, and carrying our trade to their doors, where we are in some measure obliged to comply with their customs, and all our dealings with them must be carried on by men who are not amenable to our laws, nor surrounded by the salutary restraints of public sentiment. If, on the contrary, the Indians were obliged to resort to our towns to supply their wants, and to trade with regular dealers ; and if all their negotiations with our officers were to be conducted within the boundaries of our organised governments, where the controlling influence of our laws and power should be distinctly recognised, they would not only be better treated, but would be brought into contact with the most intelligent and benevolent of our citizens, and imbibe more correct notions of us and our institutions.

There are other evils in our existing system of Indian relations, which are inseparable from it, and which imperiously indicate the necessity of an entire change.

One fruitful cause of injustice to the Indians, lies deep in the habits and interests of our people, and may be difficult to eradicate ; but it is one of grave importance, and is so involved with the public peace and the national honour, as to demand the most serious attention. The thirst for new lands is an all-absorbing passion, among the inhabitants of the frontier states, and its operation upon the Indians has been most calamitous. Although living in a country which is still comparatively new, embracing everywhere large tracts of wild land, their wandering and enterprising habits lead them continually abroad, in search of newer and fresher lands. Whenever a boundary is settled between our territory and the Indian lands, the enterprise of our people carries the population up to the line, while the Red men, shy of such neighbours, retire from the boundary, leaving a wide space of wilderness between themselves and the settlements. A class of pioneers who subsist by hunting and rearing cattle, intrude upon the lands thus left unoccupied, and establish upon them their temporary dwellings. Careless in regard to the ownership of the soil they occupy, seeking new and fresh pastures where their herds may roam at large, and forests stocked with game, they pay little regard to boundary lines or titles. Others, prompted by more sordid and deliberate purposes of wrong, and looking forward to the ultimate purchase of such territory by the United States, traverse it with the view of selecting the choice parcels, under the expectation that Congress will grant the right of pre-emption to actual settlers, and under the belief that at all events, their prior claims by occupancy will be respected by common consent, when the country shall be brought into market.

Although these intrusions are in contravention of treaties with the Indians, and against the laws of the United States, they are of frequent occurrence, and are made the basis of urgent *claims* upon the Government. Collisions occur between the intruders and the natives, most usually provoked by the artful designs of the offending parties, to accelerate the expulsion of the rightful possessors of the country. The Indians are insulted and provoked, and when such injuries are resented, however tardily, and with whatever stinted measure of retaliation, a loud outcry is raised against the savages; clamorous petitions are sent to the Government, setting forth the hostile disposition of the Indians, the terrors of border warfare, and the danger of the unprotected settlers; and insisting upon the immediate purchase of the territory, and the removal of the Indians to other hunting grounds. But one party is heard at Washington; and its bold assertions, being uncontradicted, are believed. A treaty is ordered to be held, which is equivalent to saying to the Red man, that it is the will of the American people that they should remove the lodges further to the West.

The Indians, thus urged, and soured by antecedent provocation, demand an exorbitant price; but the emergency admits of no delay, and the territory is purchased on their own terms. The scene which ensues fully discloses the moving springs of the operation. No sooner is the land brought into market, than Congress is called upon to grant *pre-emption rights* to *actual settlers*. True, these actual settlers are obviously intruders, violators of law, having certainly no title to a preference over other citizens; but their case is so stated as to make them appear a meritorious class, and their *claims* are urged with zealous pertinacity. The nation is made to ring with the merits and sufferings of the hardy men, who have marched in the van of civilisation, braving the Indian and the beast of prey; and much is said of the injustice of permitting others to purchase *the farms* of this meritorious class. Pre-emption rights are granted, and the violators of the law are secured in the fruits of their aggression. And who are the gainers by a transaction commencing in bad faith to the Indian, compromitting the justice and the honour of the nation, and ending in rewarding our own citizens for breaking our laws? When the pre-emptions come to be entered at the land offices, the larger portion of them are found to be in the hands of a few sagacious speculators, whose hands may be traced throughout the whole of this iniquitous proceeding, and who amass fortunes. And it not unfrequently happens, that before the whole of this scheme can be compassed a war must be fought—a war fraught with indescribable horrors, with domestic misery, personal sacrifice, vast loss of life, and immense expense to the public.

It is an unfortunate consequence also, inseparable from this kind of intercourse, that it gives employment to a numerous body of unofficial and irresponsible agents. At all the treaties with the Indians, especially those held for the purchase of land, a number of white men are found

present, who by some means or other have acquired
influence with the tribes, or with particular chiefs.   They
are usually traders or interpreters, who have lived long
enough among the Indians to have become familiar with
their language and customs, and personally acquainted
with the individuals composing the tribe.   A part of these
men usually advocate the treaty as proposed by the
Government, while others again oppose it, and both are
exceedingly assiduous in making converts among the chiefs
and influential braves.   The first party are those who have
been convinced by the arguments of the speculators ; the
others are those who are still open to conviction.   What
arguments are used to gain their suffrages, we are not able
from personal observation to state : but the fact is, that in
the end the treaty is usually made as proposed.

In the public councils, in which the Indians transact
their business, the chiefs and head men, who are the
ostensible actors, are merely the exponents of the public
will.   The tribe is a pure democracy, in which every
individual has a right to vote, and in which the individuals
are in fact consulted.   It is singular, that under such
circumstances, the deliberations of an Indian council are
always harmonious, and the decision almost invariably
unanimous.   These results are attributable in part to the
decorum which pervades these assemblages, in which a
speaker is never interrupted, nor contradicted, and where
no one speaks without previous careful preparation.   But
another reason for the harmonious operation of the council
is, that the business is mostly adjusted out of doors.   The
leading men consult their respective followers separately,
confer with each other, and agree on measures before going
into council ; so that the speeches uttered there, are rather
intended for effect or to announce conclusions already
formed, than to persuade or convince the audience.

This mode of proceeding affords great advantages to those who tamper with the leading men, who are easily approached by means of bribes, or warped by insidious appeals to their passions or prejudices. Some inference may be drawn as to the character of the appliances used in this diplomacy, from the procedure which is not unusual on occasions of this kind. When they first assemble, the greater number of the chiefs are commonly opposed to the cession of their lands. They sit in council with solemn and forbidding countenances, and are taciturn and inaccessible : one after another, occasionally expressing his aversion to the proposed transfer, in brief, sententious, and pithy remarks, in which the rapacity of the white man, the wrongs of the Indians, and their veneration for the bones of their ancestors, form the leading topics. Presently, during a recess of the council, one of these leaders receives a present of a gun, or a pair of pistols, from some individual, which he receives with apparent indifference, hinting at the same time that there are other articles, which he names, of which he stands in equal need ; which of course are added, until the wily savage professes to be satisfied, that perhaps, after all, it would be best for his people to agree to the treaty. The same process is repeated in regard to others, including the common Indians, and not forgetting the women and children, until good humour is diffused throughout the assemblage. After this the harangues are delivered, which sometimes appear in print, and finally an unanimous result is obtained. We do not aver that these practices obtain now, or that they are sanctioned by the commissioners who represent the Government ; but we assert that such means have been effectually employed in some instances, and that they are unavoidable under the present system of relations between the white and red men. The Government does not, and cannot control the intercourse, while a numerous band of mercenary men, not responsible to it, are permitted to influence the savage mind, and while no effectual restraint is imposed upon the fell spirit of speculation, which first intrudes on the lands of the Indian, and then institutes a series of intrigues to dispossess the savage of the soil, and defraud the Government of the price, by means of grants and pre-emptions.

As we have asserted that the policy of our Government, and the intentions of the American people towards the Indians, have been uniformly just and benevolent, we shall conclude our remarks on this branch of the subject, by quoting a few passages from the official communications of the several Presidents to Congress, which will show conclusively the tone of public feeling towards that race, and must satisfy the most sceptical, that whatever mistakes may have been made, and whatever wrong the aborigines may have suffered, no deliberate purpose to oppress or injure them has ever been entertained by the Government or people.

From President Washington's Address to Congress,
of November 6, 1792.

"You will, I am persuaded, learn with no less concern than I communicate it, that reiterated endeavours towards effecting a pacification have hitherto issued only in new and outrageous proofs of persevering hostility on the part of the tribes with whom we are in contest. An earnest desire to procure tranquillity to the frontier, to stop the further effusion of blood, to arrest the progress of expense, to forward the prevalent wish of the nation for peace, has led to strenuous efforts, through various channels, to accomplish these desirable purposes; in making which efforts, I consulted less my own anticipa-

JACK-O-PA
A Chippeway Chief

tions of the event, or the scruples which some considerations were calculated to inspire, than the wish to find the object attainable, or if not attainable, to ascertain unequivocally that such was the case.   *   *   *

" I cannot dismiss the subject of Indian affairs without again recommending to your consideration the expediency of more adequate provisions for giving energy to the laws throughout our interior frontier, and for restraining the commission of outrages upon the Indians, without which all pacific plans must prove nugatory. To enable, by competent rewards, the employment of qualified and trusty persons to reside among them as agents, would also contribute to the preservation of peace and good neighbourhood. If, in addition to these expedients, an eligible plan could be devised for promoting civilisation among the friendly tribes, and for carrying on trade with them upon a scale equal to their wants, and under regulations calculated to protect them from imposition and extortion, its influence in cementing their interests with ours could not but be considerable.   *   *   *

" When we contemplate the war on our frontiers, it may be truly affirmed, that every reasonable effort has been made to adjust the causes of dissension with the Indians north of the Ohio. The instructions given to the commissioners evince a moderation and equity proceeding from a sincere love of peace, and a liberality having no restriction but the essential interests and dignity of the United States."

From President Adams's Address to Congress, of November 23, 1797.

" In connection with this unpleasant state of things on our Western frontier, it is proper for me to mention the attempts of foreign agents to alienate the affections of the

Indian nations, and to excite them to actual hostilities against the United States. Great activity has been exerted, by those persons who have insinuated themselves among the Indian tribes residing within the territory of the United States, to influence them to transfer their affections and force to a foreign nation, to form them into a confederacy, and prepare them for a war against the United States. Although measures have been taken to counteract these infractions of our rights, to prevent Indian hostilities, and to preserve entire their attachment to the United States, it is my duty to observe, that to give a better effect to these measures, and to obviate the consequences of a repetition of such practices, a law, providing adequate punishment for such offences, may be necessary."

From President Jefferson's Message of January 28, 1803.

"These people are becoming very sensible of the baneful effects produced on their morals, their health, and existence, by the abuse of ardent spirits, and some of them earnestly desire a prohibition of that article from being carried among them. The Legislature will consider whether the effectuating that desire would not be in the spirit of benevolence and liberality which they have hitherto practised towards these our neighbours, and which has had so happy an effect towards conciliating their friendship. It has been found too, in experience, that the same abuse gives frequent rise to incidents tending much to commit our peace with the Indians."

From President Jefferson's Message of October 17, 1803.

"The friendly tribe of Kaskaskia Indians, with which we have never had a difference, reduced by the wars and wants of savage life, to a few individuals unable to defend themselves against the neighbouring tribes, has transferred its country to the United States, reserving only for its members what is sufficient to maintain them in an agricultural way.   The considerations stipulated are, that we shall extend to them our patronage and protection, and give them certain annual aids, in money, in implements of agriculture, and other articles of their choice.   *   *   *

"With many other of the Indian tribes, improvements in agriculture and household manufacture are advancing, and with all our peace and friendship are established, on grounds much firmer than heretofore.   The measure adopted of establishing trading houses among them, and in furnishing them necessaries in exchange for their commodities at such moderate prices as to leave no gain, but cover us from loss, has the most conciliatory and useful effect upon them, and is that which will best secure their peace and good-will."

Extract from President Jefferson's Message of
November 8, 1804.

"By pursuing an uniform course of justice towards them," (the Indians), "by aiding them in all the improvements which can better their condition, and especially by establishing a commerce on terms which shall be advantageous to them, and only not losing to us, and so regulated as that no incendiaries of our own, or any other nation, may be permitted to disturb the natural effects of our just and friendly offices, we may render ourselves so necessary to their comfort and prosperity, that the protection of our citizens from their disorderly members, will become their interest and their voluntary care.   Instead, therefore, of an augmentation of military force, proportioned to our extent of frontier, I proposed a moderate enlargement of the capital employed in that commerce, as a more effectual, economical, and humane instrument for preserving peace and good neighbourhood with them."

Extract from President Jefferson's Message of
November 8, 1808.

"With our Indian neighbours the public peace has been steadily maintained. Some instances of individual wrong have as at other times taken place, but in nowise implicating the will of the nation. Beyond the Mississippi, the Ioways, the Sacs, and the Alabamas, have delivered up for trial and punishment, individuals from among themselves, accused of murdering citizens of the United States. On this side of the Mississippi, the Creeks are exerting themselves to arrest offenders of the same kind; the Choctaws have manifested their readiness and desire for amicable and just arrangements respecting depredations committed by disorderly persons of their tribe. And generally, from a conviction that we consider them as part of ourselves, and cherish with sincerity their rights and interests, the attachment of the Indian tribes is gaining strength daily, is extending from the nearer to the more remote, and will amply requite us for the justice and friendship practised towards them."

Extract from President Madison's Message of
December 7, 1813.

"The cruelty of the enemy in enlisting the savages into a war with a nation desirous of mutual emulation in mitigating its calamities, has not been confined to any one quarter. Wherever they could be turned against us, no exertions to effect it have been spared. On our south-western border, the Creek tribes, who yielding to our persevering endeavours were gradually acquiring more civilised habits, became the unfortunate victims of seduction. A war in that quarter has been the consequence, infuriated by a bloody fanaticism, recently propagated among them. It was necessary to crush such a war before it could spread among the contiguous tribes, and before it could favour enterprises of the enemy into that vicinity. With this view, a force was called into the service of the United States from the states of Georgia and Tennessee, which, with the nearest regular troops, and other corps from the Mississippi Territory, might not only chastise the savages into present peace, but make a lasting impression on their fears.

" The systematic perseverance of the enemy in courting the aid of the savages on all quarters, had the natural effect of kindling their ordinary propensity to war into a passion, which, even among those best disposed towards the United States, was ready, if not employed on our side, to be turned against us. A departure from our protracted forbearance to accept the services tendered by them, has thus been forced upon us. But in yielding to it, the retaliation has been mitigated as much as possible, both in its extent and in its character, stopping far short of the example of the enemy, who owe the advantages they have occasionally gained in battle chiefly to the number of their savage associates; and who have not controlled them either from their usual practice of indiscriminate massacre on defenceless inhabitants, or from scenes of carnage without a parallel, on prisoners to the British arms, guarded by all the laws of humanity and of honourable war. For these enormities the enemy are equally responsible, whether with the power to prevent them they want the will, or with the knowledge of a want of power they still avail themselves of such instruments."

Extract from President Madison's Message of
December 3, 1816.

"The Indian tribes within our limits appear also disposed to remain at peace. From several of them purchases of lands have been made, particularly favourable to the wishes and security of our frontier settlements, as well as to the general interests of the nation. In some instances the titles, though not supported by due proof, and clashing those of one tribe with the claims of another, have been extinguished by double purchases, the benevolent policy of the United States preferring the augmented expense to the hazard of doing injustice, or to the enforcement of justice against a feeble and untutored people by means involving or threatening an effusion of blood. I am happy to add, that the tranquillity which has been restored among the tribes themselves, as well as between them and our own population, will favour the resumption of the work of civilisation which has made an encouraging progress among some tribes, and that the facility is increasing for extending that divided and individual ownership, which exists now in movable property only, to the soil itself; and of thus establishing, in the culture and improvement of it, the true foundation for a transit from the habits of the savage to the arts and comforts of social life."

Extract from President Monroe's Message,
December 2, 1817.

"From several of the Indian tribes inhabiting the country bordering on Lake Erie, purchases have been made of lands on conditions very favourable to the United States, and it is presumed not less so to the tribes themselves.

"By these purchases the Indian title, with moderate reservations, has been extinguished to the whole of the land within the state of Ohio, and to a great part of that of Michigan Territory, and of the state of Indiana. From the Cherokee tribe a tract has been purchased in the state of Georgia, &c. &c. * * *

"By these acquisitions, and others that may reasonably be expected soon to follow, we shall be enabled to extend our settlements from the inhabited parts of the state of Ohio, along Lake Erie, into the Michigan Territory, and to connect our settlements by degrees, through the state of Indiana and the Illinois Territory, to that of Missouri. A similar and equally advantageous effect will soon be produced to the south, through the whole extent of the states and territory which border on the waters emptying into the Mississippi and Mobile. In this progress, which the rights of nature demand and nothing can prevent, marking a growth rapid and gigantic, it is our duty to make new efforts for the preservation, improvement, and civilisation of the native inhabitants. The hunter state can exist only in the vast uncultivated desert. It yields to the more dense and compact form, and greater force of civilised population; and of right it ought to yield, for the earth was given to mankind to support the greatest number of which it is capable, and no tribe or people have a right to withhold from the wants of others more than is necessary for their own support and comfort. It is gratifying to know that the reservation of land made by the treaties with the tribes on Lake Erie, were made with a view to individual ownership among them, and to the cultivation of the soil by all, and that an annual stipend has been pledged to supply their other wants.

"It will merit the consideration of Congress, whether other provision not stipulated by the treaty ought to be made for these tribes, and for the advancement of the liberal and humane policy of the United States toward all the tribes within our limits, and more particularly for their improvement in the arts of civilised life."

Extract from President Monroe's Message,
November 17, 1818.

"With a view to the security of our inland frontiers it has been thought expedient to establish strong posts at the mouth of the Yellowstone River, and at the Mandan village on the Missouri, and at the mouth of St Peter's on the Mississippi, at no great distance from our northern boundaries. It can hardly be presumed, while such posts are maintained in the rear of the Indian tribes, that they will venture to attack our peaceable inhabitants. A strong hope is entertained that this measure will likewise be productive of much good to the tribes themselves; especially in promoting the great object of their civilisation. Experience has clearly demonstrated that independent savage communities cannot long exist within the limits of a civilised population. The progress of the latter has almost invariably terminated in the extinction of the former, especially of the tribes belonging to our portion of this hemisphere, among whom loftiness of sentiment and gallantry in action have been conspicuous. To civilise them, and even to prevent their extinction, it seems to be indispensable that their independence as communities should cease, and that the control of the United States over them should be complete and undisputed. The hunter state will then be more easily abandoned, and recourse will be had to the acquisition and culture of land, and to other pursuits tending to dissolve the ties which connect them together as a savage community, and to give a new character to every individual. I present this subject to the consideration of Congress, on the presumption that it may be found expedient and practicable to adopt some benevolent provisions, having these objects in view, relative to the tribes within our settlements."

Extract from President Monroe's Message,
November 14, 1820.

"With the Indians peace has been preserved, and a progress made in carrying into effect the act of Congress, making an appropriation for their civilisation, with a prospect of favourable results. As connected equally with both these objects, our trade with those tribes is thought to merit the attention of Congress. In their original state, game is their sustenance and war their occupation, and if they find no employment from civilised powers they destroy each other. Left to themselves, their extirpation is inevitable. By a judicious regulation of our trade with them, we supply their wants, administer to their comforts, and gradually, as the game retires, draw them to us. By maintaining posts far in the interior, we acquire a more thorough and direct control over them, without which it is confidently believed that a complete change in their manners can never be accomplished. By such posts, aided by a proper regulation of our trade with them, and a judicious civil administration over them, to be provided for by law, we shall, it is presumed, be enabled not only to protect our own settlements from their savage incursions, and to preserve peace among the several tribes, but accomplish also the great purpose of their civilisation."

Extract from the Message of President Adams, of
December 2, 1828.

"The attention of Congress is particularly invited to
that part of the report of the Secretary of War, which
concerns the existing system of our relations with the
Indian tribes. At the establishment of the Federal
Government under the present constitution of the United
States, the principle was adopted of considering them as
foreign and independent powers, and also as proprietors
of the land. They were moreover considered as savages,
whom it was our policy and our duty to use our influence
in converting to Christianity, and in bringing within the
pale of civilisation.

"As independent powers we negotiated with them by
treaties; as proprietors we purchased from them all the
lands which we could prevail upon them to sell; as
brethren of the human race rude and ignorant, we
endeavoured to bring them to the knowledge of religion
and letters. The ultimate design was to incorporate in
our own institutions that portion of them which could be
converted to the state of civilisation. In the practice of
European states, before our revolution, they had been considered as children to be governed; as tenants at
discretion, to be dispossessed as occasion might require;
as hunters, to be indemnified by trifling concessions for
removal from the ground upon which their game was
extirpated. In changing the system, it would seem as if
a full contemplation of the consequences of the change
had not been taken. We have been far more successful
in the acquisition of their lands than in imparting to them
the principles, or inspiring them with the spirit of civilisation. But in appropriating to ourselves their hunting
grounds, we have brought upon ourselves the obligation

of providing for their subsistence; and when we have had the rare good fortune of teaching them the arts of civilisation, and the doctrines of Christianity, we have unexpectedly found them forming in the midst of ourselves communities claiming to be independent of ours, and rivals of sovereignty within the territories of the members of the Union. This state of things requires that a remedy should be provided; a remedy which, while it shall do justice to these unfortunate children of Nature, may secure to the members of our confederation their right of sovereignty, and of soil."

Extract from President Jackson's Message of December 8, 1829.

"The condition and ulterior destiny of the Indian tribes within the limits of some of our states have become objects of much interest and importance. It has long been the policy of Government to introduce among them the arts of civilisation, in the hope of gradually reclaiming them from a wandering life. This policy has, however, been coupled with another wholly incompatible with its success. Professing a desire to civilise and settle them, we have at the same time lost no opportunity to purchase their lands, and thrust them farther into the wilderness. By this means they have not only been kept in a wandering state, but been led to look upon us as unjust and indifferent to their fate. Thus, though lavish in its expenditures upon the subject, Government has constantly defeated its own policy; and the Indians, in general, receding farther and farther to the West, have retained their savage habits. A portion, however, of the southern tribes, having mingled much with the whites, and made some progress in the arts of civilised life, have lately attempted to erect an independent government within the limits of

Georgia and Alabama. These states, claiming to be the only sovereigns within their territories, extended their laws over the Indians, which induced the latter to call upon the United States for protection.

"Under these circumstances, the question presented was, whether the general government had a right to sustain those people in their pretensions ? The Constitution declares, that 'no new state shall be formed or erected within the jurisdiction of any other state' without the consent of its Legislature. If the general government is not permitted to tolerate the erection of a confederate state within the territory of one of the members of this Union, against her consent, much less could it allow a foreign and independent government to establish itself there. Georgia became a member of the confederacy which eventuated in our Federal Union, as a sovereign state, always asserting her claim to certain limits, which, having been originally defined in her colonial charter, and subsequently recognised in the treaty of peace, she has ever since continued to enjoy, except as they have been circumscribed by her own voluntary transfer of a portion of her territory to the United States, in the Articles of Cession of 1802. Alabama was admitted into the Union on the same footing with the original states, with boundaries which were prescribed by Congress. There is no constitutional, conventional, or legal provision, which allows them less power over the Indians within their borders, than is possessed by Maine or New York. Would the people of Maine permit the Penobscot tribe to erect an independent government within their state ? and unless they did, would it not be the duty of the general government to support them in resisting such a measure ? Would the people of New York permit each remnant of the Six Nations within her borders, to declare itself an independent people under the protection of the United States? Could the Indians establish a separate republic on each of their reservations in Ohio? and if they were so disposed, would it be the duty of this government to protect them in the attempt? If the principle involved in the obvious answer to these questions be abandoned, it will follow that the objects of this government are reversed; and that it has become a part of its duty to aid in destroying the states which it was established to protect.

"Actuated by this view of the subject, I informed the Indians inhabiting parts of Alabama and Georgia, that their attempt to establish an independent government would not be countenanced by the Executive of the United States, and advised them to emigrate beyond the Mississippi, or submit to the laws of those states.

"Our conduct toward these people is deeply interesting to our national character. Their present condition, contrasted with what they once were, makes a most powerful appeal to our sympathies. Our ancestors found them the uncontrolled possessors of these vast regions. By persuasion and force they have been made to retire from river to river, and from mountain to mountain, until some of the tribes have become extinct, and others have left but remnants, to preserve for a while their once terrible names. Surrounded by the whites, with their arts of civilisation, which, by destroying the resources of the savage, doom him to weakness and decay; the fate of the Mohegan, the Narragansett, and the Delaware, is fast overtaking the Choctaw, the Cherokee, and the Creek. That this fate surely awaits them, if they remain within the limits of the states, does not admit of a doubt. Humanity and national honour demand that every effort should be made to avert so great a calamity. It is too late to inquire whether it was just in the United States to include them and their territory within the bounds of the new states whose limits they could control. That step cannot be retracted. A state cannot be dismembered by Congress, or restricted in the exercise of her constitutional power. But the people of those states, and of every state, actuated by feelings of justice and regard for our national honour, submit to you the interesting question, whether something cannot be done, consistently with the rights of the states, to preserve this much injured race.

"As a means of effecting this end, I suggest for your consideration the propriety of setting apart an ample district west of the Mississippi, and without the limits of any state or territory now formed, to be guaranteed to the Indian tribes as long as they shall occupy it, each tribe having a distinct control over the portion designated for its use. There they may be secured in the enjoyment of governments of their own choice, subject to no other control from the United States than such as may be necessary to preserve peace on the frontier, and between the several tribes. There the benevolent may endeavour to teach them the arts of civilisation; and, by promoting union and harmony among them, to raise up an interesting commonwealth, destined to perpetuate the race, and to attest the humanity and justice of this Government.

"This emigration should be voluntary, for it would be as cruel as unjust to compel the aborigines to abandon the graves of their fathers and seek a home in a distant land. But they should be distinctly informed that if they remain within the limits of the states, they must be subject to their laws. In return for their obedience as individuals, they will, without doubt, be protected in the enjoyment of those possessions which they have improved by their industry. But it seems to me visionary to suppose that, in this state of things, claims can be allowed on tracts of country on which they have neither dwelt nor made improvements, merely because they have seen them from the mountain or passed them in the chase. Submitting to the laws of the states, and receiving, like other citizens, protection in their persons and property, they will ere long become merged in the mass of our population."

Extract from President Jackson's Message of December 7, 1830.

"Humanity has often wept over the fate of the aborigines of this country, and philanthropy has been long busily employed in devising means to avert it. But its progress has never for a moment been arrested; and, one by one, have many powerful tribes disappeared from the earth. To follow to the tomb the last of his race, and to tread on the graves of extinct nations, excites melancholy reflections. But true philanthropy reconciles the mind to these vicissitudes, as it does to the extinction of one generation to make room for another. In the monuments and fortresses of an unknown people, spread over the extensive regions of the West, we behold the memorials of a once powerful race, which was exterminated, or has disappeared, to make room for the existing savage tribes. Nor is there anything in this, which, upon a comprehensive view of the general interests of the human race, is to be regretted. Philanthropy could not wish to see this continent restored to the condition in which it was found by our forefathers. What good man would prefer a country covered with forests and ranged by a few thousand savages, to our extensive Republic, studded with cities, towns, and prosperous farms; embellished with all the improvements which art can devise, or industry execute; occupied by more than twelve millions of happy people, and filled with all the blessings of liberty, civilisation, and religion.

"The present policy of the Government is but a continuation of the same progressive change, by a milder process. The tribes which occupied the countries now constituting the eastern states, were annihilated, or have melted away, to make room for the whites. The waves of population and civilisation are rolling to the Westward; and we now propose to acquire the countries occupied by the Red men of the south and west by a fair exchange, and, at the expense of the United States, to send them to a land where their existence may be prolonged, and perhaps made perpetual. Doubtless it will be painful to leave the graves of their fathers: but what do they more than our ancestors did, or than our children are now doing? To better their condition in an unknown land, our forefathers left all that was dear in earthly objects. Our children, by thousands yearly leave the land of their birth, to seek new homes in distant regions. Does humanity weep at these painful separations from everything, animate and inanimate, with which the young heart has become entwined? Far from it. It is rather a source of joy that our country affords scope where our young population may range unconstrained in body or mind, developing the power and faculties of man in their highest perfection. These remove hundreds, and almost thousands of miles, at their own expense, purchase the lands they occupy, and support themselves at their new homes, from the moment of their arrival. Can it be cruel in this Government, when, by events which it cannot control, the Indian is made discontented in his ancient home, to purchase his lands, to give him a new and extensive territory, to pay the expense of his

KEE-SHE-WAA
A Fox Warrior

removal, and support him a year in his new abode?
How many thousands of our own people would gladly
embrace the opportunity of removing to the West on
such conditions? If the offers made to the Indians were
extended to them, they would be hailed with gratitude."

III.

WHEN any reflecting man is asked, what it is that
constitutes the difference between the American people
and the subjects of an European despotism, and what is
the cause of that prosperity which has carried forward
our country with such rapid strides in her march to
greatness? he refers at once to the character of the
people as resulting from the institutions of a republican
government. Their enterprise, industry, intelligence,
temperance, and republican simplicity, and the equality
of rights secured to them in their social compact, are the
elements of their respectability as individuals, and their
greatness as a people. Our systems of public instruction,
our varied means for the diffusion of knowledge, our
religious toleration, and freedom from civil burthens,
all tend to ameliorate and refine the character, to
stimulate the enterprise, and awaken the latent energies
of the people. Do we extend these rights and advantages
to the Indian, or impart to him the virtues and the
comforts of the civilised man? In the pageantry of the
councils which are held with their chiefs, do we display
that simplicity which marks our intercourse with each
other? Do we inculcate frugality by presenting them
with loads of gaudy finery? Do we teach self-dependence,
industry, and thrift, by supplying their necessities, and
encouraging their idle habits? Do we, by any systematic

exertion, present to them the example of our virtues, and offer them inducements to cultivate peace, industry, and the arts? The replies which must necessarily be given to these questions lead inevitably to the conclusion, that we have grossly oppressed this people, or unpardonably neglected our duty towards them.

If it be inquired, what remedy can be applied to this enormous and growing evil?—we reply, that the question is one, to our minds, of easy solution. We do not believe that the All-wise Creator has doomed a race of men to a merely sensual existence. We cannot be persuaded that human beings, gifted with intellectual faculties, are destined to live and to perish like brutes, without any knowledge of the hand that created them, without any perception of a responsibility for their actions as rational beings, without any cultivation of the mind or conscience. It is altogether possible that to the different races parts have been assigned, upon the great theatre of human action, of greater or less dignity; but we cannot believe that any have been excluded from the practice and the benefits of that wide scheme of benevolence which seeks the happiness of the whole human family. We have seen no authentic version of the golden rule, to which any exception is attached. The command *to love one another*, would scarcely have been given in such broad language, if those to whom it was given were to be brought into contact and familiar intercourse with another race, who could neither excite that love, nor bear its infusion into their own bosoms. In other words, we think the Indians have souls; and that our duty towards them is plainly pointed out by the relations in which we stand placed towards them. If they are our dependents, we should govern them as dependents; if they are our equals, we should admit them to an equality of rights; if they are properly subject to the operation of our laws, we should break down the barrier which separates them from us, bring them at once into the bosom of the Republic, and extend to them the benefits, immunities, and privileges that we enjoy ourselves. If it be objected that they are independent nations, and that we cannot in good faith destroy their national character, as we should do by imposing our laws and civilisation upon them against their will; it will be necessary, before we advance any further in our argument, to examine whether the fact be so, that these tribes are independent, and to ascertain the sort of national existence which they have held.

With regard to as many of the Indian tribes as have, by solemn treaty, placed themselves under our protection, given us the right to regulate their trade, navigate their rivers, traverse their country, and punish their people in our courts, and agreed to admit no white man of any nation into their territory without our licence, there seems to be little room for discussion. Sovereign nations they are not, for they have parted with all the highest attributes of sovereignty. They have placed their destinies at our disposal for good or for evil, and whether it be for evil or good depends on the fidelity with which we shall discharge the trust. It is too late now to inquire into the validity of those transactions, or the policy which dictated them. We have accepted the trust, and are bound in good faith to exercise it in a spirit of justice and philanthropy. And if we refer to our own legislation it will be seen, that this is not confined to those tribes which have by treaty submitted themselves to our jurisdiction. The general phrases "Indian" and "Indian territory" extend the operation of those laws to all the country lying West of our settlements, and to all the tribes and individuals within that region. With what

propriety can we now pause to inquire into our right of
sovereignty over these tribes, when we have already
exercised that sovereignty to the full extent that our
own safety or interest required? If to protect or
aggrandise ourselves we have assumed jurisdiction, without a qualm of conscience, shall we become squeamish
when called upon to exercise the same power for the
benefit of the Indian? The question is not now to be
decided whether we shall extinguish the independence
of the Indians, because that point has long since been
settled, and we have, by purchase or conquest, acquired
full sovereignty. Passing over the treaties to which we
have referred, and which speak for themselves, we shall
proceed to show that we have, in various ways, asserted
an absolute and unlimited power over these tribes. To
avoid repetition, we shall pass over the statutes above
referred to, and shall proceed to notice some other
assumptions of sovereignty on our part.

It will be recollected that the European Governments
have, from the first, exerted the right to parcel out among
themselves the newly discovered territories of savage
nations, assuming the principle, that a horde of savages
roaming over a wilderness, for the purpose of hunting, did
not acquire that sort of property in the lands which should
exclude their occupancy by a permanent population. Our
Government has been more tender towards the savage in
its construction of his rights, and has always acknowledged
a qualified property in him, of which he could not be
dispossessed without an equivalent. But the policy of the
Government has always looked to the settlement and cultivation of all the lands within our boundaries, and the removal
or civilisation of the Indians, and we have steadily made our
arrangements with a view to these ends, without consulting
the aborigines, or doubting the justice of our course.

In the year 1783, Virginia ceded to the United States all her right, title, and claim, as well of soil as of jurisdiction, to that region which was afterwards called the North-Western Territory, the whole of which was occupied by the Indians, except a few spots inhabited by the French. The condition of this grant was, that the territory so ceded should "be laid out and formed into states," "and that the states so formed shall be distinct republican states, and admitted members of the Federal Union," etc. To this treaty the Indian tribes were not parties, and of course seem not to have been recognised as having any political or civil rights. They were in full possession, and had manifested no intention either to sell the lands or abandon the country; yet the territory was ceded, and conditions made in regard to its future occupancy, without any reference to the actual condition or supposed wishes of the Indians. Virginia by ceding, and the United States by accepting, both "soil and jurisdiction," and both parties by providing for the erection of republican states in this country, deny all right of sovereignty in the aborigines as effectually as if they had done so by express words.

Afterwards, and before any of this country was purchased from the Indians, an ordinance was passed by Congress for its government; and although it is provided in this Act that the Indians shall be protected in their "property, rights, and liberty," this provision is not broader than that made in favour of the French inhabitants of the same country in the Deed of Cession, and it only extends to *the people* of that territory the same "indefeasible" rights which appertain to every citizen of the United States. The terms used apply to the Indians, in their individual, not in their national capacity; and the very passing of such a law is an assumption of sovereignty, which excludes the idea of any power existing in the Indians to protect their own rights, property, and liberty.

Chief Justice Marshall, in his opinion given in the celebrated case of *Worcester* v. *The State of Georgia*, says: "The Indian nations had always been considered as distinct, independent political communities, retaining their original natural rights, as the undisputed possessors of the soil, from time immemorial, with the single exception of that imposed by irresistible power, which excluded them from intercourse with any other European potentate than the first discoverer of the coast of the particular region claimed; and this was a restriction which those European potentates imposed on themselves, as well as on the Indians." In another part of the same opinion, he defines the relation existing between the United States and an Indian tribe, as "that of a nation claiming and receiving the protection of one more powerful; not that of individuals abandoning their national character, and submitting as subjects to the laws of a master."

From this high authority we are not disposed to dissent, nor is it necessary to do so. In ascertaining the legal position of the Indian nations, the Supreme Court were guided by the treaties, charters, and other public documents, by which the character of those nations was formally recognised. That they are independent and sovereign in name, and outward seeming, and that they are treated with by our Government as distinct nations, we admit. Our argument is, that, while they are so legally and nominally independent and sovereign, they have in fact been stripped of every national attribute, and that it is a mere mockery to continue to them the shadow, when we have taken from them the substance.

The country beyond the Mississippi is of vast

importance to the American people.   It forms the Western boundary of our population, and is inhabited by hordes of savages, who, from having been our equals, our enemies, our allies, the scourge and terror of our borders, are sinking fast into a state of imbecile dependence, which must soon render them the mere objects of our compassion. Already their rights have become so questionable, as to divide the opinions of our best and wisest men.   Not that any are so bold as to deny that they have *any* rights.   Far be it from us, at least, to hint that such a thought is seriously entertained.   Their claims upon us are high and sacred ; but, unfortunately for us and for them, they have become so complicated as to be undefined, and almost undefinable.   How shall we ascertain the political rights of those who have never acknowledged any international law, whose station is not fixed by the code of empires, who have no place in the family of nations ?   How estimate the civil condition of those whose government is, if we may so express it, a systematic anarchy, in which no maxim either of religion, morality, or law, is admitted to be fundamental, no right is sacred from the hand of violence, no personal protection insured, but to strength and valour ?   What are the obligations of religion, justice, or benevolence, towards those who acknowledge neither the one nor the other, in the sense in which we understand these terms ?   How shall we deal with a people, between whom and ourselves there is no community of language, thought, or custom ; no reciprocity of obligations ; no common standard by which to estimate our relative interests, claims and duties ?   These are questions of such difficult solution, that they will at last be decided not by reason but by power, as the Gordian knot was severed by the sword of the conqueror.

We apprehend, however, that the agitation of some of

these questions would be rather curious than useful. It can be of little benefit to the Indian, at this day, to inquire what have been the rights that he has forfeited by his own misconduct and the selfish interference of pretended friends—lost by misconception, or surrendered to the hand of violence. We cannot now place him in the situation in which our ancestors found him, but must deal with him according to the circumstances by which he is surrounded. And the question now is, what, in the present condition of the Indian, is our duty to him, and to ourselves? what policy, consistent with the interest and dignity of the American people, would be best calculated to save from utter destruction the remnant of the aboriginal tribes, and elevate them to the condition of a civilised race? We say, what policy *consistent with our own interests*, because, in the exertion of our own benevolence, towards a comparatively small number of savages, we are not to overlook the welfare of a numerous civilised population, and the great interests of humanity and religion, which are now inseparably connected with the consideration of this subject.

In the first place, we cannot believe that the mere fact, that a wandering horde of savages are in the habit of traversing a particular tract of country in pursuit of game, gives to them the ownership and jurisdiction of the soil as sovereign nations. In order to sustain such a claim, it should be shown that they have, at least, definite boundaries, permanent institutions, and the power to protect themselves, and enforce their laws. These are some of the attributes of nations. To make a *nation* there must be a *government*—a bond of union by which the individual character shall, for civil and social purposes, be merged in that of the body politic; and there must be a power somewhere, either in the rulers or the people, to make and enforce laws. Other nations must be satisfied that there is a *permanent authority*, which has the right to represent, and the power to bind such a community, by treaty. They must be satisfied, that there is a legal or a moral power sufficiently strong to enforce the obligations of justice, and that there is some judicial mode of investigating facts, determining questions of right, and settling principles. There must be some known principles of political and moral action, observed alike by the people and their rulers, which shall govern their intercourse with foreigners, and render it safe and certain. A body of men, merely associated together for present security and convenience, is by no means a nation. Between such a body, and a great empire in the full exercise of all the attributes of sovereign power, there may be several grades of the social compact. States may be dependent or independent, free or tributary; the people may govern themselves, or they may acknowledge a master; the state may be well governed and prosperous, or it may be corrupt and insignificant. But between *a government* and *no government* there is but one line. There is a clear distinction between a state and a mere collection of individuals: the latter, whatever may be their separate personal rights, cannot have collectively any political existence; and any nation, within whose limits or upon whose borders they may happen to be, has a clear right to extend its authority over them, having regard always to the rights of other nations. It is necessary, for the common advantage and security of mankind, that all men should belong to some government; and those who neglect to organise themselves into regular civil communities, must expect that existing governments will impose their laws upon them.

It is very clear that the North American Indians have, at this time, no regularly organised governments. Even the sub-division of tribes is doubtful and fluctuating. They are separated into smaller, or gathered into larger bodies, as their own convenience, or the caprice of a chief may dictate. An intelligent and warlike leader may amalgamate many of these clans together, or a war may force them to unite ; but when the cause which binds them together ceases, or when rival warriors contend for the ascendancy, they separate, or form other combinations. In the *Narrative of Long's Second Expedition,* we find that the Dacotahs are divided into *fifteen* tribes, and the writer observes, "Almost every traveller, who has visited the Dacotahs, has given a different enumeration of their divisions, some reckoning but *seven,* while others admit as many as *twenty-one* tribes." Again, he remarks, "These form *two* great divisions, which have been distinguished by traders into the names *Gens du Lac* and *Gens du Large* —those who live by the lake, and those who roam over the prairies." In this instance, it would be difficult to ascertain what individuals or tribes could be classed together as a nation, and the claim of any portion to be classed together, as a body politic, would, in the technical phrase of lawyers, *be bad for uncertainty.*

John Tanner, to whose interesting *Narrative* we have had occasion more than once to refer, was the son of an American citizen residing in Kentucky, and was taken prisoner when a child by the Ojibway or Chippeway Indians. He was adopted into an Indian family, was reared in their habits, and had lived among them for thirty years, when he was found by the gentlemen engaged in the Expedition under Long, and prevailed upon to furnish a narrative of his adventures for publication. The work is compiled with great care, and may be relied upon as authentic. Tanner not only lived with the Indians, but hunted and travelled extensively among the tribes who inhabit the shores of the upper lakes; yet he does not, in his whole *Narrative* refer to anything like a government. He does not mention the name of a ruling chief, nor does he detail a single instance of the exertion of sovereign authority. In all his troubles—and he had many—when robbed, abused, and exposed to violence in various forms, he sought no protection from a chief; there was no law, no ruler, no power, that could stay the hand of the oppressor, or give relief to the injured party. It is very clear that there is no government among a people thus situated. There are divisions into *tribes*, it is true, but these are large families rather than nations, for the distinctions are those of blood, not of country or government. There are *bands* formed for occasional purposes, which are dispersed whenever the necessity ceases which brought them together. Tanner himself never acknowledged any superior, nor considered himself as belonging to any particular body, though he called himself an Ojibway. Among his tribe were many leaders. A man who became distinguished as a warrior, or hunter, was resorted to by others, who became his followers; to secure the temporary advantages of the protection afforded by numbers, remained with him as long as he was successful, and dispersed whenever he experienced a reverse, or whenever game grew scarce. These combinations seldom last more than one season; and the same chief, who now commands a hundred warriors, revels in the spoils of his enemies, is wealthy in dogs and horses, and patriarchal in the number of his wives and dependents, will perhaps spend his next year in hunting, at some solitary spot, by himself, or be wandering about at the head of a little band, composed of his own relatives. In the next great war or hunting party, he may be first, second, or third in rank, or have no rank, just as it happens. Speaking of one of

their large war parties, Mr Tanner says: " On this
occasion men were assembled from a vast extent of
country, of dissimilar feelings and dialects, and of the
whole *fourteen hundred* not one who would acknowledge
any authority superior to his own will. It is true that
ordinarily they yield a certain deference, and a degree of
obedience, to the chief each may have undertaken to
follow; but this obedience in most instances continues no
longer than the will of the chief corresponds entirely with
the inclinations of those he heads."

This may be said to be an extreme case. The northern
hordes, inhabiting a sterile country and inhospitable
climate, suffer greatly for want of food, and are necessarily
scattered in small parties over a wide region. They are
reduced by the circumstances surrounding them to the
lowest grade of wretchedness, and of course exhibit the
savage life in its most unfavourable aspect. But it is
not materially different in Florida, so far as respects the
question of government. In our late negotiations and
wars with the Seminoles, we found a people answering to
a common name, and enlisted in a common cause; but
there was no central authority, nor any ruling chief, but a
collection of independent bands, who acted separately or
in union, as circumstances dictated.

The largest of our savage nations, the Osages and
Pawnees, are those in whom the savage state is seen to
the greatest advantage. The fertility of the country over
which they roam, the mildness of the climate, and especially
the abundance of food afforded by the immense herds
of buffalo, combine to raise these people above the
hardships which assail the more northern tribes, and
enable them to live together in larger bodies. They
are a more active and more cheerful people, have more
of the comforts of life, and are under infinitely better

discipline, but it is only *discipline*, mere martial law, and not civil government.

These nations, like the Dacotahs, are divided into bands, some of which seem to be wholly independent of the original stock—such as the Pawnee Loups, the Republican Pawnees, etc., which are bands that separated from the Grand Pawnees ; and the Little Osages, who are a branch of the Great Osages. During the last war between the United States and Great Britain, a portion of the Saukies, then residing at Rock Island on the Mississippi, being unwilling to unite with the majority of the nation in making war upon the United States, removed to a point on the Missouri River. Here they have remained ever since ; the separation between the two parts of the nation has become final, yet both retain the original name. These frequent divisions add to the other proofs of the absence of a binding or permanent organisation among the Indians.

The Osages have a tradition that they came originally from the East. They were for many years at war with the Missouries, who were a powerful nation, and by whom they were gradually driven to the West,—first to the Mississippi, where they remained some time, and then to the Missouri. The Missouries settled and built villages on the Mississippi. When Charlevoix, who was sent on a tour of discovery by the French Government, came through this region, he stopped for a short time among the Missouries, and made them presents of guns, ammunition, and knives, with which they were not acquainted before that time. Thus armed, they renewed their attacks upon the Osages, who had entrenched themselves within a fortification of logs and mud. The report and the effects of the fire-arms, now witnessed by the Osages for the first time, struck a panic into them, and, believing that the Great Spirit had put his thunder into the hands of their enemies, they fled. Proceeding up the river, they came to the stream which has since borne their name, the Osage River, where they halted; while the Missouries had the honour of giving their name to the Great River of the West, upon whose banks they settled. The Osages, at that time, numbered about three thousand warriors, but there were dissensions among them, arising out of discussions of the question where they should become permanently settled. In this state of things, some of the chiefs, with a small number of followers, went back to the Missouries, with whom they made peace—the conditions being, that they should settle in adjacent villages, and defend each other in case of war. How long they remained there does not appear; but they eventually rejoined the main body of the nation, with whom they are now united, though as a separate band, called the Little Osages. Since then other bands have separated from the Great Osages, who are known as the Omahas, the Kansas, and the Arkansas—indeed the Osages consider their nation as the original stock of nearly all the tribes between the Mississippi and the Rocky Mountains.

These separations occur from various causes—sometimes from quarrels among the chiefs, but more frequently from the scarcity of game, which induces large hunting parties to detach themselves from the main body of the nation, and wander off to distant places in search of game. It is a curious, but well-attested fact, evincing the evanescent nature of an unwritten language, that when a part of a tribe is thus separated for a few years from the remainder, they become distinguished by a peculiar dialect. Each party adopts new words, and forgets some of those in use; so that, with a rapidity almost incredible, a dissimilarity of tongue ensues between those who have but recently sprung from the same stock.

Much has been said and written of the attachment of the Indians to their hunting-grounds, to the places of their nativity, and the bones of their ancestors. The sympathy of the American people has often been invoked in relation to the alleged cruelty of all attempts to promote their civilisation, by removing them to new homes, where they could be protected from the encroachment of the whites. The cruelty, of course, consists in the violence done to their local attachments; for, unless the preference for a particular spot be very strong and deeply rooted, it would seem that all places would be pretty much alike to the mere roamer of the wilderness.

We suppose that on this subject there has been much mistake and exaggeration. The Indians have a great regard for the *bones* of their ancestors, but we are not aware that this feeling extends to the *places* where those bones are deposited. As with all pagans, the want of a rational belief in the immortality of the soul, induces the affection for deceased objects to attach to the inanimate remains, instead of following the spirit to its eternal abode. But that superstitious feeling attaches itself only to those relics; it is much akin to the awe which the ignorant among ourselves feel for dead bodies and places of burial, and has no assimilation nor connection with the love of country, or with any sentiment of regard for past generations.

There is no reason why the Indian should have strong local attachments, nor have we any satisfactory evidence of the existence of that feeling. He has no permanent habitation, and does not dwell at any spot sufficiently long to become attached to it by habit, or by mere familiarity with the surrounding objects. His whole life is spent in wandering; and if, for several successive years, he returns at intervals to one place, which thus becomes a kind of permanent encampment, and is called a town, it is only because of some convenience connected with the locality, which is abandoned whenever a stronger attraction is presented at some other spot. The whole plain of the Mississippi abounds in the deserted sites of Indian towns, and in the evidences of this erratic mode of life. And why should the savage become attached to the place of his abode? He builds no house, erects nothing, plants nothing, which would afford present comfort, or remain as a memorial of his existence. There is nothing to which either the pride or the convenience of ownership can be attached. The idea of real estate is unknown to him; there is no rood of ground to which he ever attaches the idea of possession, past, present, or prospective. There is no monument which appeals to his pride, or his affections, or calls up any associations connected with the past. He inherits nothing but the arms or clothing of his ancestors, and leaves nothing to his children which is not equally perishable. The Swiss peasant, however poor, dwells in a hut which has braved the elements for centuries; the village church is hallowed by the recollections of childhood; the moss-covered walls in the neighbourhood have their legends, which have become familiar from frequent repetition; the mountain-side, though bleak and sterile, is marked with paths trodden by successive generations; these, and a thousand other memorials, have impressed themselves upon the heart and the memory, and become the landmarks of home and country. The path of the Indian is like that of the mariner upon the ocean,—his footsteps leave no print behind them. Instead of a religion, he has a superstition, which never appeals to the heart, nor awakens any of the sensibilities of his nature; his god has no visible altar, neither a temple consecrated to holy purposes, nor a hallowed spot in the bosom of the domestic circle.

A WINNEBAGO
An Orator

That the Indians have not strong local attachments, is as demonstrable from their history, as it is clearly deducible from their character. They have always been a restless, wandering people. The savage is erratic from the very nature of his life : the nomadic state affords no scope for the cultivation of the affections; and whenever the savage is restrained from wandering, he becomes, more or less, a civilised man, as water becomes clear in a state of rest. The roaming from place to place, the want of a home, the absence of property, the habit of invading without scruple the lands of others—these are the most pregnant causes of the state of barbarism, as well as the most obvious proofs of the absence of the sort of attachment alluded to.

The Shawanoe nation, when first known to the whites, were a numerous and warlike people of Georgia and South Carolina. After the lapse of a very few years, they abandoned, or were driven from that region, and are found in the south-western part of the Ohio valley, giving their beautiful name to the river, which, by the bad taste of the Americans, has acquired the hackneyed name of Cumberland. We next hear of them in Pennsylvania, participators in the tragic scenes which have given celebrity to the valley of Wyoming. Again, they recede to the Ohio valley, to a locality hundreds of miles distant from their former hunting-grounds in the West, selecting now the rich and beautiful plains of the Sciota valley and the Miamies. Here they attained the highest point of their fame. Here was heard the eloquence of Logan ; here was spent the boyhood of Tecumseh. It was from the romantic scenes of the Little Miami, from the Pickaway plains, and the beautiful shores of the Sciota—from scenes of such transcendent fertility and beauty, as must have won any *but* a nature inherently savage, to the luxury of rest and contentment, that the Shawanoes went forth to battle on Braddock's field, at Point Pleasant, and along the whole line of the then Western frontier. Lastly, we find them dwelling on the Wabash, at Tippecanoe, holding councils with the Governor of Indiana at Vincennes, intriguing with the Cherokees and Creeks of the South, and fighting under the British banner in Canada. Here we find a people, numbering but a few thousand, and who could, even as savages and hunters, occupy but a small tract of country at any one time, roaming, in the course of two centuries, over ten degrees of latitude; changing their hunting-grounds, not gradually, but by migrations of hundreds of miles at a time; abandoning entirely a whole region, and appearing upon a new and far distant scene. What land was the *country* of the Shawanoes? To what *place* could that strong local attachment, which has been claimed for the Indians, have affixed itself? Where must the Shawanoe linger, to indulge that veneration for the bones of his fathers, which is said to form so strong a feeling in the savage breast? Their bones are mouldering in every valley, from the sultry confines of Georgia to the frozen shores of the Canadian frontier. Their traditions, if carefully preserved, would have embraced a hundred battle-fields, in as many separate districts, and have consecrated to the affections of a little remnant of people a vast expanse of territory, which now embraces eight or nine sovereign states, and maintains five millions of people.

The Saukies are said to have been settled originally on the banks of the River St Lawrence, near the ocean, and were driven thence towards the Lakes. Coming into contact with the great Iroquois confederacy, they waged a long and fierce war with that powerful people, through whose territories they passed. On the southern shore of

Lake Erie, they came into collision with the Wyandots, and were again plunged into sanguinary hostilities. Reaching the borders of Lake Michigan, they rested awhile; and it was here probably that they became allied with the Musquakee, or Fox nation. Thence bending their steps to the South, they poured down upon the widespread and beautiful prairies of Illinois, at that time covered with herds of buffalo, and possessed themselves of the country on the waters of Rock River, which they held until lately.

We might speak of other migrations, but these examples are sufficient for illustration. We know of no Indian nation which has remained stationary. Their traditions invariably point to their former abodes, in far distant places, and are fraught with allusions to long and perilous wanderings.

It is necessary, as a preliminary step to the civilisation of the Indians, that this migratory disposition should be eradicated. The Indian should be confined within settled boundaries, and be taught to cherish his own rights, by being forced to respect the rights of others. He should learn to associate his name and his destiny with that of the soil on which he dwells, and thus acquire the virtue, of which he has now no conception—the love of country. The Indian loves his tribe, he loves his wild, free habits of life, he loves the wilderness; but all these feelings are personal; they travel with him in his wanderings, and abide with his people wherever they may chance to dwell. They are not attached to the soil, nor interwoven with recollections of place and scenery. They are not connected with the sacred and delightful associations of home and country. The wild man has no home nor country.

Assuming the proposition, that the United States have a clear right to establish over the Indian tribes such form of government as will be best calculated to promote the happiness of those nations, and to insure to them the highest state of civilisation of which they are susceptible, we hold that our duty to extend these benefits to them is undeniable. And this should be done without delay, as every year is diminishing their numbers, deteriorating their character, and weakening the sympathy and the moral sense of duty towards them, which is now felt by all good men.

The plan that we would propose, would be to divide the whole Indian territory into districts, as few in number as could be conveniently arranged, so that each might be brought under the subjection of a Governor, who should have ample powers, and a sufficient military force to make himself obeyed. The machinery of this government should be simple ; its character parental; its object to protect, restrain, and reform the savage. The Governors should be instructed to rule with kindness and forbearance, to use every effort to allure the savages to practise the arts of civilised life, to gain their confidence, and to restrain them with a firm hand from their present habits of rapine and violence. The subordinate officers should all be men of fair character ; they should be amply paid for their services, and strictly forbidden from engaging in any traffic other than such as it might be found expedient for the Government to sanction; and the most unceasing vigilance should be used to protect the Indians from the fell grasp of the unprincipled speculator. These conditions may be deemed impracticable in a Government like ours, subject to frequent changes, and to the demoralising influence of party violence and political intrigue. It is to these causes that most of the abuses of which we complain are attributable ; but we hope for better things ; we hope that benevolent and patriotic men may be found, who will agitate this subject until a strong public sentiment shall be brought to bear on the national legislature, and that some of the influential members of that body, who are now "giving to party that which belongs to mankind," may be induced to earn the gratitude and applause of posterity, by devoting themselves to the prosecution of this great and philanthropic reform. Under such auspices, the scheme may succeed.

The Indians should be told at once, that they are not independent; that we intend to rule, and to protect them; that they must desist entirely from war, and must cease from wandering into the territories of their neighbours. They should be admonished to learn war no longer, and every exertion be used to blunt their martial propensities; military exercises should be discouraged; marks of respect and distinction should be withheld from chiefs and others who are eminent only for their feats in battle, while the favour of the Government should be shown to those who should successfully cultivate the arts, or practise the civil and social virtues. Instead of flattering their warriors, as our public functionaries too often do, by referring to their martial exploits, and their descent from a line of warriors, they should be told that bloodshed is forbidden by our religion, prohibited by our laws, and wholly inconsistent with our state of society; that we regard with abhorrence the taking of life, permitting it only, with great reluctance, in self-defence; and that the President will, on all public occasions, distinguish and prefer those chiefs and influential men whose hands are clear of blood, and who do most to preserve the lives and elevate the character of their people.

There can be no doubt as to the ultimate effect of sincere, patient, and continued efforts to inculcate the arts of peace, by constant appeals to the interest as well as the moral feelings of those people, aided by kindness, by good example, and by salutary restraint, firmly enforced by power. But the healthful operation of this procedure and its success, depend so entirely upon the character of the agents by whom it may be conducted, that it would be useless to make the attempt unless it be committed to men of sterling integrity and genuine benevolence, who would enter heartily into the spirit of the enterprise.

A council to be selected by themselves, composed of a few of their chief men, might assist the Governor in making laws, which should be few, brief, and simple. The code should at first embrace little more than the Christian Decalogue ; and new laws might, from time to time, be added, to meet the growing exigencies of increasing civilisation. The council might at first be vested with judicial powers, the trial by jury afterwards ingrafted, and a complete organisation of courts, with all the forms of legal investigation, gradually introduced. No violent change should be attempted, no sudden reformation forced upon the unprepared mind of the savage, no abrupt assault upon ancient customs or superstitions be permitted to alarm his pride or his fears ; but improvements should be gradually, unceasingly, and almost imperceptibly introduced, until the rank productions of ignorance and heathenism should be cleared away, and the foundations of the social edifice be laid, broad, strong, and symmetrical.

The Indian Bureau at Washington should be retained with enlarged powers, and under a watchful supervision ; but the agents, the presents, the traders, the interpreters, the legion of beneficiaries, who prey upon the funds appropriated by the national bounty to the Indians, should all be withdrawn, and the practice of granting annuities be discontinued. No white man but the Governor and his subordinates should be permitted to reside or remain in the Indian country, until the condition of the people should have become such as to admit of a higher grade of government, when it might be desirable to adopt a different policy.

Instead of preventing the Indians from coming into our country to trade, they should be encouraged to do so, as this would be one of the most effectual means of inducing them to learn our language, and adopt our customs.   They would see our industry, our comforts, and our arts, imbibe our opinions, become reconciled to our manners and fashions, and especially would get definite ideas of the use and value of our various articles of property.   They would be induced to purchase articles of dress and ornament, such as are worn by us, until by degrees their costume would be assimilated to ours. Imperceptibly they would fall into the use of many things of which they are now ignorant, or which they despise as unsuited to their condition, such as mechanical tools, household furniture, and farming implements.   Every article thus adopted would be a messenger of civilisation ; every art, comfort, and luxury of social life, which the Indian should learn to appreciate, would create a new want, to be supplied by us, and add a new bond to cement our union.

But the most important end to be gained would be the protection of the savages from imposition, and from a demoralising intercourse, which, while it robs them of the petty avails of their hunting, depraves their character, and sours them against the white men.   The traders, who now purchase the furs and peltries of the Indians, under the licence of the Government, enjoy a monopoly which enables them to carry on the traffic upon their own terms, and to perpetrate the grossest frauds without the danger of detection.   The place of barter is the wilderness, where there is no competition to regulate value, no public opinion to restrain dishonesty, no law to punish violence; and the trader, who adventures life and property in a business so precarious, may not greatly strain the ordinary morals of trade in deeming it justifiable to indemnify himself for his risks by extravagant profits, and retaliate aggression by force or cunning, as opportunity may offer. Humanity shudders at the recital of the nefarious arts practised by the white traders upon the Indians; yet the half of them are not known nor dreamed of by the American people.

Some instructive facts on this subject may be gleaned from Tanner's *Narrative*—the biography of a man born in Kentucky, who was captured by the Chippeway or Ojibway Indians in his childhood, and spent his life among them—written at his dictation by one of the gentlemen connected with *Long's Expedition*. In this work, we have a minute account of Indian life through a series of thirty years, embracing all the ordinary incidents and vicissitudes of the savage state. Here we find the traders sometimes taking *by force*, from a poor Indian hunter, the produce of a whole year's hunt, without making him any return; sometimes pilfering a portion while buying the remainder; and still more frequently driving a hard bargain with the intoxicated savage, and wresting from him a valuable property for a very inadequate compensation, consisting chiefly of the poison by which his faculties were obscured. In one case, Mr Tanner tells of an Indian woman, his adopted mother, who, "in the course of a single day, sold one hundred and twenty beaver skins, with a large quantity of buffalo robes, dressed and smoked skins, and other articles, *for rum*." This property, worth several hundred dollars, was the product of a whole season of hunting of two active men, the son and adopted son of this woman, attended by dangers, difficulties, and privations, which seem to us almost incredible, and constituted the sole wealth of a family, and their only means of support during the inclemency of a long northern winter ; and the author pathetically concludes, " of all our large load of peltries, the produce of so many days of toil, of so many long and difficult journeys, *one blanket and three kegs of rum* only remained, besides the poor and almost worn-out clothing of our bodies." Repeated instances of the same kind are related by this author, exhibiting a most unfavourable view of the intercourse between the traders and the Indians, and we have ample reason, from other sources of information, to believe that the picture is faithfully drawn. These, it is true, were British traders, on the inhospitable shores of Lake Superior, far beyond the influence of law or gospel : we hope and believe that such atrocities are not permitted within the regular agencies of our Government. From a personal knowledge of some of the gentlemen engaged in the fur trade, and of many of the agents of the United States, we can say with confidence that such abuses are not practised with their sanction. But human nature is the same everywhere ; the debasing love of gain has always been found to conduce to fraud and violence, when unrestrained by law and public sentiment. Mercantile integrity alone is not a sufficient safeguard against temptation. There are abundant proofs in our own land, that men cannot be trusted unless surrounded by wholesome restraints, and held to rigid responsibility. History abounds with lamentable proofs of the bad faith of all traffic carried on between civilised and savage men *in the countries of the latter:* India, Africa, the coasts of America, and the isles of the ocean, have all witnessed the dark and dreadful effects of the lust of gain.

Not only is the trade with these people liable to abuse, but all our treaties with them afford opportunities for the practice of gross frauds, which it is almost impossible to prevent, even with the greatest care on the part of the Government. But constituted as our Government is, it would be useless to expect any great degree of vigilance on such a subject, and the only mode of preventing the abuse is to remove the occasion. We could point to a recent instance in which the United States became bound by treaty to pay a certain description of claims set up by individuals of an Indian tribe. Commissioners were appointed to ascertain and liquidate the amounts due to each person, who, in the course of their investigation, discovered that nearly the whole of those claims had been secretly purchased by speculators for trifling considerations, and that immense sums granted in a spirit of liberality by Congress were about to be intercepted by a set of mere marauders, while the beneficiaries to whom it was intended to secure a livelihood had already expended the pittances given them in exchange. We are happy to say, that, in this instance, the fraud attempted to be practised by cunning upon ignorance was prevented. We shall not attempt to expose the numerous impositions of this kind, by which the munificence of our Government has been diverted from its legitimate channels ; the purpose of this Essay does not require such disclosures. The public ear has been pained and sickened by manifold recitals of the rapacity which has first driven the Red man from his hunting-grounds, and then stripped him of the poor price of his heritage. The sending of missionaries to labour by the side of the miscreants who thus swindle and debauch the ignorant savage, is a mockery of the office, and a waste of the time of these valuable men.

If the Indians were required to trade within our States, their intercourse would be with regular traders in the bosom of organised societies, and in the light of public observation; and the same law and public sentiment which protect us would protect them. Instead of bartering peltries for merchandise, without a definite idea of the value of either, they would use money as the medium of exchange, and become accustomed to fix prices upon the articles of traffic. We attach some importance to this change. Under the present system, the Indian delivers a package of skins, and receives a lot of merchandise, consisting of blankets, cloth, calico, beads, knives, gunpowder, etc.; and a very rough estimate only can be formed of the relative values of the articles, while in regard to the quality there can be but little room for choice. The formation of provident and frugal habits depends much upon proper notions of value, and the practice of close dealing. The economical maxims of Dr Franklin could not be practised in a community in which there should be no small coins, and would not be understood by a people without money. If, for instance, there should be, in any country, no coin, nor representative of money, of a less denomination than a dollar, the fractions under that sum would, in all transactions, be thrown off, and would cease to be regarded, and the people would never become close calculators in small transactions. The maxim, "take care of pence, and pounds will take care of themselves," would have no application among them. Such was the state of things, and such the effect, a few years ago, in some of our Western States, when small bank notes were not in circulation, and scarcely any coin less than half-dollars, and when it was so customary to throw off the fractions less than a dollar, that it was thought mean to insist on the collection of a balance which could only be counted in cents. So striking was the result of this state of things to one not accustomed to it, that a sagacious Englishman remarked to the writer, as an "*alarming circumstance,* the want of small coin, and the consequent pride or carelessness of the people in regard to their minor pecuniary transactions." To estimate the force of this remark, it is only necessary to contrast the disposition alluded to with the thrift of a New England farmer, who would in a year accumulate a considerable sum by hoarding the pittances which a frontier settler would scorn to put into his pocket. If this reasoning be just, its application to our subject is easy. The change from the rude and loose transaction of bartering commodities, to the more accurate method of selling and buying for money, would be the first step in the improvement we propose; the next would be a correct appreciation of the values of money and merchandise; and we think that sagacity in dealing, frugality in expenditure, and correct notions in regard to property, would follow. The Indian at present knows nothing of money, except from seeing boxes of dollars exposed when the annuities are paid to the chiefs; but if the individuals of that race were in the habit of carrying the products of the chase to a market, where they would learn to feel the excitement induced by competition, and where, as they wandered from shop to shop, a variety of articles, differing in quality and price, would be offered in exchange, we cannot doubt that the result would be beneficial.

The Indians are prevented from keeping live stock, or making any permanent provision for the future, by the insecurity of the lives they lead. The corn raised by their women, their only grain, and often their sole provision for the winter, is kept in pits dug in the ground, which is carefully levelled over the concealed treasure, so as to baffle the search of a stranger who might seek for it. But though hidden from an enemy, a large portion of the corn is inevitably destroyed by the moisture of the place of deposit, and in some seasons but little would be saved by this rude plan of preservation. An Indian who was asked, by an inquisitive traveller, why they did not store their corn in houses as we do, instead of burying it, at the risk of having so much of it destroyed, replied, promptly, that if they were to put their corn in houses their enemies would come in the winter and kill them to get it. If they were asked, why they keep no domestic animals but dogs and horses, the reply would be similar. They have no prejudice against any means which would furnish them with a regular supply of food without labour. They build no houses, make no fields, nor attempt any provision for a permanent residence; and all for the same reason— *property* of any description would tempt the rapacity of their enemies. Security is only found in poverty and swiftness of foot, and in their happiest state they are always prepared for instant flight. The attempt to civilise a people thus situated is absurd. We have begun at the wrong end. Their habits must first be changed, and their physical wants supplied, before any beneficial effect can be produced upon their minds and hearts. The pressure of external danger, which now keeps their minds excited and their passions in a state of continual exaltation, must be removed, and the inducements to war decreased, by lessening the occasions of provocation.

When placed, as we propose, under the immediate care of our Government, and restrained from war, the first measure should be to collect them in villages, and give them *permanent* habitations. They should be encouraged to build houses, to own cattle, hogs, and poultry, and to cultivate fields and gardens. They should at first be assisted in building, and a liberal supply of domestic animals should be given to them. But this aid should be extended to them with discrimination; and, while it furnished them with the means of improving their condition it should not degenerate into a mere gratuity to support them in idleness, and to be looked for with the return of each revolving season. It should be distinctly understood that the Government would not supply them with food and clothing. The annuities, which we are bound by treaty to pay, would have to be paid in good faith; but all other gratuities, except such as their change of life might render temporarily necessary, should be withheld.

The Indians, placed under these circumstances, would soon become an indolent pastoral people. They would not at first become an agricultural or an industrious race. That change would be too violent. The transition from the chase and the war-path to the plough would be difficult. Their indolence, their pride, their martial and gentlemanly dislike of labour, and their love of sleep, would all rebel against every sort of muscular exertion which could by any means be avoided, while all their prejudices would rise up in opposition to the indignity of performing the servile offices, which they suppose to lie peculiarly within the province of the women. They would grow lazy and harmless. Prevented from going to war, they would lose their martial habits, the influence of the war chiefs would be destroyed, and the propensity for rapine would be blunted. Their cattle, roaming over the rich plains to which nearly all the tribes have now been driven, would require but little care, and would soon increase to large herds. Abundance of food would lessen the necessity for hunting; and the men, left without employ and with little necessity for mental or bodily exertion, would lose their active habits.

The women, as they now do, would cultivate corn, but

with increased encouragement to industry, for the fruits of their labour would be more abundant, and would be secured to them. In other respects their condition would be improved and elevated, and they would become important agents in the civilisation of their race. The savage woman is debarred of the prerogatives, and deprived from exercising the virtues, of her sex, by her wandering life. The fireside, the family circle, all the comforts, luxuries, and enjoyments which are comprised in the word *home*, are created and regulated by female affection, influence, and industry—and all these are unknown to the savage. He has no home. The softening and ennobling influences of the domestic circle are unknown to him; and the woman, having no field for the exercise of the virtues peculiar to her sex, never appears in her true character, nor is invested with the tender, the healthful, the ennobling influence which renders her, in her proper sphere, the friend and adviser of man. We would elevate the savage woman to her legitimate place in the social system, and make her the unconscious, but most efficient, instrument in the civilisation of her race. We feel, and see, and acknowledge, in every department of life, the ameliorating and conservative influence of female virtue, and we would give this inestimable blessing to the savage, even against his will. We would restrain his feet from wandering, and his hand from blood, and force upon him the softening and elevating endearments of *home*. Then would the Indian woman assume her appropriate station and her proper duties. The wretched wigwam, or the temporary skin lodge, afford no theatre for her ingenuity, no field for the exercise of any feminine virtue or accomplishment. The drudge, who spends her whole existence in following the savage hunter in his perilous wanderings, may learn to share his hardihood and ferocity, but can never have either the power or disposition to soften his rude nature. Mistress of a *house*, she would awaken to a sense of her own importance, and become alive to kind and generous impulses, which she knows not in her present condition. The possession of a home would suggest ideas of comfort, and bring into action the whole train of household cares. Pride and affection would unite in suggesting new wants and novel improvements. That fidelity which she now exhibits in the patient endurance of toil and danger, would expand and thrive in the more genial exercise of the domestic economy; and even her vanity, leaning to virtue's side, would exert a genial influence. One article of furniture after another would be introduced; and, as every woman desires to be as rich and as respectable as her neighbours, whatever one procured would be desired by all the others. From the mere necessaries of life, they would advance to its comforts and its luxuries. Vanity would kindle the love of dress and furniture; and rivalry, if no better feeling, would introduce cleanliness and good housewifery. The passing generation might not be materially changed; but the young would grow up with a new train of habits and associations. They would be accustomed to sleep on beds, to sit upon chairs, and, softened as well as enervated by indulgences unknown to their ancestors, they would be less fitted for the fatigue of war and the chase, and more susceptible of the enjoyments of social life.

It is worthy of observation, that those who have been most successful in gaining the confidence of the Indians have been the Quaker and the Roman Catholic;—the one displaying all the magnificence of a gorgeous ceremonial, and the other all the simplicity of entire plainness. But the success of both was attributable to the same principle.

WAA-TOP-E-NOT
A Chippeway Chief

They both secured the attention of the Indian by kindness; and their forms of faith, in both cases, appealed to the senses. The Quaker exhibited a practical demonstration of the doctrines of the Redeemer, by the observance of peace, humility, kindness, temperance, and justice; and there could be no mistake as to a faith, the effects of which were so marked and salutary. The Catholic, in his explanations to the heathen, dwelt chiefly on the moral code of the Bible, and exhibited outward forms and symbols, which awakened attention, excited the imagination, and impressed the memory. The Protestant missionary has usually proceeded upon a different plan. He attempts to explain to the uncultivated mind of the savage the scheme of salvation by a Saviour; that complex, wonderful, and stupendous plan, in the contemplation of which the highest mental powers of the philosopher find full employment; and the savage listens with incredulity, because he listens to mere abstractions which convey to his mind no definite ideas. Such teachers forget that the Creator, in revealing His will to man, gave first to the Patriarchs the simplest form of faith; to the more enlightened Hebrews a more complex system was revealed, and a wider range of thought was opened; the coming of a Divine Saviour was shadowed forth through a long series of years, and at last, upon minds thus enlightened, dawned the full effulgence of the Christian religion. The reasoning powers of the Indians have never been exercised. An acute and experienced observer of that race has said, that, in regard to the mass of the people, they give no evidence of having ever entertained an abstract idea. Thus, in their speeches, the figurative language, which some have attributed to a poetical temperament, is really used from necessity to supply the want of thought, of descriptive powers, and even of words; for they can only make themselves understood by referring to sensible objects around them. Now I humbly conceive, that, if ever the Christian system is to be successfully communicated to such a people, we must follow what I suppose to be the Gospel plan—first, teach them the simple duties and virtues of a pastoral people, then surround them with the restraints and obligations of a moral and civil law ; and, lastly, when their minds are trained to thought, to obedience, and to a sense of responsibility, unfold to them the glorious truths of the Gospel of salvation.

The almost frantic passion for ardent spirits, which is evinced by all savages, would probably be corrected by a change of life ; for we have no doubt that one of the causes of their attachment to it is that it deadens the painful sense of hunger, which among them has become constitutional. An Indian, like a wolf, is always hungry, and of course always ferocious. In order to tame him, the pressure of hunger must be removed ; it is useless to attempt to operate on the mind while the body is in a state of suffering. It is well ascertained that the Indian is for about half his time destitute of food, and obliged either to endure the pangs of hunger, or to use the most arduous exertions to procure provisions. The habitual improvidence of the savage, his wandering mode of existence, and the insecurity of property, prevents him from laying up any store during the season of plenty, and, when winter covers the bosom of the earth with her mantle of snow, hundreds and even thousands perish for want of food. Unexpected vicissitudes of the seasons, and long-continued extremity of heat or cold, sweep off these unprotected wretches with fearful havoc. A drought, which, by destroying the herbage, deprives the game of support, or a deep snow, which shuts up all the sources of supply, spreads a famine throughout the tribes, and thins their numbers with fearful rapidity.   In the inhospitable regions which border on the northern Lakes and extend thence to the Missouri, including the country of the Chippeways, Ottaways, Menominies, Winnebagoes, and a portion of the Sioux, the horrors of starvation brood over the land during the continuance of their long and dreary winters, and recur with each revolving year.

To be fully satisfied on this point, it is only necessary to read Tanner's *Narrative* which was carefully prepared by one who was capable of understanding the exact meaning of the relator, and stating it with clearness.   His whole thirty years among the Indians were spent in active exertions to get something to eat.   The *Narrative* presents an affecting picture of an active and energetic life, checkered with dangers, toils, and struggles, yet with no higher object than that of obtaining a bare subsistence. The incidents are stirring in their nature ; the adventures exhibit a boldness, a patience of toil and fatigue, and a hardihood of endurance, which exerted on a more dignified scene of action, would have elevated the actor into a hero ; but the vicissitudes are chiefly those induced by the changes of the seasons and the abundance or scarcity of game ; and the joys and sorrows of Tanner resulted from the alternations of poverty and plenty, of repletion and starvation !   Few solemnities, and fewer amusements, are spoken of throughout the volume ; of rest, domestic quiet, or social enjoyment, there is none ; and whenever a number of Indians collected together they were presently dispersed by hunger.   To live three, four, or five days without food was not uncommon.   Sometimes they subsisted for weeks upon a little bear's grease ; sometimes they chewed their peltries and moccasins.   Often they were reduced to eat their dogs, or to subsist whole days upon the inner bark of trees.

The moral influence of this mode of life, as disclosed in the volume alluded to, is most deplorable. The frequent and sudden recurrence of famine enervates the mind, and destroys its energy and elasticity. The want of employment, and the absence of a laudable object of pursuit, leaves the thinking faculty dormant, and gives place to childish desires and puerile superstitions. Good and bad fortune are ascribed to friendly or malignant spirits, and a blind fatalism usurps the place of reason. Their necessities and sufferings, and the want of social intercourse, render them selfish, and lead them to steal, to hide from each other, and to practise every species of rapacity and meanness; and this is not the tale of one day or of a year, but the disgusting burthen of a story which comprehends a series of years, and describes the people of a whole region.

Among the more Southern tribes, a milder climate, and a country more prolific in the supply of food, exempt the inhabitants the frequent occurrence of widespread and long-continued famine, but they are far from being regularly or well supplied with food. On the fertile plains —watered by the Missouri, the Arkansas, and Red River —the Indian brave, mounted on the native horse and attired in all the finery of the savage state, exhibits the most favourable aspect of the savage state, and his character rises to the highest grade of elevation attained by man as a mere animal. The great droves of buffalo that roam over these prairies supply him with food and clothing; and the use of the horse, while it adds largely to his pride and his efficiency as a warrior, contributes greatly to his success as a hunter, and his enjoyment of his wild mode of life. But the existence of the man who depends on hunting for a subsistence, is, at best, extremely precarious. The migrations of animals, though somewhat mysterious, are frequent; and the same district which at one time abounds in buffalo, deer, bear, or some other animal, is at another entirely deserted by the same description of quadrupeds. Extremes of heat and cold, and the consequent failure of subsistence, are probably the more usual causes of these movements; but there are instances in which they cannot be traced to any apparent cause.

The inhabitants of the Sandwich Islands, when first visited by the Europeans, were savages, as uncivilised and barbarous as the North American Indians, and were besides addicted to some vices which are comparatively unknown to the latter. Their insular position, their climate, their indolent and luxurious habits, and several other peculiarities of condition and character, rendered them much less likely to become the subjects of civilisation than the more hardy inhabitants of the North American continent. Yet here the experiment has been triumphantly successful. The civilisation of the Sandwich Islanders has been so complete, as to leave no room for a doubt or a cavil. They have formally abrogated their savage customs, renounced their pagan superstitions, and abandoned their former mode of life. The change has not been merely formal and theoretical, but actual, practical, and thorough; and these islanders, so lately plunged in the most brutal practices of heathenism, rank among the civilised and Christian nations of the earth. They have received the Bible, and become converted to the Christian faith. The American missionaries established among them have been eminently successful in teaching the doctrines of the Gospel, and in building up the Church of the Redeemer. The converts are numerous, embracing the majority of the population, and they give abundant evidence of sincerity, zeal, and devotion. The schools are well attended, and include as pupils the great mass of the population. So complete has been the revolution, and so rapid the progress of this amiable people in the attainment of religious instruction, and in the amelioration of their general condition, that they will probably soon become, if they are not now, an uncommonly moral and well-disciplined nation, and afford an example of piety and good government, which might be followed with advantage by some of the oldest communities of Christendom.

In marking the characteristic features of this revolution, we discover some of the elements which we have insisted upon as indispensable in bringing about a similar result among our own Indians. The insular position of the islanders restrained them from the wandering habits, which we consider peculiarly hostile to the introduction of civilisation, while it greatly curtailed their opportunities for war, and the indulgence of those propensities which are inseparable from the state of war, especially among savages —the lust for carnage, and the lust for plunder. They were free from the sinister influence of a loose population upon their borders, preying upon their substance, and demoralising their character; and, from the pressure of a superior population, exciting continually their jealousy and hatred. There was, it is true, a malign English influence, which would have kept these people savages for ever, for the worst of purposes; but this was happily overcome by the perseverance of the American missionaries, strengthened by the aid of our naval officers, and of a large portion of our commercial marine trading in those seas.

The rapid and complete revolution effected in the character of these islanders affords so apt an illustration of our subject, that we think it may not be uninteresting to quote a few paragraphs, from an authentic source, in regard to that remarkable people. Our authority is Jarves's *History of the Hawaiian or Sandwich Islands*, recently published :—

"The general cast of features prevailing among the whole group was similar to that of all Polynesia, and analogous to the Malay, to which family of the human race they doubtless belong. A considerable variety in colour existed, from a light olive to an almost African black ; the hair was coarse, and almost equally dissimilar, varying from the straight, long, black, or dark brown, to the crispy curl peculiar to the negro. This latter was comparatively rare. White hair among the children was common. A broad, open, vulgarly good-humoured countenance prevailed among the males, and a more pleasing and engaging look with the females. Both bespoke the predominance of gross animal passions. Many of the latter, when young, were pretty and attractive. Though farther from the equator, both sexes were some shades darker than the Tahitians, Marquesans, or Ascension islanders ; all of whom excel them in personal beauty. As with them, a fullness of the nostril, without the peculiar flatness of the negro, and a general thickness of lips, prominent and broad cheek-bones, and narrow, high, and retreating foreheads, resembling the Asiatics, predominated. Instances of deformity were not more common than in civilised life. Their teeth were white, firm and regular ; but their eyes were generally bloodshot, which was considered a personal attraction. The hands of the women were soft, well made, with tapering fingers. When the sex arrived at maturity, which took place from ten to twelve years of age, they presented slight and graceful figures ; which a few years settled into *embonpoint*, and a few more made as unattractive as they were before the reverse.

"No regular marriage ceremonies existed; though, on such occasions, it was customary for the bridegroom to cast a piece of cloth on the bride in the presence of her family. A feast was then furnished by the friends of both parties. The number of wives depended upon the inclination of the man, and his ability to support them. Though the common men usually lived with one woman, who performed household labours, no binding tie existed; each party consulting their wishes for a change, joining or separating, as they agreed or disagreed.

"Some doubt formerly existed, whether cannibalism ever prevailed in the group. The natives themselves manifested a degree of shame, horror, and confusion, when questioned upon the subject, that led Cook and his associates, without any direct evidence of the fact, to believe in its existence; but later voyagers disputed this conclusion. The confessions of their own historians, and the general acknowledgment of the common people, have now established it beyond a doubt; though, for some time previous to Cook's visit, it had gradually decreased, until scarcely a vestige, if any, of the horrible custom remained. This humanising improvement, so little in accordance with their other customs, was a pleasing trait in their national character. It may have resulted from instruction and example, derived from their earliest European visitors, or a self-conviction of its own abomination. Be that as it may, a public sentiment of disgust in regard to it prevailed at that period, highly creditable to them as a nation, and which distinguished them from their more savage contemporaries of New Zealand, the Marquesas, and even from the more polished Tahitian.

"The cleanliness of the islanders has been much praised, but without reason. Frequent bathing kept their persons in tolerable order; but the same filthy

clothing was worn while it would hold together.   The
lodging of the common orders was shared with the brutes,
and their bodies a common receptacle of vermin.

"The Hawaiian character, uninfluenced by either of
the foregoing causes," (civilisation and Christianity,) "may
be thus summed up.   From childhood no natural affections were inculcated.   Existence was due rather to
accident than design.   Spared by a parent's hand, a boy
lived to become the victim of a priest, an offering to a
blood-loving deity, or to experience a living death from
preternatural fears—a slave not only to his own superstitions, but to the terrors and caprices of his chief.   Life,
limb, or property, were not his to know.   Bitter, grinding
tyranny was his lot.   No mother's hand soothed the pains
of youth, or father's guided in the pursuits of manhood.
No social circle warmed the heart by its kindly affections.
No moral teachings enkindled a love of truth.   No revelation cheered his earthly course, and brightened future
hopes.   All was darkness.   Theft, lying, drunkenness,
riots, revelling, treachery, revenge, lewdness, infanticide,
murder—these were his earliest and latest teachings.
Among them was his life passed.   Their commonness
excited no surprise.   Guilt was only measured by failure
or success.   Justice was but retaliation, and the law
arrayed each man's hand against his brother.   Games and
amusements were but the means of gambling and sensual
excitement.   An individual selfishness, which sought
present gratification, momentary pleasure, or lasting
results, regardless of unholy measures or instruments, was
the all-predominating passion.   Their most attractive
quality, it cannot be called a virtue, was a kind of easy,
listless, good nature, never to be depended upon when
their interests were aroused.   Instances of better dispositions were sometimes displayed, and occasional gleams of

humanity, among which may be mentioned friendship, and a hospitality common to all rude nations, where the distinctions of property are but slightly understood, enlivened their dark characters; but sufficient only to redeem their title to humanity, not make us altogether blush and hide our heads to own ourselves their fellow-men.   Individuals there were who rose above this level of degradation, and their lives served to render more prominent the vices of the remainder.   La Perouse, though fresh from the Rousseau School of innocence of savage life, thus expressed his opinion :—'The most daring rascals of Europe are less hypocritical than these natives. All their caresses are false.   Their physiognomy does not express a single sentiment of truth.   The object most to be suspected is he who has just received a present, or who appears to be the most earnest in rendering a thousand little services.'"

The following remark conveys, in a few words, a strong picture of depravity.   "So dark were their conceptions of one of the most pleasurable emotions of the heart, grati-tude, that there was found in their language no word to express the sentiment.   While it abounded in terms expressive of every shade of vice and crime, it was destitute of those calculated to convey ideas of virtue or rectitude."

Revolting as this picture may appear, it is but a softened portraiture of the disgusting depravity of these islanders.   The details are so shocking as to be unfit for publication.   Yet this is a true representation of savage nature, as we find it exemplified in all parts of the world : it is the human heart "deceitful above all things, and desperately wicked," as described in the inspired Volume, and as it exists everywhere, when untouched by the ameliorating influence of Gospel truth.   It is modified, it is true, by circumstances. It is influenced by the climate, by the abundance or scarcity of food, and by the habit and opportunities of engaging in the pursuits of war and rapine. The North American Indian is of a colder temperament than the islander of the Pacific Ocean. He is trained to war, and his passions are disciplined to obedience. Every desire and emotion of his heart is brought in subjection to a martial police, and his individuality is to a great extent merged in a kind of military *esprit de corps*, which takes the place of patriotism. He is less sensual than the islander, constitutionally; and from his location in a colder climate, is less given to self-indulgence, in consequence of his military training, and the laborious life of the hunter; and is more manly in his bearing, from the effect of athletic exercises and frequent exposure to danger. But after these allowances are made, and the necessary deductions drawn from them, we shall find that these varieties of the savage character, however superficially different, are the same in structure, and in every elemental part and principle. The islander became by far the more depraved and vicious from the enervating influence of climate, and from a variety of degrading influences incident to his position.

Yet this people have become civilised so rapidly, that the same generation has witnessed their transit from the total darkness of paganism to the effulgence of Gospel light. They have established a regular government, and have been recognised as an independent nation by the United States and Great Britain. They are governed by the wise and equal laws of a free people. The same writer, from whose valuable work we have already quoted, says :—

"Suitable harbour and quarantine regulations are incorporated in the body of laws. The penal code recognises a just distinction between offences, and provides proportionate punishments. Courts of appeal and decision are established, in which, by the help of foreign juries, important cases, involving large amounts of property, have been equitably decided. This legislation is extended to all the wants of the native population, and regulates the landed distinctions, fisheries, transmission of property, property in trust, collection of debts, interest accounts, weights and measures; in short, is sufficient, except in complex cases, arising from mercantile affairs, to provide for all the emergencies of the civilised population.

"Taxation is rendered lighter and more equal. All taxes can be commuted for money; when this is wanting, they are assessed in labour or the productions of the soil. Foreigners pay nothing but a voluntary capitation tax of a trifling amount annually.

"A great interest is manifested in education; the law provides schools and teachers for all children; encouragement for agricultural enterprises is freely afforded, and bounties for the introduction of the useful arts and productions, and for those whose time and abilities shall be made of public benefit. An enlightened spirit pervades the whole system; in its present incipient stage, it cannot be expected to bear the fruits of maturity, but on such a foundation a fair and firm fabric will doubtless arise. The government, not to let their laws and enactments become a dead letter, have provided for their monthly exposition, by the judges and subordinate officers, to the people. If they do not eventually become what their legislators would have them, the burthen will rest upon their own shoulders; government has opened wide the door of moral and political advancement; and no more efficient aids to the cause exist than his Majesty, Governor Kekuandoa, and some chiefs of lesser degree.

In 1840, to the surprise of the foreigners, who predicted the customary leniency towards rank, the majesty of the laws was fully asserted in the hanging of a chief of high blood for the murder of his wife. Later still, in 1841, the English Consul was fined by a municipal court for riotous conduct, while the judge addressed a withering rebuke to him, as the representative of an enlightened nation, for setting aside all respect for his office or character, and appealed to the other official gentlemen present for their countenance in the support of good order.

" The annual assemblages of the king and council have been held at Lahaina, the capital of the kingdom. Every succeeding one has manifested an improvement on the last. Legislative forms are becoming better understood, and modifications of the code made to suit the necessities of the times. In 1842, a treasury system was adopted, which, in its infancy, has given a credit to the government it never before possessed. Instead of the former squandering methods, by which moneys were entrusted to courtiers or dependents, and never strictly accounted for, they are deposited in a regular treasury, at the head of which is Dr G. P. Judd, a man eminently qualified to give satisfaction to all classes. Assisted by intelligent natives, accounts of receipts for taxes, port charges, and the customs, for which, within the past year, a slight duty on imports has been laid, are kept, and from the proceeds the expenses and debts of the government are regularly paid. Instead of living upon their tenants, the officers receive stated salaries; but these and other changes are too recent to be chronicled as history; they are but landmarks in the rapid improvement of the nation.

"From the great quantity of liquors introduced, and their cheapness, it was feared, and with reason, that the old thirst for ardent spirits would be awakened. Many did drink to excess, and men and women reeling through the streets were common sights. As it was impossible to exclude the temptation, the chiefs, though partial to their use themselves, determined to restrict the sale by preventing the demand. The natives were prohibited from manufacturing ardent spirits; temperance societies were formed; and by combination and addresses the enthusiasm of the nation enkindled; thousands, particularly of the young, joined them, and finally the king, setting an example which was followed by most of the chiefs, pledged himself to total abstinence.

"In religious knowledge the progress of the nation has been respectable. In 1841, there were sixteen thousand, eight hundred and ninety-three members of the Protestant Churches, and this number was increasing. Upwards of eighteen thousand children are receiving instruction in the schools, most of which, however, embrace simply the elementary branches; these are so generally diffused, that it is uncommon to find a native who cannot read or write, and who does not possess some knowledge of arithmetic and geography. In the High School, and some of the boarding schools, a much more extended education prevails, sufficient to qualify the pupils for becoming teachers, or eventually filling more responsible professions. It is a striking fact, that of all the business documents in possession of the Hawaiian Government, accumulated in their intercourse with foreigners, *one-half* bear the *marks* of the latter who were unable to write; while there is but *one* instance of so deplorable ignorance on the part of the natives, and that was Kaikoewn, late Governor of Kanai, whose age and infirmities were a sufficient apology for his neglect. If a belief that the Bible contains the revealed will of God, the sacred observance of the Sabbath, the erection of churches, the diffusion of education, gratuitous contributious of money for charitable purposes to a large amount annually, a general attendance on Divine worship, and interest in religious instruction, and a standard of morality rapidly improving, constitute a Christian nation, the Hawaiians of 1842 may safely claim that distinction. Rightly to appreciate the change, their original character should be accurately known.

"At their rediscovery by Cook, heathenism had waxed hoary in iniquity and vileness. Little better than miserable hordes of savages, living in perpetual warfare, writhing under a despotism strained to its utmost tension, and victims to the insatiable avarice of a bloody-minded priestcraft, they had reached that period when decline or revolution must have ensued. By the adventitious aids of commerce, the aspiring Kamehamela effected the latter; blood was freely spilt; but, under his universal rule, the horde of priestly and feudal tyrants were merged into one—himself—whose justice and benevolence, imperfect as they were when viewed in the light of increased wisdom, are allowed, by the concurrent testimony of Hawaiians and foreigners, to have formed a new era in their history. During his reign, civilisation had full scope for its effect upon barbarism; good men advised, moral men were examples; and the result was in accordance with the strength of the principle brought to bear upon them. The Hawaiians became a nation of skilful traders, dealing with an honesty quite equal to that which they received; mercantile cunning succeeded former avaricious violence; good faith became a principle of interest; scepticism weakened bigotry. This was all, the spirit of gain, in its civilised costume, could accomplish; it had bettered the condition of the savage, inasmuch as it was itself superior to brute lust. It carried them to the height upon which it was itself

poised, a modern Pisgah, from which glimpses of the
promised land could be seen.   By inoculating their
minds with the desire, though crude, for better things,
it became the instrument of the rising of the spirit of
liberty, and the first step toward mental ascendancy.
Further progress could only be gained by the active
recognition of the Divine command, 'Go ye and teach
all nations.'   This was obeyed by that people who have
been most alive to its commercial advantages.   The
struggles and labours of twenty-one years of missionary
exertions, and their general results upon the political
and religious character of the nation, have been depicted.
During that time upwards of five hundred thousand
dollars have been devoted by the 'American Board of
Foreign Missions' for this purpose ; more than forty
families of missionaries employed throughout the group :
the   advantages   of   well - regulated   domestic   circles
practically   shown ;   one   hundred   millions   of   pages
printed and distributed, among which were two extensive editions of the Bible, and translations and compila-
tions of valuable school and scientific books.   The
multiplicity of religious works have been varied by
others of historical and general interest ; newspapers
printed ; in fine, the rudiments of a native literature
formed, which bids fair to meet the increasing wants of
the nation.   Several islanders have manifested good
powers of composition, and, both by their writings and
discourses, have been of eminent advantage to their
countrymen.   Neither have the mechanical arts been
neglected by their instructors.   Under their tuition, the
labours of the needle have been made universal.   Weaving,
spinning, and knitting, have been introduced.   With the
same illiberality which characterised some of the earliest
white settlers, who refused to instruct the natives for fear

PEE-CHE-KIR
A Chippeway Chief

they would soon 'know too much,' a number of the mechanics of the present day associated themselves to prevent any of their trade from working with, or giving instructions to natives. But their mechanical skill was not thus to be repressed; with the assistance of the missionaries, numbers have become creditable workmen; among them are to be found good masons, carpenters, printers, bookbinders, tailors, blacksmiths, shoemakers, painters, and other artisans. Their skill in copper engraving is remarkable. They are apt domestics, expert and good-natured seamen, hard workers as labourers, and in all the departments of menial service, faithful in proportion to their knowledge and recompense.

"It is no injustice to the foreign traders to attribute this general prosperity mainly to missionary efforts. By them the islands have been made desirable residences for a better and more refined class of whites; these have been instruments of much good, and even of counteracting the somewhat too rigid and exclusive tendencies of the mission. But they came for pecuniary gain, and the good resulting from their intercourse was incidental. The whole undivided counsels and exertions of the mission have been applied to the spread of Christianity and civilisation. How far they have been successful, let the result answer."

The question, so important to humanity, and so long considered doubtful, as to the practicability of civilising the various tribes of savages scattered over the face of the earth, may now be considered as settled. The experiment at the Sandwich Islands was commenced under the most unfavourable auspices. Human nature had reached there its lowest point of degradation. The darkness of ignorance in which they were plunged was complete—not a ray of light illumined it. They had all the vices of savages, and were destitute of that manliness of character which sometimes gives dignity to the barbarian state. They were inferior to the North American Indian in courage, in self-command, in discipline, and in decency of deportment, and far inferior in bodily activity. Yet from the first regular and sustained effort to introduce civilisation, that noble enterprise has gone forward with scarcely any interruption; and they are now a civilised people, having a written constitution, a regular government, a settled commerce, laws, magistrates, schools, churches, a written language, and the Gospel of salvation.

To produce an effect equally happy upon our own Indians only requires the same energy of effort directed by the same singleness of purpose. Whenever the civilisation of our Indians shall be undertaken by the Government, with an eye single to that object, it will be accomplished with a facility which will astonish even those who are neither unfriendly to such a result, nor incredulous as to its actual consummation. We desire to be fully understood in this proposition. We have in another place spoken of our Government and people as decidedly friendly to this humane object; they have expended millions of treasure with this avowed purpose. But this has been done without system, and much of the munificence of the Government has been wasted by careless application, intercepted by fraud, or misdirected by knavish hypocrisy. The civilisation of the Indians has been a secondary object, lost sight of in the multiplicity of other concerns, and has never engaged the share of attention demanded by its importance and solemnity. Whenever it shall be attempted with earnestness, in good faith, under the immediate sanction of the Government, and under the influence of a public sentiment fully awakened to the subject, it must succeed.

IV.

CAN the North American Indians be civilised ? Are their minds open to the same moral influences which affect the human family in common, or are they the subjects of any constitutional peculiarity, which opposes a permanent barrier to an improvement of their condition ? Perhaps the shortest reply to these questions, would be found by asking another — Is the Bible true ? Are all men descended from Adam and Eve ? If we believe that there is but one human family, the conclusion is inevitable, that however, by a long process of degeneration the race may have become divided into varieties, that operation may be reversed through the agency of the same natural causes which produced it. We cannot entertain the doctrine of multiform creations, or with any show of reason admit the existence of separate races, miraculously established after the Flood, by the same power, which brought about the confusion of tongues, and the dispersion of the inhabitants of the earth. But if we did, it would bring us back to the same point ; we should still acknowledge a common ancestry, and claim for every branch of the human family a common destiny. The promises were given to all ; no exception is made in the offers of salvation. If it be admitted that men were divided into races, and certain distinctions of colour and physical structure established, to separate them permanently, still they are all the intelligent creatures of God ; the subjects of His moral government, and the objects of a great system of rewards and punishments, which He has vouchsafed to reveal, without debarring any from its benefits, or absolving any from its obligations. We cannot, consistently with these views, give up any portion of the human race to hopeless and everlasting barbarism.

In the last number of this work we alluded to the rapid progress in civilisation, made by the natives of the Sandwich Islands, as affording ample testimony on this subject; and we shall now attempt to corroborate those views, by reference to what has been done towards reclaiming the Indians of our own continent.

In summing up this evidence, we beg the reader to bear in mind the proofs we adduced in the former parts of this Essay, of the originally favourable disposition of the savages towards the whites, as evinced by their kind reception of the first colonists. In the settlement of Pennsylvania, for instance, the most amicable intercourse was maintained between the stranger races, for a series of years, and a mutual kindness, respect, and confidence towards each other was established. This experiment must be satisfactory, as far as it goes, to the most incredulous; to our own mind it is conclusive: for we consider the question to be, not whether the Indian intellect is endowed with the capacity to receive civilisation, but whether his savage nature can be so far conciliated, as to make him a fair subject of the benevolent effort. The question is not as to the possibility of eradicating his ferocity, or giving steadiness to his erratic habits, but as to the practicability of bringing to bear upon him the influences by which his evil propensities and his waywardness must be subdued. The wild ass may be tamed into the most docile of the servants of man; the difficulty is in catching him—in placing him under the influence of the process of training. Whenever the bridle is placed upon his head, the work is done; all the rest follows with the certainty of cause and effect—in the contest between the man and the brute, between intellect and instinct, the latter must submit. So it is between the civilised and savage man. The difficulties to be overcome, are the distance by which the races are separated, and the repulsion which impedes their approach. There is no sympathy between the refinement of the civilised man and the habits of the savage ; nor any neutral ground upon which they can meet and compromise away their points of difference. They are so widely separated in the scale of being, as to have no common tastes, habits, or opinions ; they meet in jealousy and distrust ; disgust and contempt attend all their intercourse ; and the result of their contact is oppression and war. And why ? The repulsive principle is never overcome, the attraction of sympathy is never established. The parties do not gaze upon each other patiently, long enough to become reconciled to their mutual peculiarities, nor sit together in peace until they become acquainted. The habit of enduring each other's manners is not established, nor the good fellowship which results from pacific intercourse, even between those who are widely separated by character and station.

We have said that the first European visitors were kindly received. They were so : but it was not from anything attractive in their appearance, or from any love or sympathy impelling the poor savage to the practice of hospitality. Fear and wonder quelled the ferocity of the Indian, and curiosity impelled him to seek the presence of these singular beings, who came mysteriously to his shores, in human shape, but wielding apparently the powers of the invisible world. It was the white man who dispelled an illusion so advantageous to himself, by the exhibition of meanness, weakness, and vice, which demonstrated his human nature so clearly, that even the ignorant savage could not mistake.

From the general misconduct of the whites, there were some noble exceptions, and from these we select the settlement of Pennsylvania, as the most prominent. The

Quakers were sincere in their religious professions.   They did not make religion the cloak of a rapacious spirit of aggrandisement, nor murder the savage in the name of a Creator who commands love, and peace, and forgiveness. They met the savage on terms of equality, overlooking the vast disparity of intellect and education, and breaking down all the barriers of separation.   The first step was decisive ; there was no room for distrust ; no time for prejudice to rankle, and ripen into hatred.   The Indian threw aside his fears and his wonder, and met the Quaker as a brother.   They dwelt together in unity ; for more than half a century they lived in peace, in the daily inter- change of kindnesses and benefits.   The experiment was successful ; because, whenever the civilised and savage man can be brought into amicable and protracted inter- course, the latter must unavoidably and imperceptibly acquire the arts and habits of the former.

The history of the "Praying Indians" of New England is fraught with instruction on the subject of this Essay, and forms a pathetic episode in the history of this people. Although the conversion of the heathen is alleged in nearly all the royal charters and patents, as one of the pretences for taking possession of newly discovered countries, and for granting them to individuals and com- panies, it does not seem to have occupied much of the attention of the first colonists.   The name of John Eliot is justly entitled to honour, as that of the pioneer of this noble enterprise ; for previous to his day we do not find that any systematic effort was made to communicate the Gospel to the Indians of New England.   Resolving to devote himself to their service, he first proceeded to qualify himself for the office of teacher, by learning the language of the Nipmuks, and he was probably the first white man who studied the language of the Indians for their advantage. He is said to have effected this in a few months, by hiring an Indian to reside in his family. His first meeting with the natives for the purpose of conversing with them, in their own language, on the subject of religion, was on the 28th of October, 1646, which was twenty-six years after the landing at Plymouth. In this and subsequent conferences he endeavoured to explain to them the leading points in the history and doctrines of the Bible, and was met with all those popular and obvious objections which are used by the ignorant, or those who are but superficially acquainted with the sacred Volume. The chiefs and conjurers also, opposed the introduction of the new religion; for wherever government and religion are controlled by the same persons, or by persons who act in concert, all reform is objected to, as subversive of ancient usages, and dangerous to the ruling powers. The most enlightened aristocrat, and the most ignorant savage chief, are equally alive to an instinctive dread of change, and especially of changes which appeal to the reflective faculties of the people, and lead them to independent thought and action, instead of the more convenient plan for the ruler, of being wielded in masses like machines. Notwithstanding this opposition, a number of the Indians became attached to Mr Eliot, and placed themselves under his teaching, while a still larger number were willing to entrust their children to be instructed by him.

Eliot became sensible of the necessity of separating his converts from the rest of their people, as well to shield them from the bad influence of the unconverted, as to train them in the arts and habits of civilisation. It was an axiom with him, that *civilisation* was an indispensable auxiliary to the *conversion* of the savage. Proceeding upon this principle, he collected his proselytes in towns, instructed them in rural and mechanical labours, and gave them a brief code of laws for their government. Some of these laws afford curious evidence of the simplicity of the times; for instance: "If any man be idle a week, or at most a fortnight, he shall pay five shillings." "If any man shall beat his wife, his hands shall be tied behind him, and he shall be carried to the place of justice to be severely punished." "Every young man, if not another's servant, and if unmarried, shall be compelled to set up a wigwam, and plant for himself, and not shift up and down in other wigwams." "If any woman shall not have her hair tied up, but hung loose, or be cut as men's hair, she shall pay five shillings." "All men that wear long locks shall pay five shillings."

The whole of the Bible was translated into the Indian tongue by Eliot, and also Baxter's *Call*, Shepherd's *Sincere Convert*, and *Sound Believer*, besides a variety of other books, such as grammars, psalters, catechisms, etc.

Cotton Mather remarks of Eliot's Indian Bible: "This Bible was printed here at our Cambridge; and it is the only Bible that was ever printed in all America, from the very foundation of the world." The same author tells us, "the whole translation was writ with but *one pen*, which pen had it not been lost, would have certainly deserved a richer case than was bestowed upon that pen, with which Holland writ his translation of Plutarch."

That worthy and quaint compiler, Drake, from whose Book of the Indians we have taken this and some other valuable items, appends in a note the following lines, which Philemon Holland, "the translator general of his age," made upon his pen:

> "With one sole pen I write this book,
>   Made of a gray goose quill;
> A pen it was, when I it took,
>   And a pen I leave it still."

The towns established under the auspices of the missionary Eliot, are said to have been fourteen in number, and the aggregate population is stated to have been eleven hundred and fifty; but as this enumeration includes whole families, the number of converts must have been much less. At the close of Philip's war, 1677, the number of towns, according to Gookin's account, was reduced to seven, but when an attempt was made during the war, to collect the "Praying Indians" in one place for safety, but about five hundred could be found, and this number was reduced to three hundred at the close of the war. Six years after that war, there were but four towns, and the number of inhabitants are not stated.

It is difficult to ascertain with precision the results of the early efforts, on the part of the English colonists generally, to convert the Indians, because the accounts of these transactions are not only incomplete, but greatly perverted by prejudice and exaggeration. There were among the early Puritans many excellent men who fervently desired the conversion of this branch of the human family, and laboured zealously in the cause, and we have good reason to believe, in regard to some of them at least, that their zeal was according to knowledge. But we have their own testimony, that the sympathies of the public were not with them, in this good work, and that the dislike of the whites towards their red neighbours, interposed a barrier which thwarted the best exertions for the civilisation of the latter. We have before us the "Historical Account of the Doings and Sufferings of the Christian Indians in New England, in the years 1675, 1676, and 1677, impartially drawn by one well acquainted with that affair, and presented unto the Right Honourable the Corporation, residing in London, and appointed by the King's Most Excellent Majesty, for Promoting the

Gospel among the Indians in America." The author was "Master Daniel Gookin," of whom Cotton Mather wrote :

> " A constellation of great converts there
> Shone round him, and his heavenly glory were.
> Gookins was one of these."

He was superintendent of the Indians, under the jurisdiction of Massachusetts, during many years ; was a man of high standing, distinguished for his humanity, his courage, and his fidelity to the cause of the Indian. The publishing committee of the American Antiquarian Society, at Cambridge, Massachusetts, in a preliminary notice of this work, say :—

"The policy adopted by Gookin towards the Indians, did not at all times escape the censure of the public ; for during the troubles that arose from the aggressions of the hostile tribes, the people could with difficulty be restrained from involving in one common destruction the whole race ; and while it required the most determined spirit, on the part of the superintendent, to stem the torrent of popular violence, he did not fail to draw on himself undeserved odium and reproach. Gookin was eminently the friend of the Indians, and never hesitated to interpose his own safety between the infuriated white man, and the un-offending object of his vengeance."

The immediate purpose of Master Daniel Gookin, is to describe the sufferings of the "Praying Indians," in the war between the whites and Indians, during the period covered by his narrative. The Christian Indians, having nothing to expect from the savage tribes of their own race, who despised and hated them, for their adhesion to the faith of the white men, were solicitous to be received as allies of the colonists ; and as their towns lay along the frontier, contiguous to the white settlements, their friendship would have been valuable, had it been cultivated in good faith, as the towns of the friendly Indians would have covered the most exposed settlements from the inroads of the savages. The protection would have been mutual, and the community of danger, and military service, would have strengthened the bands of friendship, while the converted Indians would have been confirmed in their new faith, and the prejudices of both parties softened by an intercourse so beneficial to each. The public manifestation on the part of the colonists, of a disposition to adopt and protect the converted heathen, connected with the evidence of power to render that protection effectual, must have produced a salutary effect upon the savage mind. The policy pursued, was unfortunately the very reverse of that dictated by sound prudence and Christian charity. No sooner were hostilities commenced, than the friendly Indians became objects of suspicion and persecution from both sides. Although they volunteered their services to the colonists, and were often employed both as warriors and guides, they were continually subjected to all the insult and injury, which the petty tyranny of military officers, and the malignity of a bigoted popular sentiment, could inflict on them. Their fidelity to the whites is attested by Mr Gookin, and other men of high character, yet they were suspected to be traitors, and almost every disaster and reverse of fortune, was attributed to their agency, and drew down upon their devoted heads, the vengeance of an infuriated populace. The work of Mr Gookin is filled with incidents of this kind, of the most pathetic interest, in which these unfortunate people are seen on the one hand, warning the colonists of approaching danger; guiding them through the mazes of the wilderness, or sharing with them the dangerous vicissitudes of the battle; while on the other, we see them falsely accused, arrested, beaten, imprisoned, their property plundered, and their families turned out to starve. That the Red man should shrink with utter aversion, from a civilisation offered him upon such hard terms, and turn with scepticism and disgust from a gospel offering such bitter fruit, cannot be surprising.

We learn from this work, that the "Praying Indians" were numerous, which is a sufficient proof of their willingness to receive the Gospel, if it had been offered to them in an acceptable manner. "The situation of those towns was such," says this writer, "that the Indians in them might well have been improved, as a wall of defence about the greatest part of the colony of Massachusetts; for the first named of those villages bordered upon the Merrimack River, and the rest in order, about twelve or fourteen miles asunder, including most of the frontiers. And had the suggestions and importunate solicitations of some persons, who had knowledge and experience of the fidelity and integrity of the Praying Indians, been attended and practised in the beginning of the war, many and great mischiefs might have been (according to reason) prevented; for most of the praying towns, in the beginning of the war, had put themselves in a posture of defence against the common enemy. . . . But such was the unhappy state of their affairs, or rather the displeasure of God in the case, that their counsels were rejected, and on the contrary, a spirit of enmity and hatred conceived by many against those poor Christian Indians, as I apprehend without cause, so far as I could ever understand, which was, according to the operation of second causes, a very great occasion of many distressing calamities that befel both one and the other."

The worthy author conceiving it both practicable

and desirable to conciliate the Indians, and willing to apologise for his countrymen for their failure to discharge so obvious a duty, proceeds to argue the matter thus : "I have often considered this matter and come to this result, in my own thoughts, that the most holy and righteous God hath overruled all counsels and affairs, in this and other things relating to this war, for such wise, just, and holy ends as these :

"First.—To make a rod of the barbarous heathen, to chastise and punish the English for their sins. The Lord had, as our faithful minister often declared, applied more gentle chastisements, gradually, to His New England people ; but these proving in a great measure ineffectual, to produce effectual humiliation, hence the righteous and holy Lord is necessitated to draw forth this smarting rod of the vile and brutish heathen, who indeed have been a very scourge unto New England, and especially unto the jurisdiction of Massachusetts.

"Secondly.—To teach war to the young generation of New England, who had never been acquainted with it ; and especially to teach old and young, how little confidence is to be put in the arm of flesh. * * *

"Thirdly.—The purging and trying the faith of the godly English and Christian Indians, certainly was another end God aimed at in this chastisement. And the discovery of hypocrisy and wickedness in some that were ready to cry 'Aha !' at the sore calamity upon the English people in this war, and as much as in them lay, to overthrow God's work in gospelising the poor Indians.

"Fourthly.—Doubtless one great end God aimed at was the destruction of many wicked heathen, whose iniquities were now full." * * *

The author proceeds to state that "the Narragansetts, by their agent Potuche, urged that the English should not send any among them to preach the Gospel, or call upon them to pray to God. But the English refusing to concede to such an article it was withdrawn, and a peace concluded for that time. In this act they declared what their hearts were, viz : to reject Christ and His grace offered to them before. But the Lord Jesus, before the expiration of eighteen months, destroyed the body of the Narragansett nation, that would not have Him to reign over them, particularly all their sachems, and this Potuche, a chief counsellor and a subtle fellow, who was then at Rhode Island, coming voluntarily there, and afterward sent to Boston and there executed." It appears from other authorities, that this Potuche was an eminent warrior, that he was a prisoner of war, and that his only offence was that of being taken in arms against the enemies of his country. The whole of this account affords a singular exposition of the spirit of the times. An intolerant people, brooking no religion but their own, nor any form of their own, but that which they professed, enforcing their own harsh dogmas upon an ignorant nation by the edge of the sword, yet coolly averring themselves to be the passive instruments of Providence in this work of carnage ! An eminently religious people, actuated by a benevolent desire to convert the heathen, yet defeating their own noble purpose by the very means employed to effect it !

We find the following note attached to Gookin's History by the Committee of Publication :—" No remark on the contempt in which the poor Indians were held by men on so many accounts to be venerated, can be more appropriate than the following note by Governor Hutchinson. 'It seems strange,' says he, 'that men, who professed to believe that God hath made of one blood all the nations of the earth, should so early, and upon every occasion, take care to preserve this distinction. Perhaps nothing has more effectually defeated the endeavours for Christianising the Indians. It seems to have done more; to have sunk their spirits, led them to intemperance, and extirpated the whole race.' This remark was made upon a passage in Major Gibbon's instructions, on being sent against the Narragansetts in 1645, in these words: 'You are to have due regard to the distance which is to be observed betwixt Christians and barbarians, as well in war as in other negotiations.'"

In another note to the same book we read:—"So obnoxious were the friends of the Praying Indians to the mass of the people, that Gookin said on the bench, while holding a court, that he was afraid to go along the streets; and the author of 'A Letter to London,' says, that his (Gookin's) taking the Indians' part so much, had made him a byword among men and boys."

As a further evidence of the cruelty and bad faith which were observed towards the Indians by the people of New England, we quote the following passage from Drake's Book of the Indians :—

"On the 4th of September, 1676, according to Church's account, Tispaquin's company were encamped near Sippican, doing 'great damage to the English, in killing their cattle, horses, and swine.' The next day Church and his rangers were in their neighbourhood, and after observing their situation, which was 'sitting round their fires in a thick place of brush,' in seeming safety, the captain ordered every man to creep as he did; and surrounded them by creeping as near as they could, till they should be discovered, and then run on upon them, and take them alive, if possible (for their prisoners were their pay). They did so, taking everyone that was at the fires, none escaping. Upon examination they agreed in their story, that they belonged to Tispaquin, who was gone with John Bump and one more to Agawam and Sippican to kill horses, and were not expected back in two or three days. Church proceeds : ' This same Tispaquin had been a great captain, and the Indians reported that he was such a great powwau, priest or conjurer, that no bullet could enter him. Captain Church said, he would not have him killed, for there was a war broken out in the eastern part of the country, and he would have him saved to go with him to fight the eastern Indians. Agreeably, he left two old squaws of the prisoners, and bid them tarry there until their captain Tispaquin returned, and to tell him that Church had been there, and had taken his wife, children and company, and carried them down to Plymouth ; and would spare all their lives and his too, if he would come down to them, and bring the other two that were with him, and they should be his soldiers, etc. Captain Church then returned to Plymouth, leaving the old squaws well provided for, and biscuit for Tispaquin when he returned.'

" This, Church called laying a trap for Tispaquin, and it turned out as he expected. We shall now see with what faith the English acted on this occasion. Church had assured him, that if he gave himself up he should not be killed, but he was not at Plymouth when Tispaquin came in, having gone to Boston, on business for a few days ; ' but when he returned he found to his grief that the heads of Annawon, Tispaquin, etc., were cut off, which were the last of Philip's friends.'

" It is true," continues Mr Drake, " that those who were known to have been personally engaged in killing the English, were, in time of the greatest danger, cut off from pardon by a law ; that time had now passed away, and like many other laws of exigency, it should then have

O-HYA-WA-MINCE-KEE
A Chippeway Chief

been considered a dead letter; leaving out of the case the faith and promise of their best servant, Church. View it therefore in any light, and nothing can be found to justify this flagrant inroad upon the promise of Captain Church. To give to the conduct of the Plymouth government a pretext for this murder (a milder expression I cannot use), Mr Hubbard says : " Tispaquin having pretended that a bullet could not penetrate him, trial of his invulnerableness was resolved upon. So he was placed as a mark to shoot at, 'and he fell down at the first shot!'"

" This was doubtless the end of numerous others, as we infer from the following passage in Dr Mather's '*Prevalency of Prayer.*' He asks, 'Where are the six Narragansett sachems, with all their captains and counsellors? Where are the Nipmuck sachems, with their captains and counsellors? Where is Philip, and squaw sachem of Pocasset, with all their captains and counsellors? God do so to all the implacable enemies of Christ, and of His people in New England!'"

If the pious men of that day could thus pray for the blood of the Indian, what could be expected from the unreflecting portion of the community, and especially from that portion of them who were trained to war? And what degree of efficacy could we attribute to the prayers and efforts for the conversion of the heathen, mingled with such ejaculations of triumph for their destruction, and so prodigal a shedding of their blood?

There is not a more touching passage in the history of this devoted people, than that which records the pious labours of the Moravian brethren, and the melancholy catastrophe by which the fruits of their exertions were blasted. The Moravian missionaries seem to have been persons of irreproachable purity; humble and simple minded; who brought to their work a truly apostolic singleness of purpose.   Their preaching was not connected with any plan of colonisation, aggrandisement, or conquest; nor was it accessory to the propagation of a particular form of faith.   It did not contain within itself the elements of discord, as has been the case with too many of the professed plans for converting the heathen, even under the most imposing auspices.   The missionaries had no other object in view, than the conversion of the Indians; and we contemplate the adventures of Heckewelder, Jung, Zeisberger, Senseman, and Edwards, with sentiments of respect for them, and sorrow for the fate of their enterprise.

The missionary, Frederick Post, visited the Indians on the Ohio, in 1758, and several others penetrated into the wilderness at an early period.   The Moravian towns, whose history we learn from the publications of Heckewelder and Loskiel, were founded previous to that time. They were situated on the Muskingum River, in Ohio, and were established while that country was yet an unbroken wilderness.   Here the Moravians collected a number of converts, from among the Delaware Indians, estimated by some writers at about four hundred, and erected them into a religious community, inhabiting three villages, Salem, Schoenbrund, and Gnadenhutten.   These villages were six or seven miles apart, and were situated south from the present town of New Philadelphia, from which place the nearest of them was distant about fifteen miles. They were sixty or seventy miles west of Pittsburgh, which was then the nearest place inhabited by civilised men.   The country in that vicinity is healthful and fertile, and well adapted to agricultural purposes; and the little fraternity of believers, who separated themselves from the world, to cultivate and enjoy the peaceful fruits of religion, combined with useful labour, might have found here the happiness they sought, and have created a blooming paradise in the wilderness, had not the unsettled state of the times left them unprotected, and exposed to insult and finally to destruction. It is impossible to ascertain, what progress was made by these converts, in the arts of civilisation, as their existence was brief, and their history little known to any whites but the missionaries. It is certain that they embraced the Christian faith, abandoned war, and resorted to agriculture for subsistence. They became essentially a pacific people, and prospered so far as was dependent on their own exertions. But the times were not propitious to a fair trial of the experiment. The revolutionary war was about to break out, and the agents of the British Government were busily employed in the incendiary work of inciting the savages to war. The adventurous backwoodsmen of Pennsylvania and Virginia, had crossed the Allegheny Mountains, and were exploring the luxuriant forests of the West, in search of fertile lands. They had surmounted the barrier which the Indians had supposed would protect their hunting grounds, and which the officious foreigner had pointed out to them as a natural boundary between the white and red races. The excitement was great throughout the whole frontier, and at no time in our history have the hostilities between these parties assumed a more fierce and unrelenting character, than that which characterised the wars of this period. Two of the British emissaries, McKee and Girty, were men who to great industry and perseverance in their despicable office, added a cold-blooded and sanguinary cruelty, for which a parallel can scarcely be found in the annals of crime. The savage mind, already irritated by the encroachments of the white settlers, became infuriated by the inflammatory harangues of these agents, accompanied by presents, by promised rewards, by the hope of plunder, by the lust of revenge, and, by that most fearful engine of destruction, the intoxicating draught.

The Moravian villages were situated about midway between some of the Indian towns and the advanced settlements of the whites, and as they practised a pacific demeanour towards both parties, receiving both alike with Christian kindness and hospitality, they soon became suspected by each of secretly favouring the other. The rights of unarmed neutrals are seldom respected by warriors with arms in their hands, and with appetites whetted for plunder. The rough militia from the frontier, and the painted savage, equally despised the humble convert of the Cross, and branded as hypocrisy and cowardice that spirit of non-resistance which they could not understand.

Under all these disadvantages the community continued to flourish until the actual breaking out of the revolutionary war in 1775. Up to that period there had been encroachments, jealousy, quarrels, marauding excursions, and occasionally a petty border warfare; but now there was a general war of a bitter and unsparing character. The American colonies, barely able to maintain the contest on the seaboard, against the fleets and armies of Great Britain, had no troops to send to the frontier, where the pioneers were obliged to defend themselves against the combined British and Indian force. It was a warfare such as we trust will never again disgrace the flag of any Christian people, or pollute the soil of our country—a war against individuals, which brought distress and ruin to the fireside, without any perceptible effect upon the national quarrel, or any advantage to either of the principal parties. The burning of the settler's cabin—the murder of women and children

—the plunder of an indigent peasantry, whose whole wealth yielded to the ruffian invader nothing but the fruits of the earth and the spoils of the chase,—all this was poor game for the diplomatic skill and military energies of a first-rate European power. The backwoods-men, left to contend unaided against this formidable allied power, imbibed the bitter feeling, and adopted the savage warfare of their enemies, so that the contest became not only fierce and bloody, but was marked by cruelties of the most atrocious character.

The war parties of either side, in passing the villages of the Christian Indians, often found it convenient to stop, and were always kindly entertained, by this pacific community, who would not have dared, even if so disposed, to refuse the rites of hospitality to armed men. It was not easy under such circumstances to avoid the suspicion of partiality. Even their benevolence, and their aversion to the shedding of blood, led them into acts which, however humane, were incautious. They some-times became apprised of the plans of the Indians, to surprise and massacre the whites, and by sending secret messages to the latter, saved them from the impending destruction; and when the famished and way-worn fugitives, who had escaped from captivity, sought a refuge at their doors, they secreted and fed them, and assisted them in eluding their pursuers. The red warriors, on the other hand, were always received with hospitality, and experienced, no doubt, all the kindness which was extended to our own people. The charities of this kind people were probably numerous, for it was a rude season, and many were the sufferers driven by the blasts of war to seek shelter within their doors. It followed naturally, that whenever a secret plan failed of success, in consequence of its being discovered and

frustrated by the opposite party, the Moravians were
charged with the disclosure. Their habitual kindness
was forgotten, the benevolence of their motive was not
taken into account, and they were cursed as spies and
traitors, for actions of which they were wholly innocent,
or which were honourable to them as men and as
Christians.

The Moravian villages were called "the half-way
houses of the warriors," and this phrase was used in
fierce derision by the lawless men, who despised the meek
professors of a pacific creed, who were content to till the
soil, taking no side in the portentous war, whose thunders
were rolling on every side. The neutrality implied in
the term *half-way house*, was anything but pleasing to
warriors embittered by an implacable hatred; and the
helplessness that should have protected the brethren
only invited insult.

As early as 1754, they are said to have been oppressed
by a tribute exacted from them by the Hurons; and
about the same time a plot to remove their residence to
Wajonick, on the Susquehanna, was set on foot by the
"Wild Indians," in alliance with the French, for the
purpose of getting the Moravians out of the way, that
they might with more secrecy assail the English settlements. Many of the brethren fell into this snare, and
some of the chiefs among them were tempted to advocate
the measure, from a latent desire to return to the war-
path. The missionaries discovered the moving springs of
the intrigue, and refused to sanction the removal; but
about seventy of their followers emigrated to that and
other places.

In the spring of 1778, the English emissaries McKee,
Elliot, Girty, and others, having been arrested at
Pittsburgh as Tories, made their escape, and passing

rapidly through the tribes, proclaimed that the Americans were preparing to destroy the Indians, and called upon the latter to strike at the settlements in self-defence. The whole frontier was thrown into a ferment by this incendiary movement.

About the year 1780, a large Indian force was collected for the purpose of striking a decisive blow at the settlements of Western Virginia, but on reaching the points intended to be assailed, full of expectation, and flushed in advance with the hope of plunder, they were disappointed by finding that preparations were made for their reception. Mortified with this result, they retreated to a safe distance, and having taken a number of prisoners, they deliberately tortured and murdered them, with every refinement of savage cruelty. The sufferers were so numerous, and the barbarities practised upon them so aggravated, as to cause an extraordinary excitement in the American settlements. In 1781, Col. Broadhead, of Pennsylvania, led an expedition against the hostile Indians; and halting near Salem, directed the inhabitants to collect their people and remain within doors, that they might not be mistaken for enemies by his exasperated troops. While this officer was assuring the Rev. Mr Heckewelder that the Moravian Indians should be protected, the incensed militia were preparing to destroy the towns, and it was only by the most strenuous exertions of the officers that the poor Indians were saved from destruction.

Not long after this event, a chief called *Pach-gaut-schi-hi-las* appeared suddenly at Gnadenhutten, at the head of eighty warriors, and surrounded the village, so as to allow no one to escape. The panic-stricken brethren, expecting that the hour for their extermination had arrived, prepared to meet their fate. The chief, however, relieved their fears, by demanding the delivery of certain leading men, who were found to be absent. After consulting with the brethren, the chief greeted them kindly, spoke with respect of their pacific habits, and deplored their exposed position on the very road over which the hostile parties must pass to reach each other. They had just escaped destruction from one of these parties, and he advised them to remove to a distance from the war - path. The Christian Indians, relying upon the innocence of their lives, declined to remove.

In the autumn of 1781, "a troop of savages, commanded by English officers," surrounded and pillaged the unprotected villages of the Moravian Indians. The corn-fields, just ready for the harvest, were ravaged by the ruthless invaders, "two hundred cattle, four hundred hogs, and much corn in store," were taken from them. Their houses were broken open, their altars desecrated, and themselves treated with merciless contempt. A young Indian woman, who accompanied the warriors, was so touched by the distresses of the brethren, some of whom were her own tribe and kindred, that she left the camp secretly, and taking a horse of Captain Pipe, the leader of the marauding Indians, rode to Pittsburgh, where she gave intelligence of the misfortunes which had befallen the brethren. This spirited woman was a near relative of Glikhikan, a distinguished chief of the Delawares, described by Heckewelder as "an eminent captain and warrior, counsellor and speaker," who was now a member of the Christian community, and on him the savages determined to wreak their vengeance, on the discovery of the mission of his kinswoman. He was seized at Salem, and carried to Gnadenhutten, singing his death song. It was proposed to cut him in pieces at once; and the Delawares, who were exasperated against him for having quitted the usages of his people, were clamorous for his instant execution; but he was saved by the interposition of a chief, who insisted that he should be fairly tried. Upon examination, he was found to be innocent, in regard to the matter which had caused his arrest, and he was set at liberty, but not until his persecutors had given vent to their malignity, by loading him with the vilest epithets. Their rage was now directed to the missionaries, and the chiefs were nearly unanimous in the conclusion to put them to death. On so important a matter, it was considered requisite to consult one of their sorcerers, whose reply was that "he could not understand what end it would answer to kill them." The chiefs then held a council, at which it was resolved to put to death, not only the missionaries and their families, but those of the Indian converts who were prominently engaged in religious duties. But the sorcerer again interposed the powerful shield of his protection; he said that some of the chief men among the brethren were his friends, and that he would serve them at every hazard. "If you hurt any of them," said he, "I know what I shall do." The threat was effectual; and the Christian ministers were rescued from a cruel death, by the priest of superstition. But the sufferings of this devoted community did not end here. The missionaries were carried to Detroit, and arraigned before the British commandant, as traitors and enemies of the King. The modern Felix, after a full examination of the charges, was compelled to admit the innocence of the prisoners, and they were discharged. But the object of the instigators of this flagitious transaction, was accomplished. The Indians were driven for the time from their villages. Heretofore, though often pillaged and threatened, their lives and persons had been spared, and some respect was attached to their character: but this bold outrage, sanctioned by the British authority, destroyed all feeling of restraint on the part of the savages, and they were now continually harassed by the war parties. Compelled to quit their once quiet habitations, they wandered through the wilderness to the plains of Sandusky, distant about one hundred and twenty-five miles, where many of them perished miserably of famine, during the succeeding winter.

In the ensuing month of February, a wretched remnant numbering about a hundred and fifty of these persecuted converts, returned to their former habitations, to seek among their ruined huts and desolated hearths, some relics of the former abundance, to save themselves from starvation. Here they met with a party of militia from the settlements, who in the brutal indulgence of that hatred for the red men, which embraced every branch of that unhappy race, slew ninety of these starving fugitives. The remainder crawled back to their companions at Sandusky.

However broken and disheartened by these various calamities, the Moravian Indians still clung to their bond of union, for in 1782 they were again collected at their villages. Their previous misfortunes seem to have been attributable to the intrigues of Elliot, Girty, and McKee, the British agents, who were always their implacable persecutors. But they were singularly unfortunate in having no friends on either side, for the American borderers were not less their enemies. Exasperated by the continual incursions of the Indians, and the atrocious cruelties perpetrated by them, they imbibed a spirit of revenge, which was too bitter and too blind, to leave any power of discrimination between the guilty and the innocent. They assumed, strangely enough, that the "Praying Indians" of the Muskingum were the tools of these foreign agents, of whom in fact they were the victims, equally with themselves. Nourishing a deadly rancour against the whole race, they took no pains to inquire into the justice of their suspicions, for revenge is always blind and incapable of any just measure of retribution. In 1782 an expedition was planned by the settlers in Western Virginia, under Colonel William Crawford, against the hostile Indians, and the destruction of the Moravian towns was deliberately contemplated as a part of the plan. Unhappily the hand of desolation had already performed its work so effectually as to leave little to be done; but that little was now completed. The followers of Crawford found desolated fields and ruined habitations, tenanted by a few broken-spirited wretches, who were again driven forth into the wilderness, never to be re-assembled. While the unresisting Christian fell thus a prey to every fierce marauder, the sword of retributive justice was not sleeping in its scabbard; it was now ready to fall on the head of the offender. The ill-fated troops of Crawford proceeded to the plains of Sandusky, where they encountered a large Indian force, and a battle ensued which lasted from noon until sunset. The next day the savages increased in number, the camp was surrounded, and the most gloomy apprehensions began to be entertained. The troops were brave and hardy volunteers, but they were raw and insubordinate, and there seems to have been but little skill or firmness among the officers. A retreat was resolved upon; but hemmed in by a numerous and active foe, this measure was scarcely practicable. Discordant councils were added to the difficulties; a difference of opinion arose as to the mode of retreat, some proposing that the army should retire in a compact body, while others advised a division into a number of parties, who should cut their

way through the enemy in different directions. Both
plans were attempted, but neither of them with energy.
The troops became panic-struck, discipline was thrown
aside, and every movement was the result of mere
impulse. The routed troops retreating in disorder were
cut to pieces or captured in detail, and but few escaped
to tell the dismal story. Crawford himself was taken
prisoner, and carried to an Indian town, where he was
beaten, tortured with lingering torments, and burnt at
the stake with every indignity and aggravation of suffering which the malignity of the savage could suggest.
Girty, the British agent, witnessed these shocking rites,
laughed at the agonies of the sufferer, and was an active
party in the bloody and atrocious scene.

We have already seen that the bad faith which
marked the conduct of the English towards the aborigines,
was not confined to any locality, or to any sect of the
colonists. To show the universality of that misconduct, it
is only necessary to open at random the history of the
early settlements, which are fraught with instances of the
reckless imprudence, or desperate perfidy of the English
adventurers.

General Oglethorpe, who landed in Georgia in 1732,
was kindly received by the Indians, who professed a high
degree of veneration for the character of the English, in
consequence of the amicable intercourse which had
prevailed between themselves and a commander who had
visited them a century before, supposed to have been Sir
Walter Raleigh. Oglethorpe carried several of their
chiefs to England in 1734, where they were entertained
with great hospitality, and whence they returned with the
most favourable impressions towards the white people.
It is lamentable to remark that an intercourse commenced
under such promising auspices, should have been almost

immediately broken up by the misconduct of individuals. As early as 1743, when Georgia was invaded by the Spaniards, the natives were enlisted as auxiliaries on both sides, and thus placed in a position which must inevitably be ruinous to them, by drawing upon them the resentment of the whites.   In the expedition against Fort du Quesne the Cherokees were prevailed upon to join the English; but they became soured by the military restraints under which they were placed, by suspicions of their fidelity, which they alleged to be unfounded, and by various other injuries, either real or imaginary.   Having lost their horses, and being worn with the fatigue of a long journey, they unfortunately, on reaching the frontiers of Virginia, supplied themselves by taking some horses which were found running at large.   The inhabitants, as usual, proceeded to inflict summary justice, and about forty of the Cherokee warriors were shot down, in cool blood, in different places, as they passed through the settlements. After Braddock's defeat, the English offered a reward for Indian scalps, a cruel and inexcusable expedient, which doubtless led to the murder of many of their own allies, as their agents, in paying for the bloody trophy, could not distinguish between those taken in battle from their enemies, and those torn, for a wretched bribe, by the mercenary hand of murder, from the heads of their own friends.   Another instance occurred about the same period, in which a party of Cherokees, who had been regaled at the house of a white man, under the implied safeguard of hospitality, were surrounded, and shot down by ruffians lying in ambuscade, as they passed from the place of entertainment!   No provocation could excuse such deeds. The capture in the woods of a few wild horses of little value, by savages unskilled in the laws relating to property, afforded no just plea for the shedding of blood; and no

offence could justify a deliberate violation of good faith,
by the murder of confiding guests. In this respect the
Indians themselves displayed a more generous conduct.
When the intelligence of these massacres reached the
Cherokees, they rushed to arms, and would have slain
several Englishmen, who were then in their country on
some business connected with the negotiation of a treaty ;
but their chief Attakullakulla interfered, and secreted the
whites, until he calmed the excited feeling of his people.
He then assembled his warriors in council, and proposed
an immediate war against the English. "The hatchet
shall never be buried," said he, "until the blood of our
people be avenged. But let us not violate our faith, by
shedding the blood of those who are now in our power.
They came to us in confidence, bringing belts of wampum
to cement a perpetual alliance. Let us carry them back
to their own settlements, and then take up the hatchet and
endeavour to exterminate the whole race of them." The
Indians not only adopted this advice, but proceeded
regularly to demand the murderers from the English
authorities, who refused to comply with the request; and
the result was a war attended with the usual atrocities of
border warfare, and followed by the common, and still
more lamentable result of such hostilities, a lasting hatred
between the parties—a hatred, the more calamitous to
the Indian, as it placed an insuperable barrier between
him and all the blessings of Christianity and civilisation.

Without multiplying any further our instances from
American history, it may be perceived that the colonists
never acted towards the Indians with any system; no
rule either of justice or humanity regulated their conduct,
no limit restrained the dictate of caprice, or the hand of
violence. Every man behaved himself towards the savage
as seemed good in his own eyes : to cheat the savage was

not dishonest, to rob him not criminal, to slay him not murder ; while the attempt to protect him from injury, or to teach him the way of salvation, was scarcely deemed meritorious. For all these atrocities, the European Governments are responsible, who interposed no restraint between their own subjects who came to this continent for mercenary purposes, and the natives who were delivered over to their tender mercies. In the charters and patents granting territory to the North American colonists, extensive boundaries were set forth, but no reservation was made in favour of the ancient inhabitants, no recognition of their present occupancy, nor any mode prescribed for the purchase or extinguishment of their title. We do not assert that they were not attended to, nor deny that they were sometimes mentioned in terms of affected benevolence ; but we do say that they were not recognised in those solemn public documents, as nations or individuals having rights to be respected. The intercourse with them was left to be directed by circumstances ; and this momentous interest, fraught with consequences so portentous to them and to us, was modified and moulded, not only by the characters of the various leaders, but the caprice, the interest, and the passions of all those who came in contact with the natives. Hence the multifarious incidents, and diverse causes and influences which have operated in producing the present condition of that people, and in forming our opinions concerning them.

Previous to the revolution we find a better feeling growing up in most of the colonies. The aspirations of our forefathers for liberty enlarged their minds, and implanted noble and generous sentiments, in regard to the whole scheme of government, and the entire system of human rights and happiness. Among the first acts of the new Confederation were measures of a considerate

and just, and conciliatory character towards the Indians;
the right of the Indians to the occupancy of their lands
was distinctly avowed, and a system adopted for the
gradual extinction of their title by purchase, which, in
most cases, has been observed.

The boundaries of the colonies extended from the sea-
coast, into the interior, so far, in most cases, as to embrace
large districts of wild land, occupied by the Indians.
Some of them extended indefinitely to the West, and we
believe that none of them acknowledged any other
boundary than that of a sister colony, or some European
possession, except where the ocean set bounds to the sway
of man. The country was divided without regard to the
Indians, who were included in the new sovereignties, and
whose removal or extinction was assumed as inevitable
in the natural course of events. The newly formed
American states adopted the same boundaries, and were
obliged to take the country subject to the existing state
of things. There were the Indians, and there were the
white population, trained up in the belief that the wilderness before them was destined to be reclaimed and to
blossom as the rose, and that they were the appointed
instruments to effect the transformation. There was the
fixed and hardened public sentiment dooming the Indian
to extirpation, and decreeing the descendant of the Saxon
to a destiny as brilliant as vanity, self-love, interest, and
ambition, could imagine. What government would dare
to protect a wretched remnant of savages, by arresting the
march of improvement, and palsying the energies of a free,
great, and enlightened people? There were the prejudices, the hatred, the rankling feuds, the cherished
memory of mutual and oft-repeated injuries, transmitted
through successive generations, and gaining continual
accessions from the tributary streams of current aggres-

JOHN ROSS
A Cherokee Chief

sion. All these were encumbered upon the inheritance of our fathers, and unavoidably influenced their councils.

There was this marked difference between the policy of the new states and that of the colonial governments which preceded them, that while both contemplated the removal of the Indians from within the boundaries of their several states, that removal was on the one hand proposed to be voluntary, on the other compulsory: the European Governments took the land of the natives whenever it pleased them to do so; the American states voluntarily pledged themselves to leave the Indians unmolested until their title to the lands they occupied could be extinguished, peaceably, by purchase.

By the Union of the States the intercourse with the Indians became complicated by a further modification. In adjusting the division of power between the general government, and the several states respectively, of the Confederacy, the intercourse with foreign nations was given up to the former, while the latter reserved to themselves all their sovereignty, as regarded the internal police of their states. The intercourse with the Indians was specially delegated to the United States, embracing the whole subject of negotiating for their lands; while the respective states, members of the Union, by their own proper sovereignty, and in the necessary maintenance of their police, claimed jurisdiction over such individuals or tribes as fell within their boundaries. It is true that this jurisdiction was, in practice, seldom extended over the unceded territory of the Indians; but that states, claiming without dispute certain boundaries, might exercise sovereignty, coextensive with these boundaries, for all the legitimate purposes of government, can hardly be denied. The United States reserving the right of pre-emption to the lands of the Indians, and denying alike to foreign states, to states members of the Union, and to individuals, the privilege of purchasing such lands, or of treating with the Indians, assumed the immediate guardianship over the latter, and became bound to the states to remove them from within their boundaries, whenever that desirable measure could be effected by peaceable negotiation.

The system that embraced the removal of the Indians from their ancient hunting-grounds to lands allotted them west of the Mississippi, was, as a system, doubtless, a humane one. While within the jurisdictive limits of states, they were subject to the action of the anomalous relations growing out of such a position. Beyond those limits, and away from the consuming effects necessarily attendant upon a close approximation of the two races, a season of rest has been afforded them, in which to improve themselves, and be benefited by the agency of those Christian labours, which, if their present possessions are secured to them, by a title as indestructible as a fee-simple right can make it, and the appropriate relations are established between them and the United States, will result in their preservation as a race, and in advancing them to the high destiny of a civilised and Christian people.

Notwithstanding the angry contentions which were continued, down to the period of the removal of the Indians, between citizens of the states, and in some instances, state governments and themselves, several of the tribes, especially the Cherokees, had resorted to agriculture ; some were converted to Christianity, schools were established, and missionaries kindly entertained. Their improvement was rapid, and there was a gratifying prospect of an auspicious result. They had even invented an alphabet, established a press, and given to themselves a written language. They adopted a written constitution, and organised a regular government. Here the state of Georgia interposed her authority. The Cherokees were within the limits claimed by her, and recognised by the other states and the Union, and she could not be expected to consent to the erection of an independent state within her boundaries. The formation of such a state would be inadmissible under the Constitution of the United States, each member of which, as well as the Confederacy, would be bound in good faith to protest against it. The United States especially, being bound to the state of Georgia, to extinguish the title of the Cherokees to their land, by purchase, as soon as the same could be done " peaceably, and upon reasonable terms," could neither consent to, nor connive at, a proceeding which would render the performance of her own undertaking impossible. Nor do we understand that this view of the case necessarily involved the expulsion, as individuals, of such portion of the Cherokees as were engaged in agriculture, or the mechanic arts. As a people they were denied a political existence within the state of Georgia ; they were offered a price for their lands, and other lands with full territorial jurisdiction and a national organisation, beyond the limits of the states of the Union. But any individual who chose to remain, to submit to the laws of Georgia, and to live the life of a civilised man, might have done so.

We shall now speak of the condition of the South-Western tribes of the United States, for the purpose of showing the actual amount of civilisation existing among them, previous to their removal, and the causes, so far as we can ascertain them, of the changes which have taken place, in the mode of life, and especially of such of these causes as bear upon the future prospects of these tribes.

The advances in civilisation made by the Creeks, Cherokees, Chickasaws, and Choctaws, afford ground for strongest encouragement on this subject. These were among the most powerful and warlike of the aboriginal tribes—as wild, as ferocious, as untameable as any of their race.   Driven across the Allegheny Mountains by the pressure of the white population, they became stationary in the fertile country lying between those mountains and the Mississippi, and within the boundaries of Tennessee, Georgia, Alabama, and Mississippi.   The tide of civilisation, pressing to the West, rolled over them, and left them in an insulated position : Missouri, Arkansas, and Louisiana became interposed between them and the native tribes lying still farther to the West, leaving them surrounded by a white population.   Their hunting-grounds were still sufficiently extensive, to keep up around them an immense wilderness, and to afford room for the free exercise of savage customs; but there were countervailing causes, which gradually restrained and limited the nomadic habits and propensities, and brought about a great revolution.   The first of these we have alluded to ; the geographical position of the tribes, obliged them to become stationary ; their villages became permanent; and their warlike propensities were curbed. Their rich country and fine climate tempted a number of traders to settle among them, who married Indian women, and became identified with the tribes.

The first and most effectual of the causes which have been brought to bear upon this portion of the Indian race, has been the mixture of whites—the introduction into the tribes of persons already civilised.   We have elsewhere remarked upon the singular facility with which the Indians admit the naturalisation of foreigners among them. Jealous as they are, and as all ignorant people are, of strangers, yet when a white man settles among them, and adopts their mode of life, he soon gains their confidence, and ceases to be in any respect an alien. Cautious and suspicious in all their doings, they receive such persons with hesitation, and watch their conduct narrowly for a while, but their confidence, when given, is without reserve. The adoption of white prisoners into the Indian families is not an uncommon occurrence; the person adopted takes the place of one who has been lost, succeeds to all his rights, and in all particulars is treated precisely as he would have been whom he represents. They seem to be wholly unconscious of that prejudice of colour, which is so strong with us; and the superior knowledge of the white man, instead of causing dislike, recommends him to favour.

The children of the intermarriages between the whites and Indians are not placed under any disability, nor does any dislike or prejudice attach to them. On the contrary they are usually a favoured class, and the only observable distinction is to their advantage. Their position places them a little in advance of the Indian; they have the advantages of speaking two languages, and of being taught by one parent the warlike habits and manly exercises of the savage, and by the other the arts of civilised life; and they thus become the orators, the interpreters, the counsellors, and the influential men, in the negotiations between the Indians and the white men. From one of their parents they imbibe notions of property, and being more provident than the savage in his natural state, are better provided with the means of subsistence, and often become wealthy.

Several of the most distinguished chiefs among the southern Indians were the descendants of white men, and nearly all of those whose influence has been actively and effectually exerted in advancing civilisation, have been of the mixed blood, and enjoyed, to a greater or less degree,

the advantages of education.   Not to mention others, we
may point out Alexander McGillivray as an example.
He was the head of the Creek nation, and was considered
the most conspicuous of the southern chiefs.   He succeeded
to the chieftaincy in right of his mother, a woman of
energy and talents, who ruled before him ; but he was
also, according to the Indian rule, freely elected by the
nation.   His father was a Scotchman, a trader, who, by
the thrift of his fatherland, made himself an influential man
among the Creeks.   Young McGillivray was born about
1739, and educated, from the age of ten years, under the
care of Mr Farquhar McGillivray, a relative of his father,
in Charleston, South Carolina.   He learned the Latin
language, was much addicted to literature, and devoted
himself assiduously to study.   In the revolutionary war he
espoused the British cause, but after the peace became
reconciled to the American Government, visited President
Washington, and was much noticed in our eastern cities.
He was young when elected chief, and died in 1793, at the
age of about fifty-four, so that he must have been in
power about thirty years, with the exception of a short
period, during which he was expelled from authority by
an adverse faction, headed by one Bowles, a white man,
and whose temporary success affords a further illustration
of the extent of that influence to which we allude.

The white men who settled among the Southern tribes
of the United States were traders, whose business was a
traffic in furs and merchandise ; but who became attached
to the savage mode of life, and becoming stationary in the
wilderness, adopted the dress and many of the habits of
the Indians, while they also devoted themselves, in some
degree, to agricultural and pastoral pursuits.   They
introduced the domestic animals, which running at large
in the range, as the luxuriant wild pastures are called,

multiplied rapidly, with but little care or expense to the owners, who soon became the proprietors of large droves of horses, cattle, and swine. These alone, in the sylvan state in which they lived, constituted wealth, and gave importance. They erected large and comfortable houses, and became surrounded with the comforts of life. Living on the borders of the slave states, they were enabled to purchase and hold slaves, who were employed in agriculture, in the cultivation chiefly of corn. Having all the means of living in great abundance, they lived rudely, but plentifully, and practised a generous hospitality. Their women, elevated from a wretched servitude, to be the companions of their husbands, relieved from the drudgery of cultivation, and the toil of following the hunter in the chase, and surrounded by the conveniences and luxuries of houses, furniture, and domestic servants, experienced a rapid improvement in character. The domestic virtues were developed, and the kindly affections appropriate to the sex, were expanded so luxuriantly, that even in the first generation, the offspring of these marriages exhibited an amelioration of character which left little of the original savage peculiarity perceptible.

One of the causes of the partial civilisation of the southern Indians, to which we have alluded, is pointed out in an admirable work, by one of the most learned men and sagacious statesmen of our country, the venerable Mr Gallatin, in his *Synopsis of the Indian Tribes*, a work of unsurpassed research, published in the Transactions of the American Antiquarian Society, at Cambridge, Mass. He says : " The only well ascertained instance, among our own Indians, of their having, at least in part, become an agricultural nation, meaning that state of society in which the men themselves do actually perform agricultural labour, is that of the Cherokees. And it is in proof, that in this case

U

also, cultivation was at first introduced through the means of *slavery*. In their predatory excursions they carried away slaves from Carolina. These were used to work, and continued to be thus employed by their new masters. The advantages derived by the owners were immediately perceived. Either in war or peace, slaves of the African race became objects of desire; and gradually, assisted by the efforts of the government, and the beneficial influence of the missionaries, some among those Indians, who could not obtain slaves, were induced to work for themselves." We only differ from this distinguished writer, in supposing slavery to have been one of the causes, instead of the only or chief cause, of the partial civilisation of the southern Indians.

The pastoral, rather than the agricultural mode of life, was that which succeeded the barbarism of these people—the rearing of large herds of domestic animals, and the cultivation of grain to the extent only which was required for bread and provender. The wealth and comfort, which a few individuals acquired in this way, afforded strong allurements to others, to follow their example; while the growing obstacles to war, and to those distant and great hunting expeditions, which were so fruitful of adventure and excitement, were every day rendering the people more indolent and less warlike, and leading the reflecting men of the tribes to see the necessity of resorting to agriculture. The rapid decay and extinction of many other tribes was not unknown to them. The melancholy truths were admitted, which pointed out the superiority of the whites, and the fatal results which invariably followed the contact of the two races. It was evident that the civilised and savage man could not live together, and that the latter would be continually encroached upon and crushed by the former. There was but one way in which this fate could be avoided, and that was, to cease to be savages. The many could not perceive the correctness of this conclusion, or received it with a disrelish which closed their minds against it; but the better class of intellects saw it, and prepared with more or less cordiality to obey the law of their destiny.

The missionaries found the Cherokees thus prepared to receive them favourably. The white men and their descendants, and all who had ceased to subsist by hunting, gladly received the schoolmaster, and offered every facility to the introduction of that education, and those arts, which would enlighten and elevate their children. These formed, it is true, a small party, and opposed to them, on this subject, stood the main body of the unreclaimed natives, united into a firm phalanx by their hereditary dislike of the whites, and the force of inbred prejudices. On both sides were arrayed men of influence : on the one hand were the chiefs distinguished in war, and eloquent in council, who exhibited their wounds, and appealed to the recollection of the many wrongs inflicted on their people by the whites ; on the other were the wealthy, the civilised and partly civilised, and some who possessed hereditary and personal popularity. On the one side were numbers, on the other property and intelligence, together with the influence of the American Government. Thus commenced those parties, so little understood by the American people, which for so many years divided these unfortunate tribes, and in which, unhappily for the cause of humanity, the missionaries themselves became involved. The good work, however, went on with unexampled success ; schools were established in which the children of mixed blood generally, and some from among the natives, were taught, and numbers were converted to the Gospel, and gave good evidence of sincere piety.

The invention of the Cherokee Alphabet was a fortuitous incident, a Providential element in this revolution, which exerted great influence. It gave them a written language, and greatly enlarged the means of addressing their minds, while it furnished an appeal to their pride, and afforded the teacher a medium through which he approached them, with less violence to their established prejudices, than if the only mode of teaching had been through a foreign tongue. (*See* Biography of Sequoyah, Vol. I., pp. 130, 141, this work.)

The attempt to establish an independent government among the Cherokees was not without its good effect. The plan was conceived and advocated by the men of mixed blood, by those who had been taught to read and write, who had abandoned the savage life, and some of whom had embraced the doctrines of Christianity. They sought earnestly the means of information, in regard to the science of government, and its practical forms in the United States; and in the endeavour to introduce this revolution among their people, it became necessary to discuss the principles of free government, and to point out the advantages of the civilised over the savage state. They became thus the most potent missionaries of civilisation. Councils were held in which the proposed reforms were discussed by the ablest men, and the best orators, who explained many of the abstract principles of political science, while they contrasted the degraded condition of the savage, with the power, the comforts, the security, and the intelligence of the civilised man. They were opposed by influential and eloquent chiefs, who appealed to the prejudices of the people, and indignantly spurned at every attempt to change the ancient customs of the nation. The whole ground was canvassed, with zeal and ability, the public mind was agitated and awakened to new subjects for thought and conversation, and all this could not be done without a general and gradual dissemination of intelligence. The missionaries and the agents of the United States threw all their influence into the scale of civilisation, and those who could not officially countenance the scheme of framing an independent government, within the limits of Georgia, did what they could to urge the moral reformation which accompanied that movement. The party opposed to reformation were compelled reluctantly to make concessions; laws were made for the protection of life and property; patrols were established to scour the country, to arrest offenders, and to preserve the peace; the schools were taken under the public protection, and the germs of a regular government widely scattered. In the meanwhile, such men as John Ross, Elias Boudinot, John Ridge, and others, whose minds had been enlarged by education and travel, laboured assiduously with the pen, and by their personal influence, not only to disseminate information among their countrymen, but to enlist the sympathies of the American Government and people.

The most prominent man of this movement was JOHN Ross, a Cherokee of the mixed blood, whose portrait is contained in this number of our work, and who is now at the head of the confederated Indian nation west of the Mississippi. We regret that the want of materials for a separate memoir of this chief has prevented us from giving him the place in the biographical portion of our work, to which his eminent services, and conspicuous position, entitle him. But this has been prevented by the difficulty of procuring authentic information, and by our reluctance to enter in detail upon a life so eventful and important, without such full and accurate materials, as would enable us to do justice as well to him, as to the numerous friends and enemies, who have acted with and against him. We must

speak of him in general terms as the leader of his people in
their exodus from the land of their nativity to a new
country, and from the savage state to that of civilisation.
Through the whole of this interesting and exciting movement he has been an efficient actor, and of some of the
most important events the prime mover. He has no fame
as a warrior, nor do we know that he has ever been in the
field. His talents are those of the civilian. Plain and
unassuming in his appearance, of calm and quiet deportment, he is a man of great sagacity and of untiring energy.
Assiduous in the pursuit of his objects, he has spent many
of his winters at Washington, where he was well known
to all the leading statesmen, and to the philanthropists
who concern themselves about the affairs of the neglected
aborigines, while the remainder of his time has been
actively employed among his own people. So far as we
can judge of his character, by his acts, we believe him to
be an able man, who has done good service for his people.

It could hardly be expected that a leader and chief of
such prominence would escape the missives of those with
whom he differed. Many and varied as had been the
excitements prior to the conclusion of the treaty of New
Echota, of 29th December, 1835, they bore no comparison
to those which grew out of this transaction. The party to
this treaty, which at no time, it is believed, exceeded a
hundred Indians, was headed by Major Ridge, his son
John, and Elias Boudinot; and against them was the
entire remainder of the Cherokee nation, at the head of
which was John Ross. These excitements would have
been of short duration, had not the Ridge party been
recognised and sustained by the United States Government.
We have no desire to introduce into this work, the
elements, even, much less the details of this controversy,
or, if we had, the entire history would be too voluminous

for this work.* We cannot refrain, however, from introducing in this place, because it illustrates not only the ability of Ross, as a writer, but the nature and grounds of the controversy itself, the following touching remonstrance, in the form of a memorial, addressed by Ross and those whom the Cherokees had associated with him, for the purpose,—"To the honourable, the Senate and House of Representatives of the United States of America." This memorial was transmitted from Red Clay council ground, Cherokee Nation, East, and bears date September 28, 1836; it is signed by 1,245 male adults. After a few preliminary remarks the memorial proceeds :—

"By the stipulations of this instrument, (the treaty of New Echota,) we are despoiled of our private possessions, the indefeasible property of individuals. We are stripped of every attribute of freedom and eligibility for legal self-defence. Our property may be plundered before our eyes. Violence may be committed on our persons ; even our lives may be taken away and there is none to regard our complaints. We are denationalised! We are disfranchised! We are deprived of membership in the human family! We have neither land, nor home, nor resting-place, that can be called our own. And this is effected by the provisions of a compact which assumes the venerated, the sacred appellation of treaty. We are overwhelmed! Our hearts are sickened! Our utterance is paralysed, when we reflect on the condition in which we are placed by the audacious practices of unprincipled men ; who have managed their stratagems with so much dexterity as to impose on the Government of the United States, in the face of our earnest, solemn, and reiterated protestations.

* For detailed information, see Doc. No. 286, House of Reps., 24th Congress, first Session.

"The instrument in question is not the act of our nation. We are not parties to its covenants. It has not received the sanction of our people. The makers of it sustain no office or appointment in our nation, under the designation of chiefs, headmen, or any other title, by which they hold or could acquire authority to assume the reins of government, and to make bargain and sale of our rights, our possessions, and our common country. And we are constrained solemnly to declare, that we cannot but contemplate the enforcement of the stipulations of this instrument on us, against our consent, as an act of injustice and oppression, which we are well persuaded can never, knowingly, be countenanced by the Government and people of the United States; nor can we believe it to be the design of those honourable and high-minded individuals, who stand at the head of the Government, to bind a whole nation by the acts of a few unauthorised individuals. And, therefore, we, the parties to be affected by the result, appeal with confidence to the justice, the magnanimity, the compassion of your honourable bodies, against the enforcement on us of the provisions of a compact, in the formation of which we have had no agency. In truth, our cause is your own. It is the cause of liberty and of justice. It is based on your own principles, which we have learned from yourselves! for we have gloried to count your Washington, and your Jefferson, our great teachers. We have read their communications to us with veneration. We have practised their precepts with success. And the result is manifest. The wilderness of forest has given place to comfortable dwellings and cultivated fields—stocked with the various domestic animals. Mental culture, industrious habits, and domestic enjoyments have succeeded the rudeness of the savage state. We have learned your religion also. We have read your sacred books. Hundreds of our people have embraced their doctrines, practised the virtues they teach, cherished the hopes they awaken, and rejoiced in the consolations which they afford. To the spirit of your institutions and your religion which has been imbibed by our community, is mainly to be ascribed that patient endurance which has characterised the conduct of our people under the lacerations of their keenest woes. For assuredly, we are not ignorant of our condition: we are not insensible to our sufferings. We feel them! We groan under their pressure! And anticipation crowds our breasts with sorrows yet to come. We are, indeed, an afflicted people! Our spirits are subdued! Despair has well nigh seized upon our energies! But we speak to the representatives of a Christian country; the friends of justice; the patrons of the oppressed. And our hopes revive, and our prospects brighten, as we indulge the thought. On your sentence our fate is suspended. Prosperity or desolation depends on your word. To you, therefore, we look! Before your august assembly we present ourselves, in the attitude of deprecation and of entreaty. On your kindness, on your humanity, on your compassion, on your benevolence, we rest our hopes. To you we address our reiterated prayers.

"SPARE OUR PEOPLE! Spare the wreck of our prosperity! Let not our deserted homes become the monuments of desolations! But we forbear! We suppress the agonies which wring our hearts, when we look at our wives, our children, and our venerable sires! We restrain our forebodings of anguish and distress, of misery and devastation and death which must be the attendants on the execution of this ruinous compact."

The foregoing sentiments were afterwards, viz. 30th of

September, reiterated, in a letter to General Wool, then commanding United States troops in the Cherokee nation, to which the General thus replied :—

" Head Quarters Army E. T. & C. N.
Fort Cass, November 3, 1836.

"I am instructed by the President of the United States, through the War Department, to make known to John Ross, and all others, whom it may concern, that it is his determination to have the late treaty, entered into between the United States and the Cherokee people, and ratified by the Senate the 25th of May 1836, religiously fulfilled in all its parts, terms, and conditions, within the period prescribed ; and that no delegation which may be sent to Washington with a view to obtain new terms, or a modification of those of the existing treaty, will be received or recognised, nor will any intercourse be had with them, directly or indirectly, orally, or in writing ; and that the President regards the proceedings of Mr Ross and his associates in the late council held at Red Clay, as in direct contravention of the plighted faith of their people, and a repetition of them will be considered as indicative of a design to prevent the execution of the treaty, even at the hazard of actual hostilities, and they will be promptly repressed," etc.

Thus circumstanced, it was thought by the Ross party that their brethren on the west of the Mississippi, who had emigrated under the treaties of 1817 and 1819, might take an interest in this question ; and that probably if they should view the question in the light they did, and so express themselves, the Government at Washington might be induced to listen to them. Whereupon a deputation was sent to lay the subject of the existing embarrassments before the councils of the Western Cherokees. A council

APAULY TUSTENNUGGEE
A Creek Chief

was convened, and their brethren from the east showed the authority under which they had come, and made known the object of their visit. Among the resolutions adopted on the occasion was the following :—" The course adopted by the general council of the Cherokee Nation, East, in regard to the instrument, aforesaid (the treaty of New Echota,) is hereby approved; and inasmuch as the said instrument is equally objectionable to us, and will, in its enforcement, also affect our best interests and happiness —Resolved, etc., that a delegation be, and hereby are appointed to represent the Cherokee Nation, West, before the Government of the United States, and to co-operate with the delegation east of the Mississippi, in their exertions to procure the rescinding of the aforesaid instrument ; and also with full powers to unite with the delegation aforesaid, in any treaty arrangement which they may enter into with the Government of the United States for the final adjustment of the Cherokee difficulties, and to promote the advancement of the best interests and happiness of the whole Cherokee people, and to do all things touching the affairs of the Cherokees, West, for their welfare."

We will let Mr Ross speak in his own language in regard to this joint mission. We copy from a letter addressed by him to Job R. Tyson, Esq., of Philadelphia.

" We departed with the members appointed to serve upon this delegation, but the severity of the winter, and the obstruction of our route by the ice in the rivers, prevented our arrival at Washington, until the 9th February, 1837, within a month of the close of General Jackson's Presidency. We attempted to obtain access to the President, but were denied an official interview with the President or his secretary. We then memorialised the Senate, which memorial was presented, but owing to the press of business, no opportunity occurred for presenting

that which we addressed to the House. In this memorial
we exhibited an account of the treatment we had experienced, and urged our claims in the most earnest and
respectful manner. We selected what we considered the
strongest arguments in support of our application. We
adverted to the extraordinary and inexplicable change
which had taken place in the mode of receiving us, and
our appeals. Among other things, we said—'We have
asked, and we will reiterate the question—*How have we
offended?* Show us in what manner we have, however
unwittingly, inflicted upon you a wrong, you shall yourselves be the judges of the extent and manner of compensation; show us the offence which has awakened your
feelings of justice against us, and we will submit to that
measure of punishment which you shall tell us we have
merited. We cannot bring to our recollection anything
we have done, or anything we have omitted, calculated to
awaken your resentment against us.'

"All, however, was vain. It may be observed that our
appeal to the Senate was necessarily presented so late in
the session, that we could not have been fairly heard,
whatever disposition may have existed in that honourable
body to give their full attention to our case.

"On the 4th March, (continues Mr Ross,) Mr Van
Buren assumed the Presidential Chair. On the 16th of
March we addressed the new President, stating to him
fully our position and wishes, reviewing the circumstances
which had occurred, and the hopes we entertained of
receiving redress at his hands. We entreated the
President to examine for himself into the ground upon
which we rested our charge; that the document called a
treaty was fraudulent, and equally an imposition upon the
United States, and upon ourselves. We asked—'Will the
Government of the United States claim the right to enforce

a contract, thus assailed, by the other nominal party to it ? Will they refuse to examine into charges of such grave import ? Will they act in matters so momentous, involving consequences so awful, without inquiry ? ' Such an inquiry we earnestly courted, saying to the President,— ' We do not arrogate to ourselves so high a standing in your estimation as to authorise us to ask that you will rely implicitly upon our statements ; but we have deceived ourselves most egregiously, if we have not presented to the consideration of the Government sufficient grounds to induce hesitation and inquiry. You have at your command hundreds of individuals, to whom you may confide the duty of making the investigation, which we solicit. Select such as you can implicitly believe, associate with them but a single individual to be approved by us, to direct to the sources of information, and if we fail to establish the truth of our allegations, we shall no longer ask you to delay exercising your power in the enforcement of your rights. Should it, however, appear, from such investigation that this instrument (the New Echota Treaty) has been made without authority, that it meets with the almost unanimous reprobation of our nation, that you have been deceived by false information, we cannot, and we will not believe, that under its colour, and under the sanction of those principles of justice which impose an obligation faithfully to perform our contracts and our promises, we shall be forced to submit to its iniquitous provisions.' "

Mr Ross then states under three several heads, the propositions made by the delegation to the Government. The *First* was that the President would enter into a negotiation with them, as the duly authorised and regularly accredited representatives of the Cherokees.

Second, That a full and thorough examination be instituted into the New Echota Treaty,—to see if any of the forms long recognised by the United States had been regarded in making it,—or,

Third, That the instrument itself be submitted to the whole Cherokee nation, for its admission or rejection. " To this proposition," proceeds Mr Ross, " we received for answer from Mr Poinsett, dated March 24th,—That the President regarded himself as bound to carry into effect all the stipulations of the document in question, because it had been ratified according to the forms prescribed by the Constitution, under a full knowledge of the conditions now urged against it, and must, therefore, be considered as the supreme law of the land. The two other propositions could not, therefore, be entertained. We were promised a candid examination of any measure we should suggest, if not inconsistent with, or in contravention of, the determination to enforce the treaty against which we had protested.

" It is due to Mr Secretary Poinsett to say, that in accordance with his professions, every courtesy was extended to us in our intercourse with him."

Mr Ross then proceeds to examine the objections raised by the authorities at Washington. In justice to him, we continue to quote his words :

" It may not be amiss, however, at this time, to make one or two observations upon the grounds taken by the Government, and upon which it appears to have finally resolved to act.

" In the first place it appears to us an extraordinary ground, that because a treaty has actually been made, which the one party deems to be of perfect obligation upon both, that, therefore, no further official intercourse shall take place between the parties. It is obvious that the instrument in question is ambiguous, and of doubtful construction, and it is well known that objections have been made to it on behalf of the Western Cherokees, who think, and we think justly, that it most seriously impairs their rights, although we believe it has not *yet* been assumed that they are bound by its provisions, having not, thus far, at least, been considered as parties to it.   These are questions still open between the parties, which, under any view of the case, it appears to us, can only be settled by negotiation and further treaty.

" *Secondly*, It strikes us as equally extraordinary, that because our avowed object was to make a treaty which should annul the provisions of this spurious compact, no negotiations would be opened with us.   Had such a ground ever been presumed to present an obstacle to negotiations, why was it not discovered when the treaty of Holstein, and every succeeding treaty ever formed with us, was under consideration.   The stipulations of each and every of them, abrogate to a greater or less extent those which preceded it.   How insuperably might it have been urged against the pretended treaty itself, which professes to annul and abrogate pre-existing treaties, to annihilate public rights held under its sanction.

" *Thirdly*, The idea that the ratification of the Senate, under the circumstances, had at all impaired the rights of either party, is equally incomprehensible.   It was the act of one party alone.   It was an act required by the Constitution of the United States, to give legal effect to a compact, which, until that was consummated, was inchoate and imperfect.   But if no treaty had in fact ever been signed, if the instrument was in truth fraudulent or unauthorised, we are not aware that the action of the Senate could make that valid which before was void, could impose any obligation upon us who were not previously bound.   Indeed, if this doctrine be true, to the extent it has been pressed, the Cherokee nation, or even their self-constituted representatives, need never have been consulted, or their signatures obtained. The President himself, might of his own mere motion, dictate the terms of a treaty to the Senate, and by the ratification of that body, it becomes binding upon all who never saw or assented to it.

"*Fourth*, But this doctrine, which we candidly confess to be beyond our comprehension, does not seem, to our feeble intellects, to have any bearing upon the question. For surely, if the President and Senate are empowered to negotiate and make our treaties for us, without our assent or knowledge, it does not seem very clear, how this power, in this particular so unlimited, can be prevented from at least listening to our objections, and at their good pleasure substituting one less offensive, if they please."

Fifth. Under this head, Mr Ross refers to the act of the United States in annulling the Creek treaty made in February, 1825, at the Indian Springs, in which he takes occasion to say, that if a like course had been taken in another, meaning the treaty of Payne's Landing with the Seminoles, and against which the body of the tribe protested, the blood and treasure expended in Florida would have been saved.

Mr Ross proceeds :—"This last treaty, which may be found in the seventh volume of the laws of the United States, page 782, contains this remarkable preamble :

"'Whereas a treaty was concluded at the Indian Springs, on the 12th day of February last (1825), between Commissioners on the part of the United States and a portion of the Creek nation, by which an extensive district of country was ceded to the United States :

"'And whereas, a great majority of the chiefs and warriors of the said nation have protested against the execution of the said treaty, and have represented that the same was signed, on their part, by persons having no sufficient authority to form treaties, or to make cessions, and that the stipulations in said treaty are therefore wholly void :

"'And whereas the United States are unwilling that difficulties should exist in the said nation, which may eventually lead to an intestine war, and are still more unwilling that any cessions of land should be made to them, unless with the fair understanding and full assent of the tribe making such cession, and for a just and adequate consideration, it being the policy of the United States in all their intercourse with the Indians to treat them justly and liberally, as becomes the relative situation of the parties.'"

Such was the preamble of the treaty of January 24th, 1826 : the first article of which declared the previous treaty to be "null and void to every intent and purpose whatever, and any right and claim arising from the same is hereby cancelled and surrendered."

"These were historical facts with which we were familiar, and we had not been informed what had occurred since that period to prevent a similar action under circumstances not similar, only because the case more imperatively demanded such action. We could not understand why the Creeks should be relieved from the burden of an unjust, and illegal, because unauthorised compact, and we should be held to one even more destitute of any semblance of authority. We could not understand why, if President Adams possessed the constitutional power to negotiate such an arrangement as we have just adverted to, how, or why, President Jackson or President Van Buren, would transcend their legitimate functions by instituting an inquiry into the truth of our allegations, and laying the result of such investigation before the Congress of the United States.

Nor could we comprehend, what there was so irregular or improper in our requests, as to furnish a reason for debarring us from our accustomed official intercourse with the President, or War Department.

"You will perceive that our only object has been, to obtain a fair arrangement upon terms which our nation can approve, to be negotiated with persons whom they have authorised to act on our behalf. Our object has been an honest one and sincerely expressed. We had hoped that the Government of the United States would listen to our representations. We knew that they had been led by similar false suggestions and fraudulent devices, into the expenditure of four times the amount of money, in attempting to settle their differences with the Indians by force of arms, which would have sufficed to accomplish all our desires, without exasperation of feeling, and without bloodshed. We asked that an instrument should not be called a treaty obligatory upon us, to which we never yielded, directly or by implication, any assent. We asked if we were to be driven from our homes and our native country, we should not be denounced as treaty breakers, but have at least the consolation of being recognised as the unoffending, unresisting Indian, despoiled of his property, driven from his domestic fireside, exiled from his home, by the mere dint of superior power. We ask that deeds shall be called by their right names.

"We distinctly disavow all thoughts, all desire, to gratify any feelings of resentment. That possessions acquired and objects attained by unjust and unrighteous means will, sooner or later, prove a curse to those who have thus sought them, is a truth we have been taught by that holy religion which was brought to us by our white brethren. Years, nay centuries may elapse before the punishment may follow the offence; but the volume of history and the sacred Bible assure us, that the period will certainly arrive. We would with Christian sympathy labour to avert the wrath of Heaven from the United States, by imploring your Government to be just. The first of your ancestors who visited, as strangers, the land of the Indian, professed to be apostles of Christ, and to be attracted by a desire to extend the blessings of his religion to the ignorant native. Thousands among you still proclaim the same noble and generous interest in our welfare; but will the untutored savage believe the white man's professions, when he feels that by his practices he has become an outcast and an exile? Can he repose with confidence in the declarations of philanthropy and sincere charity, when he sees the professors of the religion which he is invited to embrace, the foremost in acts of oppression and outrage?

"Most sincerely and ardently do we pray that the noble example of William Penn may be more generally followed, and that the rich rewards which attended his exertions may be showered upon the heads of those, who like him, never outraged the rights, or despoiled the property of the Indian. To such, among their highest earthly comforts, and among the assurances of still higher enjoyments hereafter, will be the blessing and prayer of the friendless native.

"I have the honour to be, sir,
most respectfully your ob't servant,
"JNO. ROSS."

We have considered it due to the Cherokees, in this afflicting crisis of their affairs, to let their chief be heard.

Happily for the parties the removal was effected without an appeal to arms. This harmonious result was produced by the parties agreeing to adopt such modifications in the offensive instrument, as to make it, if not altogether acceptable to the Cherokees, yet preferable to the alternative of a bloody conflict, and perhaps their extermination.   Omitting any reflections of our own, upon the means adopted to carry out the policy of removing the Cherokees, and the other south and southwestern tribes from the east to the west of the Mississippi, we stop long enough to express our opinion that their present position is better adapted, under every view which we have been able to take of the subject, to their advancement in civilisation, in the arts, and in religion, than was their former one, on this side the Mississippi.   But we are no less sincere in our belief, that before these remnants of a noble race can be thoroughly imbued with the elements essential to work out such a change, an indispensable one must be superadded—and that is, the element of *equality with ourselves.*   Their right in the soil must be made indestructible, and their relations to this Union must be so changed as to bind their territory, and themselves, to our Union, and to our people, by precisely the same ties that connect Iowa, or Ouisconsin to it, including the same constitutional privilege of an ultimate annexation to the United States, as a member of the Confederacy.   Such relations, and such only, it is our firm conviction, can perpetuate the Indians as a race, and produce upon their future destiny all those blessings which the just and the humane, have been engaged for more than two hundred years, but in vain, in endeavouring to confer upon this hapless race.   And unless our present relations with the Indian Confederacy, for such it is at present, are changed, and some such new ones are adopted as we have glanced at, it requires no very great foresight to see that a heavy retribution awaits us, in the longest, most costly, and bloodiest war, that has ever yet afflicted us.

The Seminoles, after a long and bloody conflict with us, arising on their part out of a like cause of discontent—viz.: the recognition of a treaty by the United States, which the body of that tribe assert they had no agency in making, and to the terms of which they refused to submit, and against the demand for their acquiescence of which they rebelled—have also gone West, and now form an integral part of the Indian territory west of the Mississippi.

The Creeks had previously emigrated, and though reluctantly, yet without resistance. The map of the Indian Territory which is appended to this work, will point out the location of their present abode, its length, breadth, etc., and number of Indians within it ; as will another map the positions occupied by the various tribes on this side the Mississippi prior to their removal.

The actual condition of the tribes who have been removed to the Western territory, is in the highest degree flattering. The Superintendent of the territory in his Report for 1837, in speaking of the Creeks in the vicinity of Fort Gibson, says : " They dwell in good, comfortable farm houses, have fine gardens, orchards, and raise forty to fifty thousand bushels of corn more than is sufficient for their own consumption. They furnish large quantities to the commissariat at Fort Gibson annually, and contributed greatly in supplying the late emigrants. They raise also more stock than is necessary for their own use, and carry on a considerable trade with the garrison, in grain, stock, vegetables, poultry, eggs, fruit, etc. There are several traders among them to supply their wants, which are as many and as various as those of the most comfortable livers of our own citizens. Two of these traders are natives, who do considerable business, selling eighteen or twenty thousand dollars' worth of goods annually." Of the Cherokees, he says: "They are more advanced in agriculture than the other tribes of the Superintendency. The number of farms in this nation is estimated at between ten and eleven hundred. *There are no Cherokees who follow the chase for a living;* the nation is divided into farmers, traders, stock-raisers, and labourers. The productions of the farms are, corn, oats, potatoes of both kinds, beans, peas, pumpkins, and melons. The great profit of a Cherokee farmer is from his corn, his horses, his cattle, and his hogs. Some of the Cherokees have taken and fulfilled contracts for the garrison at Fort Gibson, and for subsisting emigrant Indians, to the amount of forty to sixty thousand dollars, without purchasing any article except in the Indian country.

"They have several valuable salt springs, but for want of capital and skill they are not profitable. At the Grand Saline, on the River Neosho, forty miles above Fort Gibson, they are making eighty bushels of excellent salt per day, for five days in the week; but the manufacture is carried on at a considerable expense for fuel, labour, hauling, etc.

"The Choctaw nation, including the late Chickasaw emigrants, white men married in the nation, and negroes, number about fifteen thousand. It affords me pleasure to say that this nation is still in a state of rapid improvement. They almost all have *given up the chase* for a living, and are engaged principally in the cultivation of the soil and raising stock. It would be impossible to estimate the number of acres or farms in cultivation, as nearly all have fields well enclosed, and raise corn, potatoes, peas, beans, pumpkins, melons, and those settled along Red River raise large quantities of cotton, more than sufficient for their own consumption.

" It would be impossible to estimate the number of horses, cattle, sheep, and hogs, owned in the nation. The country is so well adapted to the raising of stock, and so prolific has been the increase, that they have furnished large quantities to the Creek contractors, without apparently diminishing the main stock, and they assure me they have an abundance to stock the Chickasaws, upon their arrival at their new homes.

" There are six native traders, all of whom appear to be doing considerable business ; and as the natives appear to be turning their attention to these pursuits, there will soon be enough native traders in the nation to be able to dispense with white ones altogether. There are several native mechanics who have learned their trades in a regular way, some of whom have been furnished by the Choctaw Academy. There are a few very ingenious men, wholly self-taught, who work well in wood and iron, make waggons, wheels, chairs, etc., and do coarse iron work. One public blacksmith, and three strikers, and two public teachers are natives ; and as the Academy is sending home some well-educated men, most of the schools will soon be taught by natives.

" The Choctaw nation embraces a large tract, affording a superabundance of rich soil, well adapted to the cultivation of cotton, tobacco, corn, wheat, rye, oats, and every kind of vegetable. The country is variegated with prairies and woodlands, swamps, barren ridges, and cane-brakes. The timber is ash, oak, hickory, walnut, gum, hackberry, cotton-wood, cedar, bois d'arc ; on the ridges grow immense quantities of pine, of an excellent quality for building. Coal abounds in great quantities in various parts of the nation.

" The Senecas, and mixed bands of Senecas and Shawanoes are labouring together, and without the

fostering care of an agent, they exhibit great signs of
improvement. They cultivate the soil and raise stock;
they make corn, oats, wheat, rye, and garden vegetables.
No tribe owns more horses, cattle and hogs, than these
people, in proportion to their population. They live in
good hewed log cabins; their gardens and fields are
enclosed with rail fences. They have some merchants and
mechanics among them, and under the care of a good
agent, promise to become, in time, a prosperous and
intelligent community. The grist and saw-mill erected
by the government, is in fine condition, since it has been
repaired, and more than supplies the wants of these two
bands."

The following extracts are from the report of the
principal distributing agent, for the same year :—

"The country inhabited by the Choctaws is extensive
and exceedingly fertile; the face of the country is generally
high, or what is termed rolling; some parts of it are
mountainous; the whole is well watered and has plenty of
timber; there are some prairies, which, as well as the
timber lands, are a first rate soil. The whole country is
adapted to corn and stock; the northern and western
portions to corn and wheat, and other small grains; the
southern part to cotton. Many of them have become
extensive farmers, cultivating cotton and corn, and
possessing large stocks of cattle; they have cotton gins,
mills of different kinds, as well as shops and mechanics;
in fine, it may be truly said, that the Choctaws are rapidly
advancing in agricultural knowledge and in the mechanic
arts.

"In travelling through the Choctaw country, one sees
little, if any difference, in an agricultural point of view,
from new frontier white settlements; their cabins are
constructed with equal order and substantiality, and

apparently, with as many comforts and conveniences; their fields are under good fences; they have gardens and cultivate fruit trees, are civil and attentive to travellers, understand the value of money, and all of them, or nearly so, have in their houses the common luxuries of coffee, tea, sugar, etc. I have no hesitation in saying that, for all the comforts of domestic life, their residences are ample and abundant, and far better than could possibly have been anticipated, prior to their removal, in so short a time."

Of the Cherokees, he says: "This tribe has been allotted a very extensive as well as a very fine tract of country. Those parts over which I have travelled possess a soil of very superior quality, adapted to the production of wheat, small grain of various kinds, and corn of the largest growth. The whole country is finely and abundantly timbered, and well watered, and the climate is exceedingly favourable to stock.

"The greater portion of the Cherokees, West, are farmers, have good and comfortable houses, and live, many of them, as well, and as genteelly, as the better class of farmers in the United States. Their resources are equal, if not superior, to one-fourth of the tillers of the soil in the United States.

"The section of country set apart for the Creeks and Seminoles, is about the same in extent with that of the Choctaws, but not so mountainous. The soil is considered to be equal in fertility, to any in the south-western section of the country. It is well watered, and has plenty of timber; there are some prairies, which however are of great advantage to the settler, the soil being rich and easy to cultivate, and they are very profitable for raising stock.

"The Creeks are a corn-growing people. Those that have been in the country some years, raise corn in large quantities; some of the principal farmers crib from five to ten thousand bushels in a season. They do not raise much stock, nor are they, as a people, so far advanced in civilisation as the Cherokees and Choctaws, though, as agriculturists, so far as raising corn, they excel either of the above named tribes. They raise stock sufficient for their own consumption, but none of any consequence for sale."

Of the Senecas and Shawanoes, the same officer reports: "These tribes inhabit a high, healthy, well-watered and timbered country; the soil rich and productive. They emigrated in 1832, are agriculturists, and are mainly engaged in that pursuit; they raise wheat and corn, and their country is well adapted to raising stock, of which they have considerable herds. Being remote, however, from a market, their cropping is confined to their own wants, and for these they provide liberally of all the substantials of life. The use of coffee, tea, and sugar, is common among them. Their cabins are well constructed, combining both comfort and convenience; and their arrangements in farming have the appearance of neatness and order; they have mills, shops, and some good mechanics. Their resources are abundant, and their condition apparently happy."

The Quapaws "emigrated in the fall of 1834; their country, in point of soil, water, timber, and health, is similar to, and equally as good as that of their neighbours the Cherokees, Senecas, and Senecas and Shawanoes. They are not so far advanced in civilisation as the several tribes of Indians above named; but a more honest, quiet, peaceable people, are not to be found in any section of the Indian country. They are industrious, and exceedingly desirous of making for themselves a comfortable home."

The Osages have "made but little progress towards civilisation; their subsistence mainly depends upon the game of the country. They raise some corn and beans, but the culture is rude. They raise no stock; they obtain their horses from those Indians residing far to the south and west of them. Their country possesses excellent soil, is well watered and timbered."

The sub-agent on the Osage River reported within the same year: "The Potawattimies are now in the act of emigrating to their land on the Osage River. Such of them as have arrived, are preparing to erect log houses, to fence and plough their fields, and show a disposition to adopt exclusively agricultural habits.

"The Weas and Piankeshaws have generally comfortable log cabins, fields fenced and ploughed, cultivated by animal power; own oxen, cows, hogs, horses, fowls, etc.; also agricultural implements and domestic utensils. They are rapidly improving in comfort and agricultural pursuits, and show a disposition to wholly abandon the chase as a means of subsistence.

"The Peorias and Kaskaskias have better houses than those above named; own more domestic animals, have a greater proportion of ploughed land, etc., but are, perhaps, in regard to general improvement, more stationary.

"The Ottawas, recently arrived in their country, have neat, hewed log cabins, fields fenced and ploughed, own domestic animals, agricultural implements, domestic utensils, etc., and are rapidly improving. Of all these tribes it may be remarked, that they raise a surplus of produce, increase in the acquisition of useful property, and evince a desire to adopt the manners and customs of the whites."

These data, selected from the earliest evidences of the prosperity of the emigrated Indians, show with what facility they adopted the new life, appointed them in their new homes. Subsequent accounts show that their improvement has been progressive. The Choctaws have a printing press, from which they have issued, up to September, 1842, thirty-three thousand impressions, or more than three millions of pages, consisting of translations of books, pamphlets, etc. They have also contributed ten thousand dollars to the building of a Central College, where they intend to complete the education of the Choctaw youth, and prepare teachers for their primary schools. Their country is divided into four judicial districts, in each of which there are judges inferior and superior, with all the necessary officers of justice. Religious and temperance societies abound, and trade is carried on with spirit. The population of the four districts which comprise their territory, is seventeen thousand. There are many missionaries among them, who are well supported. In one district there are eighteen, of whom fourteen are of the Methodist Episcopal Church.

The Western Territory is now peopled by a number of tribes:—the Choctaws, Creeks, Seminoles, Cherokees, Chickasaws, Senecas, Shawanoese, Quapaws, Weas, Piankeshaws, Peorias, Kaskaskias, Ottawas, Delawares, Kickapoos, Iowas, Saukies and Foxes, Kansas, Ottos, Missouris, Omahas, Pawnees, and Osages. The last six named tribes, were occupants of parts of the country before it was selected as a permanent residence for the Indians, and all the others are emigrants removed thither by the Government. Each tribe has a separate district, guaranteed to it forever, and over which it exercises a local jurisdiction, through its own chiefs and council; and there is a confederated government over the whole, administered by a general council, to which each tribe sends representatives, and whose laws are binding when sanctioned by the President of the United States. An advisory power is exercised by the United States, through her agents; but this interference will be gradually withdrawn, as the Indians acquire skill in legislation. Thus far the plan has succeeded well, and the experiment may be considered as having resulted satisfactorily.

In the suggestions we have thrown out, we have purposely avoided burthening our plan, for the improvement of the condition of the Indians, with details, because we are indifferent as to the measures that may be employed, provided the principles be observed; and also because the extreme simplicity of our scheme is such as to require but little legislation. The difficulty lies, not in planting, but in clearing the ground. The field is occupied by a bold and well organised corps who will resist all change. The numerous body of stipendiaries and speculators, who find a profitable, and some of them an honest, employment, under the present state of things, would throw every obstacle in the way of reform. Thousands of individuals would be ejected from the Indian country, whose interest it is to keep the savage in his present condition; and hundreds of thousands of dollars would be retained in the treasury of the United States, which are now used to debauch the Indian, or to enrich those who thrive upon his ignorance and his ruin. We should not be particular as to the form of the remedy, provided it be such as would wholly withdraw the patronage of the Government from this class of persons, and oblige them to abandon the Indian country.

We have supposed that the pastoral state would be that which would at first be adopted. But we do not propose to keep the tribes in that condition. From feeding herds to cultivating the soil, the transition is easy and obvious, and we have seen, in the example of the

Indians in the Western Territory, that it is rapid. The Indian women already raise corn, beans, and pumpkins. If restrained from wandering, provided with permanent habitations, and secured from being plundered, their industry would be quickened and their economy improved. The products of their husbandry would become more various ; they would rise in usefulness, importance, and influence ; and as the inducements to train the boys from infancy to the use of arms shall be decreased, the mothers would lead them into the fields, and they would learn the use of the axe, the hoe, and the plough.

Among the men there would be some who would immediately turn their attention to rural employments. We have seen that this has been the case whenever a tribe has become stationary, and enjoyed a season of repose from war. However repugnant the toils of husbandry may be to the majority, there are always some men of pacific disposition, who would slide easily into the habits of civilisation. There are also in all our tribes, men of superior capacity, persons of sagacity and prudence, who would adapt themselves to any circumstances in which they might be placed. The annals of these tribes exhibit, in a wide expanse of moral darkness, many gleams of the most exhilarating intellectual light. There have been among the Indians, examples of genius, of vigorous thought, of patriotism, and of sound moral feeling, which commend this race to our sympathies, as men of like passions with ourselves, and as possessed of capacities susceptible of the highest degree of refinement. Such men as Brant, Red Jacket, Tecumseh, and Corn Plant ; Ongpatinger, chief of the Omahas, and the gallant Young Pawnee, Petalesharro ; Major Ridge, John Ridge, Elias Boudinot, the Hickses, and John Ross ; Sequoyah and Opothle Yoholo, would never sink into idle drones.

We have an example of that benevolence which assimilates so beautifully with true courage, and which occurs in the history of Tecumseh, who when a young man, on one of his earliest warlike expeditions interfered with his companions to save a prisoner from torture, and through whose influence, it is probable that the practice of torturing captives was discontinued among the North-Western tribes.

The affecting story of Totapia, a Choctaw mother, known to the whites by the name of Jenny, related by the Rev. Dr Morse in his report, exhibits a touching example of the strength and sensibility of maternal affection, and shows a depth and tenderness of feeling in the Indian woman, which, in a Roman, or a Grecian matron, would have been rendered immortal by the poet and historian. She was the widow of a Choctaw, who, having slain one of his own tribe, was pursued by the relatives of the deceased, and put to death according to the Indian law. After the death of her husband she settled near St Francisville, in Louisiana, where she lived reputably with four or five children, of whom Hoctanlubbee or Tom, her son, was the eldest.

At the age of twenty-five her son murdered an *old* Indian ; for which act, according to the unalterable law of the nation, his life was demanded, and he was sentenced to die.   The day of his execution was fixed, and had arrived, and the relatives and friends both of the murdered and of the murderer, with others, a mingled throng, were assembled after their usual manner, and all things were ready for inflicting the criminal sentence of the law.   At this moment of strong and mingled feeling, Jenny, the mother, pressed through the crowd, to the spot where her son stood, by the instruments prepared to take from him his life.   She then addressed the chiefs and the

company, demanding the life of her son, offering in its
stead her own. Her plea was this: "He is young. He
has a wife, children, brothers, sisters, all looking to him for
council and support. I am old. I have only a few days
to live at most, and can do but little more for my family.
Nor is it strictly just—it is rather a shame—to take *a new
shirt for an old one.*"

The magnanimous offer of the devoted mother was
accepted, and a few hours were allowed her to prepare
for death. She repaired immediately to the house of a
lady, Mrs T., who had been her kind and liberal friend,
and without divulging what had occurred, said she came
to beg a winding sheet and coffin for her son. Not
suspecting the arrangement of Totapia, to preserve her
son, the lady acceded to her request. When asked in
relation to the length of the coffin and grave-clothes,
the Choctaw mother replied, "Make them to suit my size,
and they will answer for my son."

"Soon after Jenny had left Mrs T. for the camp,
where all things were ready for her execution, a messenger
arrived in haste, and informed Mrs T. of what was passing
in camp, and that Jenny was immediately to die. She
hastened to the scene with the intention of rescuing her
friend; but Jenny the moment she saw her carriage
coming, at a distance, imagining doubtless what was
her object, standing in her grave, caught the muzzle of
the gun, the prepared instrument of her death, and
pointing it to her heart, entreated the executioner to do
his duty. He obeyed, and she fell dead."

We are not told how it happened that the son suffered
his mother to die for him, or whether he could have
prevented it. It seems, however, that he was despised
for permitting it, and that his own conscience goaded
him. The friends of the old man whom he had murdered,

taunted him : "You coward ! you let your mother die for you ; you are afraid to die." Unable to endure all this, he stabbed a son of his former victim ; but not until five years had elapsed since the death of his mother.

"He returned home with indications of triumph, brandishing his bloody knife, and without waiting for inquiry, confessed what he had done. He told his Indian friends, that he would not live to be called a coward. 'I have been told,' he said, 'that I fear to die. Now you shall see that I can die like a man.' A wealthy planter whose house he passed, he invited to see how he could die. This was on Sunday. Monday, at twelve o'clock, was the hour he appointed for this self-immolation."

"Here," says the lady who gives this information, who was present and relates what she saw, "a scene was presented which baffles all description. As I approached, Tom was walking forward and back again, still keeping in his hand the bloody knife. With all his efforts to conceal it, he discovered marks of an agitated mind. The sad group present consisted of about ten men, and as many females ; the latter with sorrowful countenances, were employed in making an over-shirt, for Tom's burial. The men, all except two brothers of Tom, were smoking their pipes with apparent unconcern. Several times Tom examined his gun, and remained silent. His grave had been dug the day before, and he had laid himself down in it, to see if it suited as to length and breadth.

"No one had demanded his death ; for all who were interested, and would have considered their honour and duty concerned in it, resided at a distance of forty or fifty miles. The death song was repeated, as was the shaking of hands. Both were again repeated, the third and last time. Immediately after Tom stepped up to his wife, a young woman of eighteen, with an infant in her arms, and another little child two or three years old, standing by her side, and presented to her the bloody knife, which till now he had kept in his hand. She averted her face to conceal a falling tear; but recovering herself, with a faint forced smile, took it. His sister was sitting by the side of his wife, wholly absorbed in grief, apparently insensible to what was passing; her eyes vacant, fixed on some distant object. Such a perfect picture of woe I never beheld. His pipe he gave to a young brother, who struggled hard to conceal his emotions. He then drank a little whisky and water, dashed the bottle on the ground, sung a few words in the Choctaw language, and with a jumping, dancing step, hurried to his grave. His gun was so fixed by the side of a young sapling as to enable him to take his own life. No one, he had declared, should take it from him. These preparations and ceremonies being now completed, he gave the necessary touch to the apparatus, the gun was discharged, and its contents passed through his heart. He instantly fell dead to the earth. The females sprang to the lifeless body. Some held his head, others his hands and feet, and others knelt at his side. He had charged them to show no signs of grief while he lived, lest it should shake his resolution. As far as possible they obeyed. Their grief was restrained until he was dead. It then burst forth in a torrent, and their shrieks and lamentations were loud and undissembled."

These scenes are fraught with melancholy interest and instruction. To the philanthropist and Christian they depict in glowing colours the debasing and destructive influence of that superstition, which pervades the savage mind, and offers the most formidable barrier to the reception of the principles of social improvement, and appeal most eloquently in behalf of this deluded race; while they show in the neglected waste of the savage mind a soil rich in the native elements of a noble character. The woman who with such prompt courage and devoted fondness could lay down her life for her son, was capable, under a better culture, of the noblest sacrifices of patriotism or Christian duty. The man who, though he faltered in principle in permitting his mother to die for him, showed in the sequel, the same keen sense of shame and desire of public approbation, which leads, in the most refined communities, to the sacrifice of life, under mistaken notions of honour; and the bereaved women who wept over his corpse, evinced all the sensibility which characterises the most tender of the sex. Deluded as they all were, we recognise in their acts and their affliction, natures kindred to our own, and impulses in which we sympathise.

We have already commented on the beautiful display of feminine loveliness in the character of Pocahontas; but that instance is not without a parallel. We quote the following incident from the *Baltimore American.*

"The committee on Indian Affairs, in the late House of Representatives, reported a Bill allowing a pension for life to Milly, an Indian woman, of the Creek tribe, daughter of the celebrated prophet and chief Francis, who was executed by order of General Jackson, in the Seminole war of 1817-18. The subject was brought to the notice of the committee by the Secretary of War, at the instance of Lieut. Col. Hitchcock, who communicated the particulars of the incident upon which the recommendation to the favour of the Government was founded.

"Milly, at the age of sixteen, when her nation was at war with the United States, and her father was one of the most decided and indefatigable enemies of the white people, saved the life of an American citizen, who had been taken prisoner by her tribe. The captive was bound to a tree, and the savage warriors, with their rifles, were dancing around him, preparatory to putting him to death. The young Indian girl, filled with pity for the devoted prisoner, besought her father to spare him; but the chief declined to interfere, saying that the life of the prisoner was in the hands of his captors, whose right it was to put him to death. She then turned to the warriors, and implored them to forbear their deadly purpose. But she was repulsed; and one of them, much enraged, told her that he had lost two sisters in the war, and the prisoner must die. Her intercession, however, continued. She persevered in entreaties, and used all the arts of persuasion which her woman's nature suggested; and she finally succeeded in saving his life, on condition that the young white man should adopt the Indian dress, and become one of the tribe.

"It appears from the information communicated by Col. Hitchcock, that some time after this event, the white man sought his benefactress in marriage, but she declined, and subsequently married one of her own people. Her husband is now dead. Her father was put to death in the war of 1817-18, and her mother and sister have since died. She is now friendless and poor, residing amongst her people in their new country, near the mouth of Verdigris River. She has three children (a boy and two girls), all too young to provide for themselves, and consequently dependent upon their mother for support.

"The committee thought that the occasion presented by this case was a suitable one, and not only to reward a meritorious act, but also to show the Indian tribes how mercy and humanity are appreciated by the Government. The grant of a pension, with a clear exposition of the grounds of its allowance, would have a salutary influence, it was believed, upon savage customs in future. A Bill was accordingly reported, to allow to Milly a pension of ninety-six dollars per annum, or eight dollars per month, for life."

We shall not multiply these instances, but refer the reader to the Biographical sections of our work, where abundant evidence will be found of the capacity of the aboriginal American. By carefully comparing these, it will be seen, that not only in boldness and cunning, but in all the nobler attributes of wisdom and generosity, the Indian mind has given evidence of a congenial soil.

These instances show that there are intellects among the Indians, not only capable of civilisation, but eminently qualified for the civil state. One or more such men would be found in every tribe, who, perceiving that the warpath was no longer the road to distinction, would aim at acquiring superiority through some other avenue. The season for political competition not having yet arrived, the only means of distinction would be wealth; and the glory of accumulating the bloody trophies of the battlefield would be exchanged for the boast of broad fields and numerous herds. The few, possessed of prudence and foresight, or desiring eminence, would see at once the advantages of agriculture, and would become farmers. The example would be salutary, and one after another would desire to possess the comforts and the independence which crown the labours of the husbandman. The best and most influential men would be the first to lead the way in this reformation; and every man who became a farmer would be a powerful advocate of the cause, because it would be his interest to diminish the number of the idle and non-producing class, who must depend on the public for subsistence, or disturb the peace by crime and violence.

To hasten this result, to hold out a reward for industry, and to provide for a more advanced state of society than that which we have been contemplating, it should be provided that whenever an Indian should have actually become a farmer, and should for a specified number of years have tilled the soil, a tract of land should be granted to him, the title to which should be a life estate to himself, and a fee-simple to his descendants. By this provision portions of the land would be converted into private property, and the remainder might be vested in the nation whenever they should have a government capable of properly disposing of it.

In this way the Indian would be allured by his interest, and led to self-elevation. We would deprive him of his natural liberty only so long as should be necessary to bring about that lucid interval, in which he would become sensible of his true condition, and apprised of the means held out for his redemption; and we would leave it to himself to seek out his own further advancement in his own way. In this we should pursue the plan of Nature. The primitive nations were not precociously instructed by their Creator in the whole circle of human knowledge, but it was left for them and their descendants to discover gradually the wealth and resources of the world benefi-cently given them, and to increase in learning by an easy and healthful gradation.

The attempt to civilise the roving bands, by reason, by the mere force of truth, or by any abstract sense of duty, has always been, and will continue to be abortive. The physical impediments must first be removed. Among white men, Christianity, literature, and the arts have never flourished during a period of anarchy, or civil war. In those countries where the peasantry are oppressed, and have no rights, property, or education, they are degraded and ferocious; and if the passions of their savage nature are not developed in deeds of carnage, it is because they are bridled by the strong arm of power. If we trace the nations of Europe from their former state of barbarism to their present moral elevation, we shall find the same causes to have always operated. The first step has always been the acquisition of permanent habitations, and the consequent love of country, and of home. Domestic comforts warmed into life the social virtues. The possession of property followed, and then personal and civil rights one after another were conceived. Then emancipation from their chiefs ensued; and political rights began to be demanded. The state of war became inconvenient. It was now the interest of the honest and industrious to protect themselves against plunder and violence; and deeds of murder and robbery ceased to be considered heroic. Commerce between nations softened prejudice, produced the interchange of commodities, encouraged the arts, and enlarged the stock of knowledge. And lastly, hand in hand, came education and religion.

The ministers of the Gospel and the schoolmaster have been powerful agents in these changes; but they have never marched in the van. They form an efficient corps in the main body, but their business is to secure and improve the acquisitions which bone and muscle, and skill and courage, have obtained. As the rifle and the axe must first subdue the forest, before the husbandman can cultivate the soil, so must the strong arm of the Government produce *peace*, enforce obedience, and organise a system of civil rights and restraints, before the mild precepts of the Gospel and the fructifying streams of knowledge can be made to pervade the wilderness, and teach the desert to blossom as the rose.

The spirit of the age calls aloud for a change in

relations with the Indians.   There is a general movement
throughout the civilised world, in favour of liberal thought,
free principles, and the dissemination of knowledge.
Every Government in Europe is trembling, and some of
them are convulsed with actual revolution, in consequence
of the universal spread of intelligence among the people.
The contest between ignorance and light, and between
despotism and liberty, is going forward throughout
Christendom.   Everywhere the spirit of improvement is
abroad; and the same spirit pervades all ranks, and every
department of human thought and industry.   In religion,
politics, literature, and the mechanic arts, men have
resolved to think for themselves.   They will neither be
machines to do the work that steam-engines can do for
them, nor will they be slaves of idle, nor the instruments
of artful rulers, in Church or State.

Ours is moreover an economical age, when nothing is
valued that is not useful or practical, and when little value
is placed upon mere names.   At such a time, with the
eyes of the civilised world upon us, we cannot believe
that a people, such as we are, can deliberately propose
to consign a vast region to eternal sterility, and to support
a multitude of human beings in idleness, ignorance,
intemperance, and bloodshed.   We are not so wedded to
names, as to believe that we are obliged to keep up
a state of things which we know to be wrong and
impolitic, merely because it exists, and has existed; nor
can we adopt the maxims of legitimacy so far as to feel
ourselves bound to respect that which has nothing to
recommend it but its long continuance, and nothing to
support it but the prejudices of ignorance and the
selfishness of interested individuals.

This whole subject must soon occupy the serious
attention of Congress and the people; and when all the

facts shall be presented, in a connected view, it will be seen that our existing policy must be radically changed or wholly abandoned; and the question to be decided will be, whether the savage tribes shall be driven beyond our frontiers, and left to their fate, or be subjected to the wholesome constraint of our laws, or connected, by ties of a territorial sort, such as connect Iowa, Ouisconsin, etc., to this nation.   The indolent and the timid may shrink from the second alternative, because it is novel, and bears the semblance of violence; humanity shudders at the former, but greets the latter as the only scheme in which justice and mercy meet and mingle, and which has in it all the elements required for the preservation and happiness of the remnants of the aboriginal race.   The statements of the interested, or the apprehensions of honest prejudice, may for a while embarrass the decision; but a magnanimous people will hear the evidence on both sides; and we have no fears as to the wisdom or the justice of the nation, in any case where its verdict shall be deliberately made up, and solemnly recorded.

INDEX

A

Adair, English trader and author, 74
Adams, President, 71, 166, 212, 321;
  addresses Congress on Indian
  affairs, 203-4. See also Index,
  Vols. I. and II.
Agawam, 282
Agriculture, advance of, 300, 305 *et seq.*
Alabama, 214. See also Index, Vol. II.
Alcohol, introduced, 167; evil effects of
  on the Red man, 242, 264
Algonquin tribe, 10, 27, 29, 56, 61.
  See also Index, Vol. II.
Alphabet, Cherokee, 300, 308. See
  also Index, Vol. I.
American Government's friendly rela-
  tions with the tribes, 184, 185, 187,
  202
Amherst, Sir Jeffrey, at "Bloody
  Bridge" Battle, 39
Amidas, Captain Philip, 112
Ancestors' bones, Indian regard for, 233
Annawon, executed, 282
Annuities to Indian tribes, 194-96
"Anonymous Conqueror" (quoted), 100
Argall, Captain, captures Pocahontas,
  120
Arichares, 58
Arkansas, 232. See also Index, Vol. II.
Articles of Cession, 214
Assiniboin River, 58
Assiniboins, 57, 58
Atkinson, General, 66; and "Red
  Bird's" surrender, 71. See also
  Index, Vols. I. and II.
Attakullakulla, Cherokee chief, 296
Axajacath, King, 100

B

"Backwoodsmen," 155; life of, 156-158
Barbour, Hon. James, U.S. Secretary
  of War, 66. See also Index, Vols.
  I. and II.
Barlow, Captain, 112
Barter, mode of, 245, 246

Battles of—
  "Bloody Bridge," 39
  Braddock, 236, 295
  Point Pleasant, 43
  Sandusky Plains, 293
  The Thames, 44
  Tippecanoe, 45. See also Index,
    Vols. I. and II.
Baylie's *Memoir of Plymouth* (quoted),
  123
Bible, influence of, on Indian character,
  260, 264, 266, 269, 272, 273;
  translated into the Indian tongue,
  274
"Blackbird," Maha chief, burial place
  of, 86. See also Index, Vol. I.
Blackfeet, 11. See also Index, Vol. II.
"Bloody Bridge" Battle, 39. See also
  under "Battles," Vol. I.
Blue River, 190
Bolling, John, and Pocahontas portrait,
  x.
Bolling, Col. Robert, ix.
Bolling, Thomas, of Cobbs, x.
Boudinot, Elias, 309, 310. See also
  Index, Vol. I.
Boundaries, State, 299
Bowles, and Chief McGillivray, 304.
  See also Index, Vol. I.
Braddock, Battle of, 236, 295. See also
  under "Battles," Vol. I.
Bradstreet, General, relieves Detroit,
  38, 39
Brant, Joseph, Mohawk chief, 153; his
  patriotism and intrigues, 169, 173.
  See also Index, Vol. II.
Brierton, John (quoted), 115
British agents and intrigues, 164, 168,
  285, 288, 292
British conquests in India, 106
British forces at "Bloody Bridge"
  Battle, 39; Lake Huron, 51; de-
  feated, 184
British Government and U.S., 142, 152,
  165, 170
British military posts, 38, 168
Broadhead, Colonel, 289
Brownstown, 36

"Buckingham and Solebury," Watson's (quoted), 132
Bump, John, 282
Bureau, Indian, 240
van Buren, President, 316. See also Index, Vol. II.
Burial mounds, 85, 86, 233
Burk and Pocahontas (quoted), 120
Burning prisoners, 181
Butte des Morts, 53; Council at, 65. See also Index, Vol. I.

C

Cahokias, 47, 136. See also Index, Vol. II.
Canards River, 36
Canepitigo, Chief, 34
Cannibalism, 258
Cape Girardeau, 41
Cape of Good Hope, discovery of, 98
Caraminie, Chief, 67. See also "Caromanie," Vols. I. and II.
Careta, Indian Prince, and Vasco Nunez, 104
Carleton, Sir Guy, 174. See also Index, Vol. II.
Carolina, South, 235
Cartier, 16
Carver, celebrated traveller, 63, 73
Catawbas, 73. See also Index, Vol. II.
Catholic influence, 250
Cayugas, 30. See also Index, Vol. I.
Chalmer's *Political Annals* (quoted), 117
Champlain, 29, 30
Chandler, Mrs, 133
Charlevoix, French Government agent, 46, 231
Charters and Patents, 297
Chegoimegon Point, 40
Cherokee Alphabet, 300, 308. See also Index, Vol. I.
Cherokees, 10, 73; location, 77; language, 78; join English forces, 295; and independent government, 308; sign New Echota Treaty, 315. See also Index, Vols. I. and II.
Chew, Joseph, 171
Cheyenne, 11
Chickasaws, 10, 73, 78, 301. See also Index, Vol. I.
Chillicothe tribe, 43; Council of, 182. See also Index, Vol. I.
Chippeways, 39, 40, 56, 63. See also Index, Vols. I. and II.
Choctaw Academy, 327

Choctaws, 10, 73, 78, 301, 326-28; their Printing Press, 332. See also Index, Vols. I. and II.
Cholula City, 101, 102
"Christian Indians in New England," 275
Church, Captain, 281; and Tispaquin, 282
Civilising Indians, 268, 269 *et seq.*
Colden, 33
Colonies, boundaries of, 298
Colonists, Charters granted to, 297
Columbus, 99
Confederation, American, 297
Congress and Indian laws, 159-61, 162
Connecticut, Puritan colony, 124, 125
Converts, Indian, 255, 264, 273, 284, 285
Corn, Indian mode of growing, 246, 247
Cortez, Herman, 23, 99, 100, 101
Council Bluffs, 50. See also Index, Vols. I. and II.
Crawford, Col. William, 293; and Battle of Sandusky Plains, 293; burnt at the stake, 294. See also Index, Vol. I.
Creator, the, Indian concept of, 19
Creeks, 10; definition of name, 75; location, 73, 75, 325. See also Index, Vols. I. and II.
Cumberland, 235

D

Dacotahs, 57, 58, 228. See also Index, Vol. I.
Declaration of Independence, 192
Delawares (*Lenne Lenape*), 12, 32, 33, 35. See also Index, Vols. I. and II.
Descent, tribal, 17
Des Moines, 49
de Soto, 74. See also Index, Vol. II.
Detroit, British military post, 38; siege of, 38, 39. See also Index, Vol. I.
Detroit River, French established on, 51; Council of, 176
Dialects, Indian, 10, 12, 232
Diaz, Bernal, 102
Dickeson, Captain, 67
Discoverers, early, 97, 98, 99
Don Henry, Portuguese discoverer, 96
Dorchester, Lord (Sir Guy Carleton), 166; his speech to Indian Deputies, 174
Drake's *Life of Tecumseh* (quoted), 180; *Book of the Indians*, 274, 281, 282
Dubuque Mines, 50. See also Index, Vol. I.

E

Eahpawaunetoter, 59
" Eagle " family, 43. See also Index, Vol. I.
Echota Treaty, 310, 311, 317. See also Index, Vol. I.
Edwards, Territorial Governor, 176. See also Index, Vol. I.
Edwards, Moravian Missionary, 284
Eliot, John, Missionary, 272, 273, 274, 275. See also Index, Vol. I.
Elizabeth, Queen, grants Letters Patent, 112
Elliot, John, British agent, 172, 288, 292
Emigration, early Indian, 22
English colonists, 143, 275
Engraving, Indian, 267
European settlers, 271

F

Falls of St Anthony, 2 ; *Minnehaha*, 2, and *note*.
" False oats," 55
Famine among the tribes, 252, 254
Federal Union, 212, 214
Female chiefs, 73
Feuillestirees, Gens de la, 58
Five Nations, 30, 31. See also Index, Vol. I.
Flattening heads, 79. See also Index, Vol. II.
Folles Avoines, 53, 55. See also Index, Vol. II.
Foreign Missions, American, 266
Fort Chartres, 136
   Gibson, 325
   Meigs, 181
   Miami, 181
   de Quesne, 295. See also under " Forts," Vols. I. and II.
Fortifications, ancient, 88
Fox River, 52, 53
Foxes, location, 49, 50 ; war with Illini, 50 ; early accounts of, 51 ; join English forces, 51 ; attack French garrison on Detroit River, 51, 52 ; allied with Saukies, 237 ; in Western Territory, 332. See also Saukies
Francis, Chief, executed, 339
French Settlements at Kaskaskia, 135 ; in Illinois, 135, 136, 137, 138
French troops on the St Lawrence, 24, 29 ; on Detroit River, 51 ; at Natchez, 77
Fur traders, 143, 147, 241 ; dishonesty of, 242

G

Gagnier, murder of, 68, 71. See also Index, Vol. II.
Gallatin's *Synopsis of Indian Tribes*, 305
Gens de la Feuillestirees, 58
   du Lac, 58, 228
   du Large, 228
Georgia, 214, 215, 235 ; and Spanish invasion, 295 ; relations with Cherokee nation, 301
Georgia v. *Worcester* case, 224
Gesnall, Captain, 115
Gibbons, Major, 127, 281
Girardeau, Cape, 41
Girty, British agent, 166, 285, 288, 292. See also Index, Vol. II.
Glikhikan, Delaware chief, 290
Gnadenhutten village, 284, 289
Gomara, historian, 100
" Gookin, Master," historian and Indian Superintendent, 127, 276, 280
Gordon, Colonel, British officer, and Joseph Brant, 170
Government, Indian, United States scheme of, 237 *et seq.*
Grand Saline, 326
Grangranaemeo, 113
" Great Sun," 76
Gregory, Major, 51
Green Bay, British military post, 38. See also Index, Vol. I.
Greenville, Treaty of, 45, 161. See also Index, Vols. I. and II.
Grenville, Sir Richard, 112 ; sails for Virginia, 115

H

" *Ha, Ha* " (Falls of St Anthony), 2, and *note*
Hall's Essay on North American Indians, 83
Hammond, Mr, British Minister, 175
Harmar, General, 161. See also Index, Vol. I.
Harrison, General, 162, 176, 179. See also Index, Vols. I. and II.
Hartshorne, William, 172
Hawaiians, 257-265
Heckewelder, Moravian Missionary, 284, 289
Hennepin, 137. See also Index, Vol. II.
Hieroglyphical Pictures, Mexican, 7
Hitchcock, Lieut.-Col., 339
Hochelaga, primitive fortified village, 16
Hoctanlubbee (" Tom "), story of, 335
Hohay, 57

Holland, Philemon, translator, 274
Holmes, William, of Plymouth, 124
Holstein, Treaty of, 319
Howard, Territorial Governor, 176
Hubbard, historian, 283
Huron, Lake, 51
Hurons, 10, 56, 288
Hutchinson, Governor, 127, 280

I

Illinois, French Settlements in, 135, 136, 138. See also Index, Vol. II.
Illinois Indians, tribes, 47, 48; at war with Winnebagoes, 49. See also Index, Vol. II.
Illinois River, 48
Immigration, Indian, route of, xiv., 1, and note
Indian Bureau, 240
Indian Department, 195
Indian Springs, Treaty of, 320. See also Index, Vol. II.
Indians, origin and descent, xiv., 1, 2; early history, 83 et seq.; character and superstitions, 83, 84; burial places, 85, 86; their primitive fortifications, 90, 91.
Inkle and Yarico, story of, 148
Intermarriage of Whites and Indians, 302, 303
Iowas, 332. See also Index, Vols. I. and II.
Iroquois, 23; and Wyandot war, 24, 29, 30; conquer Delawares, 33, 34; Confederacy, 236. See also Index, Vol. I.

J

Jackson, President, 213; addresses Congress on Indian affairs, 217. See also Index, Vols. I. and II.
Jarves's History of Sandwich Islands, 257
Jefferson, President, letters of, 163; addresses Congress on Indian affairs, 204-6.
Jefferson Barracks, 65. See also Index, Vol. II.
" Jenny" (Totapia), story of, 335
Johnson, Sir John, 171. See also Index, Vol. I.
Johnson, Dr, on the early discoverers, 97, 98
Johnston, Sir Guy, 155. See also Index, Vol. II.

Johnston, Col. R. M., at Battle of The Thames, 44. See also Index, Vol. II.
Judd, Dr G. P., 263
Jung, Mr, Moravian Missionary, 284

K

Kaikoewn, Governor of Kanai, 264
Kamehamela, Hawaiian ruler, 265
Kames, Lord (quoted), 31
Kanai, 264
Kansas nation, 189, 232, 332. See also Index, Vol. II.
Kaskaskias, 47, 135, 204, 331. See also Index, Vol. II.
Kekuandoa, Governor, 262
Kickapoos, 12, 43, 46, 332. See also Index, Vol. II.
Kinnakanic, 69
Knox, General, 169

L

du Lac, Gens, 58
Lafiteau, 97
Lahaina, 263
Lake Huron, 51
Lake St Clair, 33, 52
Lake of the Woods, 39
La Salle, 137
Lascalteca City, described, 101
"Leaf Shooters," 58. See also Index, Vol. I.
Le Bœuf, British military post, 38
Ledyard, John, celebrated American traveller, 3; extracts from his Journal on Tartar language, 3-5
Lenne Lenape, 32. See also Index, Vol. I.
Limestone (Maysville), 180
Lincoln, General Benjamin, 171
Lindlay, Jacob, 172
"Little Turtle," 174. See also Index, Vol. II.
Locke, Dr John, geologist, 88
"Long Knives," 138. See also Index, Vol. II.
Long's Rocky Mountains Expedition, 150; Second Expedition, 228 (quoted)
Loskiel, 284

M

McArthur, General, 182
McKenney's account of " Red Bird's " surrender, 66-71

McGillivray, Alexander, Creek chief, 304
McGillivray, Farquhar, 304
McKee, Colonel, British agent, 166, 167, 285, 288, 292
Madison, President, 184; addresses Congress on Indian affairs, 206-8. See also Index, Vol. II.
Makostrake tribe, 43
Mandan village post, 210. See also Index, Vols. I. and II.
Mandans, 58
Man-eating Society, 47
Manitou, 13
Manitoulin Islands, 29
Marquette, 137
Marriage, and Indian women's devotion, 148-151
Marsh, Mr, Government sub-agent, 67
Marshall, Chief Justice, on *Worcester* v. *State of Georgia* case, 224. See also Index, Vol. II.
Mascontires, 48. See also Index, Vol. II.
Mather, Cotton, 274, 276
Mathers' (Dr), *Prevalency of Prayer*, 283
Matoaka (Pocahontas), 119. See also p. ix.
Maumee River, 37, 38
Maysville, 180
Mendewahkautoan Band, 58
Mengue, 49
Menominies, 12, 53; dialect, 54; location, 56. See also Index, Vols. I. and II.
Mexico, early history and conquest of, 99, 100, 102, 103; and hieroglyphical pictures, 7
Miami, Little, 235
Miama River, Council at, 173
Miamies, 25, 46, 235; treaty, 171
Michigamies, 47
Michilimackinac, 35; British military post, 38
Migration, Indian, xiv., 1, and *note*, 31, 235-37
"Milly," daughter of chief Francis, story of, 339; granted pension, 340
Minataree dialect, 10
Mingoes, 29. See also Index, Vol. I.
Minnehaha, 2, and *note*
Missionaries, 141, 332; American, 255; Moravian, 32, 283; Protestant, 251; R. C., 35, 40
Mississippi Boundary, 224
Missouri River, 232
Missouries, 231, 332
Mohawks, 30, 153, 154; described by Baylie, 123. See also Index, Vols. I. and II.
Mohegans, 28

Monroe, President, addresses Congress on Indian affairs, 208-11. See also Index, Vol. I.
Montezuma, 100
Moore, Joseph, 172
Moravian Indians, 289 *et seq.*
Moravian Missionaries, 32, 283: towns and villages, 284, 286, 288, 289, 290
Morse, Rev. Dr, and "Jenny," 335
Muskingum River, 33, 284
Muskogee tribe, 10, 75. See also Index, Vols. I. and II.
Musquakees, 237. See also Index, Vols. I. and II.
Mythology, 18

N

Nanibujo, 19
Narragansetts, 28, 127, 279, 283
Natchez, characteristics of the, 76, 77
Naudawessie (Sioux), 57
Newcalenous, 46
New England, founders of, 121, 122, 123; "Historical Account," 275
New Orleans, American victory at, 184
Niagara, British military post, 38; American victory at, 184
Nipmuks, 272
Nomenclature, Indian, 2, 4
Northern Indians, 230
Nunez, Vasco, 103

O

Oglethorpe, General, 294
Ohio Boundary line, 172, 173, 176, 179
Ojibways, 229. See also Index, Vol. I.
Omahas, 58, 232. See also Index, Vols. I. and II.
Onalaska Island, 4
"Onas, the Great and Good," 131, 138
Oneidas, 30. See also Index, Vol. I.
Ongpatinger, 334
Onondagoes, 30. See also Index, Vol. I.
Ore, lead, 50
Origin and descent of American Indians, xiv., 1, 2, 4
Osage River, 232, 331
Osages, 230, 231, 331; traditions, 231. See also Index, Vols. I. and II.
Osages, Great, 231, 232
Osages, Little, 231, 232
Ottagamies (Foxes), 49
Ottawas, 12, 37, 331. See also Index, Vol. II.
Ottoes, 332. See also Index, Vol. I.

P

Pach-gaut-schi-hi-las, and the Moravian Missionaries, 289

Padouca, 11

" Panther " family, 43

Parish, John, 172

Patronymic appellations, 12

Pawnee Loups, 231. See also Index, Vols. I. and II.

Pawnees, 10, 230, 332; Grand, 231; Republican, *ibid.* See also Index, Vol. II.

Payne's Landing, Treaty of, 320. See also Index, Vol. II.

Peace chiefs, 17

Penn, William, 129; Pennsylvania Constitution, 130; patent, 134; pacific government, 138. See also Index, Vol. I.

Pennsylvania, founding of, 130; settlements, 270, 271

Pennsylvania, Historical Society of, 132

" People Who Never Fall," 59

" People Who Shoot the Leaves," 58

Peorias, crusade against, 39, 47; extinct, 163, 331. See also Index, Vol. II.

Pequots, 28, 123; massacre of, 126

Perouse, La, 260

Perrot, Sieur, 25, 46

Petalesharro, 334. See also Index, Vol. I.

Philadelphia, Council of, petitions the King, 134

Philip, Chief, 28

Philip's War, 275

Piankeshaws, 48, 331. See also Index, Vols. I. and II.

Pickaway Plains, 235

Pickaways, 43

Pickering, Colonel Timothy, 171

Piekann Indian Encampment, *Frontispiece*

Pipe, Captain, 290

Pittsburgh, British military post, 38

Pizarro, 99

Plattsburgh, American victory at, 184

Plymouth Landing, 273

Pocahontas (Princess), romantic story of, 117; at British Court, 118; intercedes for Captain Smith, 119; birth of, 120; captured by Captain Argall, 120; baptized Rebecca, 121; marries John Rolfe, ix., 121; death of at Gravesend, 121. (*For Notes on her Portrait, see pp. ix.-xii.*)

Pocasset, 283

Poinsett, J. R., U.S. Secretary and Chief John Ross, 318. See also Index, Vol. II.

Point Pleasant, Battle at, 43, 236

Pontiac, Ottawa chief, 28; hostile to the British, 37; attacks British military posts, 38; at " Bloody Bridge " Battle, 39; assassinated, 39. See also Index, Vols I. and II.

Portuguese discoverers, 96, 97, 98

Post, Frederick, Missionary, 284

Potawattimies, location, 40; characteristics, 41, 331. See also Index, Vol. II.

Potuche, 279; executed, 280

Powhattan, 119

Prairie du Chien, 63; massacres at, 64 (*note*), 65, 66. See also Index, Vol. II.

Prairie du Rocher, 136

" Praying Indians," 127, 272, 275, 276, 278, 292

Pre-emption Rights, 199

Presque Isle, British military post, 38

Printing Press, Choctaw, 300, 332

Proctor, General, British commander, his compact with Tecumseh, 179, 181; condemned by Tecumseh, 182. See also Index, Vol. I.

" Prophet, The," 43, 44, 45. See also Index, Vols. I. and II.

Protestant Missionaries, 251

Puans, 63

" Pueblo " peoples, xiii.

Pukeshinwau, 43

Puritans, settlement of, 124, 125, 275

Q

Quakers, 129; pacific government, 130, 133, 134, 138, 171, 172; influence of on Indians, 250; Settlements, 272

Quapaws, 330. See also Index, Vol. II.

du Quesne (Fort) expedition, 295

R

Raisin River, 183

Raleigh, Sir Walter, 112, 294

Randolph, Beverly, 171

Randolph, D. M., and Pocahontas portrait, xi.

Randolph, Richard, of Curles, and Pocahontas portrait, x.

Randolph, Ryland, x.

"Red Bird," Winnebago chief, and Prairie du Chien murders, 64 (*note*); surrenders, 65, 66, 70; death of, 71. See also Index, Vols. I. and II.

Red Clay Council, 311, 314

"Red Jacket" and the missionaries, 141. See also Index, Vols. I. and II.

Religion and Indian Mythology, 18, 19

Republican States, 223

"Reservations." *See Map at end.*

Revolutionary War, 286

Ridge, Major, 310. See also Index, Vols. I. and II.

Robertson, Dr, and Mexican hieroglyphical pictures, 7, 100

Robinson, Dr T., and Sully's Pocahontas portrait, xi.

Robinson, Mrs Anne, and Sully's Pocahontas portrait, xi.

Rock Island, 231

Rocky Mountains, Long's Expedition to, 150

Rogers, Major, and Chief Pontiac, 37

Rolfe, Henry, 121

Rolfe, John, marries Pocahontas, ix., 118, 121

Rolfe, Thomas, son of Pocahontas ix., 121

Ross, John, Cherokee chief, 309; his Memorial to the Senate, 311 *et seq.* See also Index, Vol. I.

Ruland, Mrs, 183

S

St Anthony's Falls, 2, and *note.*

St Clair, General, 161, 171. See also Index, Vols. I. and II.

St Clair, Lake, 33, 52

St Joseph, British military post, 38

St Joseph River, 167

Sacs (Sauks), 50

Saginau Bay, 51

Saint Phillippe, 136

Salem Village, 284

Salt Springs, 226

Sanderson, William, 112

Sandusky Plains, 36, 292; Battle of, 293

Sandusky River, 36

Sandwich Islanders, 255; Jarves's *History*, 257

Sarstantzee, Wyandot chief, 36

Sassacus, 126

Sauk Town, 51

Saukie now, 51

Saukies, 231, 236; at war with Iroquoi and Wyandots, 236; allied with Musquakee, 237. See "Foxes," and Index, Vols. I. and II.

Savannah River, 42

Savery, William, 172

Schoenbrund Village, 284

Sciota River, 42; Valley, 235

Seminoles, 75, 320, 325; war, 339. See also Index, Vol. II.

Senecas, 327, 330. See also Index, Vol. I.

Senseman, Moravian Missionary, 284

Settlers, European, 271

Shawanese (Shawanoe), 12, 29; location, 41; migration of, 42; claim foreign origin, *ibid.*; division into tribes and families, 43, 179, 189, 235, 327, 330; at Braddock Battle, 236. See also Index, Vol. I.

Simcoe, Governor, 172, 175, 176

Simpson, W. F., letter of, to Sully, *re* the Pocahontas portrait, x.

Sioux, 10, 30, 53; location, 56, 57, 62; families, 57, 58; characteristics, 61; religious opinions, 61, 62. See also Index, Vols. I. and II.

Sioux, Lower, 58, 59

Silliman's *Journal* (quoted), 88

Sippican, 281

Sistasoons, 58

Six Nations, 29, 154; Confederacy, 31, 32. See also Index, Vol. I.

Smith, Captain John, historian, 112, 116, 120

"Snow feather" (Pocahontas), 119

"Society of Friends," 171, 172

Solebury, 132

de Soto, 74. See also Vol. I.

Southern Indians, 73, 74, 254, 305

South-Western Indians, 301

Spanish invasion, 99; of Georgia, 295

Sparks' *Life of John Ledyard* (quoted), 4

Spring, Cornelius, interpreter, 34

Steukley, Sir Lewis, 121

Stevens, Mr, 103

Stickney, Mr, Indian agent, 23

Stith, historian, 120, 121

Stone's *Life of Joseph Brant* (quoted), 169, 171

Stoughton, Captain, 126

Sully, R. M., and his portrait of Pocahontas, ix.-xii.

Swedes, 132, 133

T

Tamorias, 47. See also Index, Vol. II.
Tanner, John, adopted by Indians, 228, 253; his *Narrative on Indian Life*, 228-30, 242
Tartar stock, and language, 2, 3, 5
Tecumthe (Tecumseh), Shawanee chief, 28, 43; killed at Battle of the Thames, 44; designated "Napoleon of the West," 177; his hatred of the whites, 178; advocates one great Indian Confederacy, *ibid.*; maintains Ohio River boundary, 179; compact with General Proctor, *ibid*; against torture of prisoners, 180, 181; *Life* by Benjamin Drake (quoted), 181-83; rescues American prisoners, 182; his humanity, 183. See also Index, Vols. I. and II.
Tens-kwau-ta-waw, "The Prophet," 43, 44
Teton tribe, 59. See also Index, Vol. I.
Thames, The, Battle of, 44. See also Index, Vol. I.
Thames River, American victory at, 184
Timons, William, historian, 116
Tippecanoe, Battle of, 45. See also Index, Vols. I. and II.
Tispaquin, executed, 281, 282
"Tom" son of "Jenny," story of, 335
Totapia ("Jenny"), story of, 335
Totem, 13
Tour to the Lakes (McKenney's), quoted, 19
Traders, and dishonest barter, 241, 242
Traditions, Indian, 22
Treaties of—
    Cherokee, 314, 315, 320
    Greenville, 161
    Holstein, 319
    Indian Springs, 320
    New Echota, 310, 311, 315, 317
    Payne's Landing, 320
    U.S., text of, 187-90. See also "Treaties," Vols. I. and II.
Tribes of the Central and Eastern States, xiii. ; List of, 7-9; dialects, 10-12; divisions of, 13; aboriginal, 30, 228
Trumbull, historian (quoted), 123
"Turtle" tribe, 42, 43
Tuscaroras, 30, 31. See also Index, Vol. I.
Twighwees, 47
Tyson, Job R., and Chief John Ross, 315. See also Index, Vol. I.

U

Uchees (Uchi), 77. See also Index, Vol. II.
Union of the States, 299
United States Government, pacific policy of, 161 *et seq.;* and Great Britain, discontent between, 176, 177; Treaties, text of, 187-90; Scheme of Indian government, 237 *et seq.;* and Pre-emption Rights, 299

V

de la Vega, historian, 75
Villages, primitive, 16
Verdigris River, 340
Virginia, discovery of, 115, 116; Western Settlements attacked by Indians, 289; cedes her rights, 223

W

Wabanocky tribe, 67
Wabash River, 236
Wabenauki, 27
Wah-kon, 62
Wajonick, 288
Wampum belts, significance of, 22, 23, 34, 296
War of 1815, 184
Warren Hastings, 106
Washington, President, 161; complains to British Government, 166; his Address to Congress on Indian affairs, 202-3
Watson's "Account of Buckingham and Solebury" (quoted), 132
Wauphauthawonaukee, 43
Waupaukonetta, 41
Waukpakoote, 58
Waukpatone Band, 58
Wayne, General, 169, 175; and Greenville Treaty, 161. See also Index, Vols. I. and II.
Weas, 46, 331. See also Index, Vol. I.
We-Kaw, implicated in Prairie du Chien murders, 65; surrender of, 66, 71
Wesir, Conrad, interpreter, 34
Western Tribes, 332
Wheeler, John, and Pocahontas portrait, xii.
Whistler, Major, 66, 67; and "Red Bird's" surrender, 70. See also Index, Vol. II.

White River, 35, 40
Whites and Indians, intermarriage of, 302, 303
Williamson, Dr, historian, on Indian migration, 31, 115
Windsor, 124
Wingandacoa (Virginia), 115
Winnebagoes, location, 12, 63; dialect, 64; at war with Illini, 49, 64, 72; manners and customs, 72, 73. See also Index, Vols. I. and II.
Winthrop's *Journal* (quoted), 125
Wool, General, U.S. Commander, 314
Worcester v. *State of Georgia* case, 224
Worthington, General, 182

Wyandots, 10, 12, 23; and Iroquois war, 24, 29; head of Indian Confederacy, 35, 56

Y

Yanctons, 59
Yarico and Inkle, story of, 148
Yellowstone River post, 210
Yuchi (Uchi) tribe, 77. See also Index, Vol. II.

Z

Zeisberger, Moravian Missionary, 284